Getting Competitive

Getting Competitive

Middle Managers and the Cycle Time Ethic

By **Philip R. Thomas**

With **Kenneth R. Martin**

McGraw-Hill, Inc.

New York St. Louis San Francisco Auckland Bogotá
Caracas Hamburg Lisbon London Madrid
Mexico Milan Montreal New Delhi Paris
San Juan São Paulo Singapore
Sydney Tokyo Toronto

Library of Congress Cataloging-in-Publication Data

Thomas, Philip R.
    Getting competitive : middle managers and the cycle time ethic /
by Philip R. Thomas with Kenneth R. Martin.
        p.   cm.
    Includes index.
    ISBN 0-07-064325-3
    1. Product life cycle.   2. Product management.   3. Competition.
4. Time management.   I. Martin, Kenneth R., date.   II. Title.
HF5415.155.T48   1991
658.5 – dc20   90-20319
                                                                                    CIP

Total Cycle Time, TCT, Cycles of Learning, Total Competitiveness
Management, TCM, and The Five I's Process are trademarks of
Thomas Group, Inc.

1 2 3 4 5 6 7 8 9 0   DOC/DOC   9 6 5 4 3 2 1 0

ISBN   0-07-064325-3

*The sponsoring editor for this book was James H. Bessent, Jr., the
editing supervisor was Scott Amerman, and the production supervisor
was Suzanne Babeuf. It was set in Baskerville by McGraw-Hill's
Professional Publishing composition unit.*

Printed and bound by R. R. Donnelley & Sons Company.

Contents

Preface

My total absorption with short cycle times began a generation ago. I was then managing a small electronics firm in England, and I discovered that my company's ability to bring new products to market ahead of our giant competitors gave us an enormous advantage. Time, not size, was the crucial factor in determining cost, productivity, and asset utilization.

Another lesson I learned back then was that Cycles of Learning — the number of opportunities to improve performance in a given year — had an enormous impact on the rate of change. I devised a systematic method to exploit those lessons of experience and accelerate response to market opportunities. Shorter response time, of course, produced more Cycles of Learning, which pushed my company's entitled performance level ever higher.

That was a long time ago. Over the next thirty years, moving up in the electronics industry, I applied and refined my cycle time concepts in many different businesses and locales. Eventually, I was able to predict accurately just how much better an operation might perform if it applied short cycle time thinking to its available resources. The improvement potential was almost always startling.

To a large extent, cutting cycle times is a systematic exercise in spotting and removing barriers to high performance; outmoded procedures, for instance, or irrelevant measurements, or unnecessary processes, or corporate myopia. As I became adept at spotting and removing such obstacles, I realized that aside from the quirks particular to any specialized operation, there existed a world of generic barriers which were very similar from industry to industry. Furthermore, it became obvious that the ethic of short cycle time transcended the manufacturing floor. It could, for example, produce a profound improvement in the white-collar sector of any company. This bigger picture pointed the way toward the culture of performance improvement that I call Total Cycle Time. Meanwhile, I had decided that short cycle time thinking was an idea whose time had come for all of American industry. Accordingly, in 1978, I founded Thomas Group, Inc. (TGI) to spread the word.

Thomas Group was and is a problem-solving company. We apply time-based management to improve corporate competitive performance. From the start, I and my colleagues had a mission and a message for industry at large. But at first, we had a hard time selling that message because most of our customers were convinced that such techniques were strictly for manufacturing lines, no more. Others, preoccupied with improving product quality, had difficulty appreciating the complementary connection between Total Cycle Time and their quality objectives. As the competitiveness crisis worsened in America during the 1980s, more and more companies began to listen—with impressive results.

Thomas Group was making real headway and growing by leaps and bounds, but I was still frustrated by our low visibility in a time that seemed critical for American industry. To address this challenge, I published my first book, *Competitiveness Through Total Cycle Time*, in 1989. That volume, aimed at CEOs, was largely a fictionalized scenario devised to provide a readable example of how any company might improve its performance by undertaking Total Cycle Time. The book achieved its objective: Many industries far and wide have adopted the concept, and I am delighted to note that many of my customized terms and phrases have become household words in American business.

The message of that book—and this one—is that Total Cycle Time drives improvements in a company's competitiveness by shortening its response time to market opportunities, by accelerating desired results, and by increasing the effective use of resources. Changing to a Total Cycle Time culture will permit any company to realize significant gains in profit and quality while reducing the amount of requisite cash tied up in inventory, all without the addition of any new resources. Implementing and institutionalizing Total Cycle Time is not easy, but it works.

Because Total Cycle Time amounts to a fundamental cultural change for any company, it must have the full support of top management, which is why my first book was directed toward CEOs. But as Thomas Group's client base widened, I realized that middle managers face a number of hard choices when they try to adopt Total Cycle Time thinking. I was thus prompted to write the book you are reading, the second in a proposed series.

Getting Competitive consists of several short stories in which a variety of middle managers in different functional areas grapple with the kinds of problems common to their management level and discover the exponential role of cycle times in enhancing performance. While the characters and companies are fictional, the situations are based on my actual experiences. The results, positive and otherwise, are likewise closely based on real incidents. I hope that this book will cause many middle managers, frustrated by insufficient empowerment, corporate mindset, or bureaucracy to take heart—and action. Having covered the management spectrum from the very top through the mid-levels, I am now at work on a third book, scheduled for 1991 publication, that will cover the individual's approach to Total Cycle Time.

Applying and refining Total Cycle Time has been a long, arduous, but fascinating process. To me, it has been and still is the most interesting thing, period. It has also been gratifying to watch as venturesome clients provide real-world, hands-on opportunity while members of Thomas Group work creatively and tirelessly, coaching customers toward their entitled performance levels. My fellow TGIers have added continuously to the storehouse of problem-solving expertise, barrier removal skills, and our Cycles of Learning database plus developing the unique set of tools we use to deliver measurable results on an incentive basis.

To return to the theme of this book: Middle and top managers alike must realize that there is no simple way to make a

company competitive. Furthermore, getting competitive requires more than competence and attention to detail. It requires guts. It demands the willingness to breach functional
divisions and attack performance barriers wherever they may
be lurking inside a company. Easier said than done. But if
done, the results can propel a business to world leadership.
In today's world, does a good middle manager have a choice?

PHILIP R. THOMAS

Getting
Competitive

Introduction

As it struggles to regain its competitive edge, American business recognizes the urgency of reducing the time required to respond to customer needs and to bring new products to market. Recently, trade journals and conferences have been full of talk about the ways and means of "time-based management," "cycle time management," and "quick response."

The pathway to competitiveness in any business lies in reducing the time to respond to change. That is accomplished by a process which systematically removes barriers and effectively exploits the learning opportunities provided by shortened cycle times. Such a process is called Total Cycle Time.

Here is the second book in a series that explains this business approach in detail. The first, Competitiveness Through Total Cycle Time: An Overview for CEOs, *addressed the issue from top management's perspective, although it was designed to be readable at all levels. This volume seeks to inspire middle managers to get busy and make a difference in their companies by implementing Total Cycle Time wherever the opportunity arises.*

If you are only slightly curious about the fundamentals and potential of Total Cycle Time, you will find this volume interesting. In fact, as a how-to book it is more interesting than most, because it is a series of anecdotes, not a textbook. Each chapter involves a middle manager whose company is faced with the opportunity to significantly change its competi-

tiveness through time-based management. The focus is on the problems and solutions as seen through the middle manager's eyes.

Each chapter is structured to present a situation in which time-based management could have a significant effect. The middle manager faces a dilemma and approaches the situation by identifying barriers and, in some cases, successfully removing them. In order to guide the reader to better understand the direction toward the problems, solution subtitles, which telegraph a sense of functional focus, have been added. At the end of each chapter, some theoretical specifics of Total Cycle Time related to the chapter are included so that middle managers can adapt and apply these concepts to their own companies and functional areas.

In order for readers to relate more directly to each chapter, the situations discussed—the kinds of people, and the barriers met, the solutions that work, and the tools that should be applied—are extracted and modified as appropriate from real-life incidents encountered over the last 20 years. Such situations will undoubtedly hit home.

When the competitiveness of many companies is being changed, managers frequently ask: "How do you inspire people?" The answer is worth repeating here, as it is an underlying theme for the book: "People are inspired to improve if they believe the performance improvement goal is desirable and realizable, and if they can see a believable methodology to reach that goal in a reasonable time." This says it all.

Whether at the top of a company or in the middle ranks, all managers want to see their companies more profitable and more effectively utilizing their resources. What are the potentials that can emerge when the concepts of Getting Competitive—Middle Managers and the Cycle Time Ethic *are applied? Experience teaches that manufacturing-based companies may expect an increase in pretax profit by more than 10 percent of sales, with improved cash positions of similar magnitude through reduction of inventories. Such* *changes could be accomplished within a two- to five-year time frame, depending on the position of the company in the $200 million to $5 billion size range.*

The critical and generic concepts of competitiveness through Total Cycle Time that drive significant financial improvement, which in this book are applied to the various middle-manager functional areas of a company, occur throughout each of the six situations that are given. These fundamental generic concepts include first, the recognition that there are two levels of performance available with current resources. These are baseline (a company's present condition) and entitlement, or realizable performance (the level of performance that can be achieved through Total Cycle Time). The second important concept is that of Cycles of Learning, in which, as business processes are simplified and shortened, feedback loops are applied around these processes in order to create Cycles of Learning. The third concept is the necessity of viewing everything done within the company as a business process that can be defined, analyzed, simplified, streamlined, and eventually made competitive. The fourth major point is that achieving performance change requires a disciplined process (the Five I's Process) which carries the change from baseline to continuous improvement at the realizable performance level. The most significant part of this process is the Implementation phase, wherein barriers are defined and removed, leading to the Institutionalization of the improved competitive posture of the company.

To a middle manager, effective utilization of time, both personal and within the company, is of the utmost importance. Time is the most precious commodity there is. How then do you work within the constraints of time to make yourself and your company more effective? Within a book of this length, not all the answers can be given; however, when you are all through reading, each of you should ask yourself one simple question: "Why not?" The characters in this book are not in the top of the management group; they lack the know-how to implement the necessary reforms, or so it seems. But they take action. And, as in real life, some make a big differ-ence, others don't. But all learn a great deal about how to get and stay competitive, and all come to realize that they are more empowered than they thought. They also come to realize that there are a great many middle managers—people like you, perhaps?—who are in the same boat.

There is a double-barreled moral to these stories. First: Total Cycle Time is easier to grasp philosophically than to implement, but it works. Second: middle managers can make a difference.

You *can make a difference. Read on.*

1
Where
Do You Fit?

Lessons in the Basics
of Cycle Time Management

It is late winter and you are on a plane to New York to attend a two-day "Executive Shakedown" conference. The program promises to shed light on the latest trend in American business strategy: making business more competitive by improving response to customers and shortening time to market. This trip is going to cost your company a bundle, but, you hope, it will be worth it if you can get some practical tips.

You spotted the ad for the conference in *Fortune* magazine just a day or two after a confab with your division manager during which he announced a new, all-out program whose objective was to improve the company's competitiveness and regain its eroding market share. The program would be companywide, your boss told you and your middle-management peers, and the key to success lay in reducing the time needed to get products to market while concurrently improving quality. He somberly assured you that the company's top brass were determined to improve those areas and were prepared to take extreme measures. "Times are changing," he said, "and for keeps." Better response to customers, shorter time to market, and higher quality had become the critical tools for corporate survival.

Well and good, you thought as the meeting broke up. Who, after all, would be opposed to increased market share, better quality, or happy customers? And there was no question that the company was being outmaneuvered by competitors here and there, so some remedial measures were long overdue. Furthermore, you had been seeing more and more articles in trade magazines and the photocopy grapevine extolling the virtues of short cycle times, timely introduction of new products, and the clearing away of unnoticed obstacles to upgrade quality. "Time to market," "speed management," "Total Cycle Time," and other buzzwords were ricocheting around the office even before your boss gave you the high sign. Now you were supposed to climb on the bandwagon.

Buzzwords. Over the last few years, you had heard so many of these, all of them denoting urgent, cure-all programs. Last year's was "total quality," wasn't it? Or was it "profit improvement"? Before that, the company had breathlessly embraced "inventory turns," which had followed "participative management," which was mixed up somewhere in the past with a program of "people involvement." You could remember the buzzwords, but what had happened to the programs? Here we go again, you thought.

Except that your division manager, who was as jaded as you about fad-of-the-year miracle cures, seemed to have gotten religion this time around. It was a sure thing he'd been briefed by senior management, which meant that the CEO had already authorized a program to shorten the time necessary to develop, make, and market products while improving quality. The writing, therefore, was on the wall, at least for a while. Where you fit into such a program was anybody's guess.

Which is why, having read that "Executive Shakedown" blurb, you signed up for the conference and wrote yourself a ticket to Manhattan to find out more about exploiting time and timing to boost competitiveness. The program promises a cavalcade of advice and testimonials from industry gurus and born-again executives. What can you lose? You ought to gain enough familiarity with time-oriented management to at least make a presentation or two to your own people upon your return.

Getting There Isn't Half the Fun

It's good to get away from the rat race for a while, but you have mixed feelings about Manhattan, which surface on the eve of the conference as your plane circles LaGuardia Airport. Out the window are intermittent glimpses of Gotham by night, one thing about New York that, you have to admit, exceeds expectations. It's all downhill from there, however. Because you've learned better than to check luggage, you wrestle your oversize carry-on bag outdoors only to find that there's not a cab in sight. The cab line consists mostly of people who look like you, edgily peering into the drizzly darkness for the sign of approaching headlights and furtively checking each other out as they switch their two-suiters from hand to hand. For an instant you're convinced that all these people are bound for the same conference.

Tomorrow's meeting is to take place in the posh midtown Bermuda House Hotel, but you've reserved a room at the Belfast, a less expensive, barely respectable establishment several blocks away. At last it's your turn, and you crawl into a taxi of sorts. How can a car this young be so grungy and loose? Your driver, who may or may not understand English, is almost incommunicado behind his protective shield of thick, finger-smudged plastic. He hears your shouted destination and, peeling rubber, sets a hair-raising course for the Triboro Bridge—the long way. Welcome to the Big Apple.

Later, alone in your room at last, you dial CNN on your TV and call room service. When it arrives, your chef salad, which you ordered to play it safe, is large enough to feed the Dallas Cowboys (provided they were not too finicky) and the tab is four times the going rate. Between pecks, while catching the news highlights, you review a few notes in preparation for tomorrow's conference.

A last-minute memo from your boss endorses your decision to do some field study and reassures you that your company is in a make-or-break mode. The phrase he uses to describe the corporate plan is Total Cycle Time, which, he assures you, is *not* a flash-in-the-pan quick fix. Maybe not, but the small library of how-to books in the bottom drawer of your desk had nothing to say on the subject, nor could you find a single title on that concept among the scores of business paperbacks you perused at the airport newsstand. A glance at tomorrow's prospectus, however, reveals that the keynote speaker will address the issue of "Total Cycle Time and International Competitiveness." That, then, will have to be your starting point. Suddenly, you're too sleepy for TV.

The next morning, you skip the Belfast's overpriced continental breakfast and hoof it over to the Bermuda House, where you can stoke up on the complimentary sweet rolls and coffee promised by your conference prospectus. You arrive early, register at the hotel's Paget Room, and choose an aisle seat near the refreshments table.

The Bermuda House's rose, green, and mouse-gray decor, replete with brass ornamental fixtures and oversize tropical greenery, makes for pleasant surroundings. The coffee is very good, as well it should be at $900 tuition per person. There are seats in the conference room for about 300 people, many of whom have now arrived. Most of these, you notice for the second time in 12 hours, look disturbingly familiar. Sure enough, their identifying nametags proclaim middle-management positions in a variety of industries; some attendees work for your competitors. Aha! You begin to feel better about the day ahead.

Cycle Time Thinking: The Nuts and Bolts

The conference begins at 9 a.m. sharp. The chairperson's opening remarks stipulate in no uncertain terms that "time is the most potent weapon in the arsenal of competitiveness." Then the keynote speaker from Dallas, Mr. Total Cycle Time, is introduced: dark suit and tie, white shirt, and an armful of transparent foils that he projects on a screen as he talks.

The speaker begins by saying that Total Cycle Time is a system of utilizing efficiently the time that elapses from the moment a customer expresses a need until that need is satisfied. "Within that time span," he explains, "are many individual cycles — discrete tasks — that collectively get the job done. In most businesses, cycles of activity fall within three interlocking areas: manufacturing and marketing, design and development, and strategic thrust [*as shown below*].

"The relative importance of these three loops varies from company to company. Each loop, of course, contains a number of cycles. In every case, identifying and eliminating performance barriers in each of these cycles will streamline effort and improve precision. The result is faster response to customers, better product quality, and more efficient use of resources."

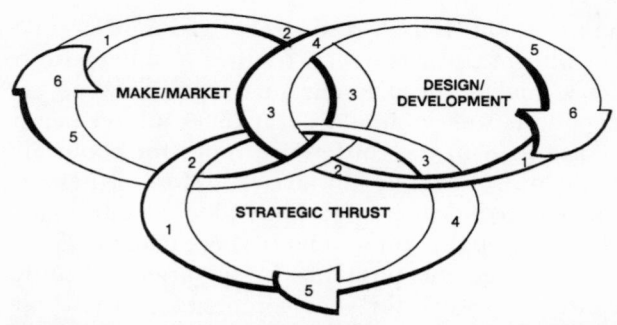

MAKE/MARKET	DESIGN/DEVELOPMENT	STRATEGIC THRUST
FROM CUSTOMER NEED IDENTIFICATION TO PRODUCT/SERVICE DELIVERY	FROM NEW PRODUCT CONCEPT TO COST-EFFECTIVE PRODUCTION	FROM NEW-BUSINESS IDENTIFICATION TO BUSINESS AS USUAL
1. ORDER ENTRY	1. CONCEPT	1. RESEARCH
2. PLANNING	2. PRODUCT/PROGRAM CONTRACT	2. ANALYSIS
3. PROCUREMENT	3. DESIGN/DEVELOPMENT	3. PLANNING
4. DOCK-TO-STOCK	4. INTEGRATION/VALIDATION	4. NEW BUSINESS START-UP
5. MANUFACTURING	5. CUSTOMER VALIDATION	5. *TOTAL CYCLE TIME INSTITUTIONALIZATION*
6. DISTRIBUTION	6. GENERAL AVAILABILITY	

Elements in the make/market, design/development, and strategic thrust loop.

A Short Course in the Basics of Time-Oriented Management

You find the next few points disturbing and a little hard to swallow. The speaker insists that in almost every company there is a substantial gap between its accustomed performance, which he calls baseline, and its achievable performance, which he calls entitlement [*as shown below*]. "Achieving entitlement does not require the addition of new resources. It is a matter of eliminating barriers to responsiveness and time to market.

"Barriers come in three types [*as shown on the following page*]. One is subject matter: counterproductive activity or processing problems peculiar to a company's specialty. A manager who knows his product and is determined to cut cycle times can often expose these by a critical evaluation of every step in a cycle.

"The second type of barrier lies in the business process itself: the detailed steps a company follows to complete the business process. Process barriers can be very tough to detect because they are part of a company's accepted procedures. Some—fancy software, for example—may even have been in-

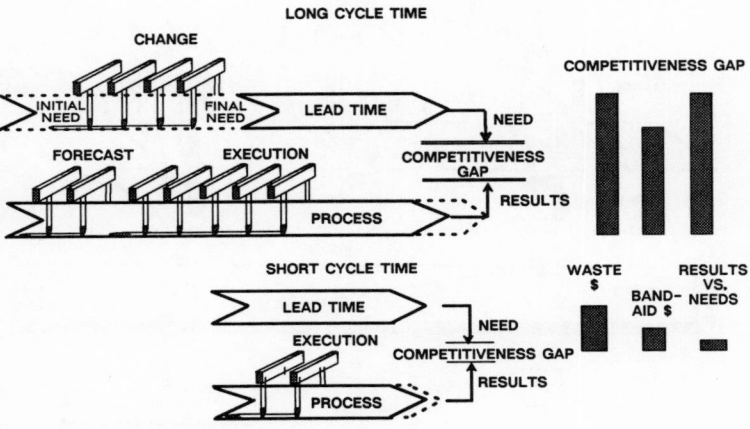

Competitiveness gap for make/market process.

tentionally installed to accomplish some positive objective but in fact prove disruptive or obstructive to other parts of the process.

"The third type of barriers are cultural: accepted corporate mindset — measurements, controls, incentives, values, or mythology that prevents decision makers from seeing the woods for the trees. Many companies are beset by a cultural myopia that impels them to cling to irrelevant procedures, to measure themselves by the wrong indices, or to use up cash in ill-advised attempts at self-medication. Getting rid of cultural barriers is most often the hardest part of a company's search for entitlement and usually requires objective assistance from outside.

"Eliminate those barriers — they're everywhere in a business — and your company can dramatically improve its performance."

"How much is dramatically?" someone asks. Another foil flips onto the screen [*as shown on the following page*]; it is an itemized bar graph showing 10 to 20 percent improvements in blue-collar productivity, 20 to 100 percent improvements

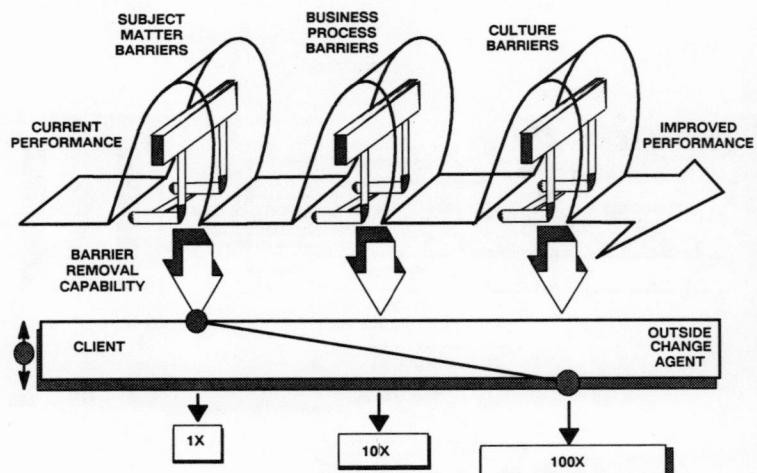

The three categories of barriers.

in white-collar productivity, 30 to 70 percent reductions in time to market, and 20 to over 100 percent increase in return on assets. In the audience, eyes roll upward and a wave of murmured disbelief sweeps the room. Too good to be true, you say to yourself.

Unruffled, the speaker continues: "I knew I'd get that reaction. I always do at first. These numbers are derived from more than a hundred cases of companies, plants, or other operations that moved from baseline to entitlement performance or got awfully close to it — all sorts of businesses, big and small, high-tech and low, old and new. The before and after figures are consistent because, in each case, the entitlement measurements were the same as those used to determine baseline. The numbers look dramatic because of the gap between baseline and entitlement. Although it often comes as a surprise, the gap is very large in any company that hasn't made a religion of time-oriented operation. I'm not suggesting that such companies are deliberately neglectful, you understand, but no matter how dutiful and attentive they may be, they're laboring under significant disadvan-

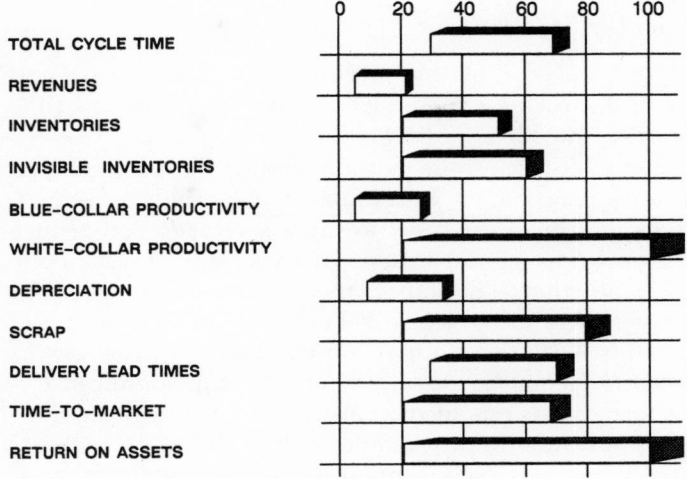

Typical ranges of improvement (by percent).

tages. No wonder so many are losing market share. Small wonder there are more and more remedial conferences like this one. But look at the opportunity for improvement!"

The speaker then rattles off several personal experiences in helping to solve cycle time problems at major corporations. Each describes a barrier to performance improvement that the company leadership could not see or did not recognize as an obstacle: excessive inventory, improper lot sizes, redundant signoffs, incorrect measurements, overzealous controls.

"At this point," he continues, "the hard part for many of you will be to admit that your company's accustomed practices are a long way from entitlement. For those of you who elect to do something about it, the *really* hard part will be to implement and institutionalize the procedures and mindset that move you to entitlement and keep you there. But all of you should be intrigued by the fact that Total Cycle Time requires no speeding up of effort nor additional resources. Instead, it's a matter of using what you have more effectively.

Cycles of Learning: The Key to Barrier Removal

"Now, one purpose of this meeting is to discuss ways and means of improving competitiveness by reducing cycle time in the make/market and design/development loops.

"You reduce cycle time by eliminating the barriers that make work take longer. You improve response by eliminating steps in a process where no value is added. You reduce cycle time by using the lessons of experience to cut cycle times even further. The shorter the cycle times, the more opportunities there are to learn from experience and make improvements. I call those opportunities Cycles of Learning [*as shown on the following page*]. Systematic exploitation of Cycles of Learning is one of the most potent, yet neglected, areas of opportunity in any company. It is therefore essential that every business cycle contain a relevant system of measurements, ongoing feedback loops to apply the lessons of

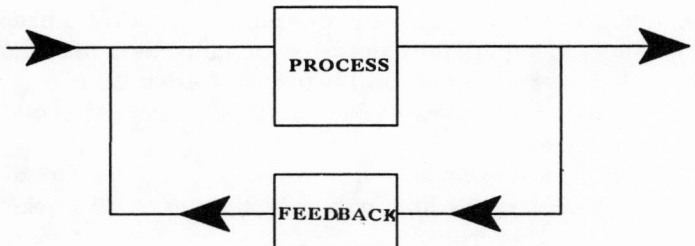

Cycles of Learning: To convert opportunities to learn into increased Cycles of Learning, both a creative element and a management-forcing function are needed in order to reap the potential benefits of lower costs and higher quality through faster learning.

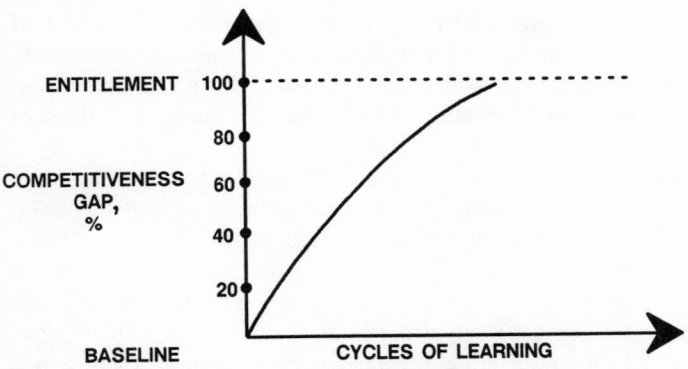

Business process improvement driven by Cycles of Learning.

experience, and management-forcing functions. Cycles of Learning are a way of life in any entitlement company. They improve upon themselves, pushing performance higher and higher [*as shown above*].

The Three R's of Total Cycle Time

"Let me close my remarks with a quick comment on the Three R's. By the end of this conference, you'll all be up to here in jargon but you really ought to think about the Three R's, because together, they define competitiveness and the relationship between speed and better performance.

"Here they are: responsiveness, results acceleration, and resource effectiveness.

"Responsiveness is a matter of a company being able to react to customers' needs precisely, economically, and quickly with minimum resources.

"Results acceleration is a matter of a company systematically using its Cycles of Learning to continuously improve its performance, particularly in the areas of quality and cost, and shorten its cycle times.

"Resource effectiveness, which results from short-cycle-time thinking, simplified business processes, and Cycles of Learning, is a matter of getting the most performance with the least capital, people, and inventory. There is a tremendous opportunity in the white-collar productivity area of business.

"The Three R's are mutually supporting. They are the very essence of competitiveness. Any company that has used Total Cycle Time to move from baseline to entitlement has a grip on the Three R's that need never loosen. Remember that competitiveness is achieved by using Total Cycle Time as the driver to accomplish the Three R's."

Despite your resistance to buzzwords and catch phrases, you find yourself jotting down the Three R's for future reference.

Cycle Time Thinking: Does It Work for You?

Meanwhile, this lecture has been a long one, and because the conference chairperson is obsessive about his time schedule, he eliminates the question-and-answer period. The next speaker, a senior executive at Motorola, describes some of the corporate resistance he encountered while implementing short-cycle-time culture. You only half listen because you're still wrestling with your own resistance to the possibility that you and your company are performing far below — what was the word?—entitlement. And then there is the matter of those promissory statistics: How could white-collar productivity in any viable company be operating at half its entitlement? It doesn't seem possible, but you haven't a clue about how to measure such a thing. You make a mental note to sign up for a set of conference cassettes and graphs.

You're feeling pretty frustrated when, mercifully, lunch is served: a decorative but largely inedible buffet of red and yellow cold cuts, indeterminate hot dishes in various shades of brown, and something quivery and pastel for desert. The coffee is still good. You're sure you won't doze off after such a lunch.

The afternoon session begins with another corporate testimonial: the quality director of a major appliance company excitedly relates how shortening design and manufacturing cycles actually improved product quality. It is almost impossible to listen to his talk because he clears his throat repeatedly and fumbles his arcane flowcharts, but the gist of his message is that reducing the required steps in both loops increased his company's opportunities to learn from experience, with good result. Uncomplicating the manufacturing cycle, for instance, reduced the number of defective products (with corresponding improvement in customer service) and permitted designers to work the bugs out of new items by running them through the line more rapidly. Better quality was achieved all round. You can't accept the implications of this talk because it contradicts your instinct that better quality is a function of painstaking care and usually requires adding steps to a process, not subtracting them. Hour by hour, this conference is becoming an increasingly confusing experience.

It's also very frustrating. While you're willing to concede that some of these unorthodox ideas may have merit (it's hard to dispute the word of Motorola bigwigs and starry-eyed quality experts), you still cannot see what all this has to do with your particular place in the corporate chain of command.

Neither can your dinner companion, a dapper, fortyish male operations VP from Atlanta who adopts you during a coffee break. You and he figure you both deserve at least one first-class meal on the town (and on the expense account). You are joined by an editor of business books who came to the conference "to get an angle on the problems of middle management." So far as you can see, the "problem of middle management" is its powerlessness to effect change. With the afternoon session over, you adjourn to an Afghan restaurant near Central Park South that your new friend has heard about. The place is larger than you expected and for some reason furnished in potted lilies, Oriental rugs, smoked mirrors, and ranks of glass-topped tables loaded with highly polished stemware that reflect a thousand points of light from wall to wall. Very tasty, and very pricey.

It turns out that you and your Atlanta buddy have little in common. He is familiar with the basics of Total Cycle Time and boasts that his company's four glass plants are "the fastest in the business." His big problem is how to motivate a newly acquired plant without having to clean house. "Looking down from above," he says, "I can see that some people have to be forced to give up their old ideas."

Looking up from below, you can see that the right way to improve competitiveness is by systematically shortening response time. But you can't pinpoint the barriers within your own area of responsibility. That being the case, what are you supposed to take home from this conference besides the conviction that cycle time reduction is an idea whose time has come? You all decide to sleep on your anxieties and, in the meantime, enjoy the food and ambience.

Some Tough Questions From the Ranks

The second day of the conference is largely devoted to a panel discussion at which attendees are invited to address questions to the participating VIPs. On your way over to the Bermuda House, it dawns on you that the source of your frustration is your feeling of powerlessness. The theories expounded and the applications described all pertained to decision making at the senior management level, not down in the corporate trenches where you live. It is also obvious that managing to short cycle time involves a major commitment by any company, a fundamental change of culture that is beyond your control.

Which brings you to your second area of frustration: Even if your company goes all out for this new nostrum, how are you as an "underling" going to be affected? Specifically, what kinds of changes are you going to have to make in your accustomed procedures? And at what point does such action simply become suicidal for a middle manager?

The morning's Q&A session helps a little because you see that you're in the same boat with dozens of other attendees. "Suppose," someone asks the panel, "my company is one of those whose baseline performance is low, and that reaching entitlement will increase white-collar productivity 100 percent. What is the company supposed to do with all the surplus people? Can them? That looks to me like a helluva reward for improving performance."

The pundit for Total Cycle Time answers: "Moving to entitlement is not simply the imposition of techniques to reduce the work force, inventory, and expenditures of a company. It includes a growth plan and an attrition plan. The combination should provide for the redeployment of people whose jobs become redundant. In most cases, performance improvement will accelerate at a faster rate than growth plus attrition, so there may indeed be lean periods. Operating with fewer people is one of the common results of business process simplification. But the reduced numbers need to be in the right places, places that are often elsewhere from where they were at baseline. That is one reason why, as much as possible, cycle time reduction should involve the entire company from the top down. And to succeed, that plan must include the mechanisms to recognize the creative input of middle managers throughout the company."

Another voice from the audience: "Making time a primary measurement of performance would be a big jump for a company like mine. We have all kinds of measurements and controls, some of which look to me to be at cross purposes to

each other. In any case, cycle time is not among them. Fixing
all that would, to use your words, require a major culture
change, not a few repairs here and there. What am I as a
middle manager supposed to do? Everyone here has heard
how important it is to put Cycles of Learning to good use;
how Cycles of Learning are integral to any system of responsive management. But to use Cycles of Learning in my department, I've got to know how to set up the right mechanisms for getting feedback from experience. And unless I
make proper use of Cycles of Learning part of my criteria for
evaluating subordinates, it just won't happen. I'm not sure
that I can do that on my own. By the same token, it's a cinch
that unless higher-ups make short cycle time a point on
which *they* evaluate people like me, my peers and I won't assign it a high priority. Speaking personally, I doubt if my superiors have grasped even basic concepts like those Three R's
we heard about yesterday."

Amen. Those remarks unleash a general discussion about
how to get all levels of the managerial hierarchy to interface.
Not much is decided because everyone's professional circumstances are different. The VIPs on the panel are convinced
that any company worth its salt will take note of a middle
manager's improved performance and consider any techniques she has found helpful, especially if she champions
them to her superiors. If that manager's measurements and
controls get results, others up and down the line will want to
give them a try, whether or not they are unorthodox.

At this point the chairperson, himself a senior manager, attempts to bring matters to a close: "You middle managers are
understandably perturbed about your small power base. But
I think you're looking at things too narrowly. Each of you
must look beyond your specific responsibilities and see how
your tasks merge with the rest of the company. Start with
that. You and all the other decision makers in a company
must learn to view the entire business as a seamless process,
not a series of loosely connected functions. Wherever you are
within that process, you should be able to count on the fact
that the person ahead of or behind you likewise sees the busi-

ness as a single process. And, wherever you are in that process, you should view whoever preceded you as your *supplier* and whoever succeeds you as your *customer*."

This comment, intended as a benediction, brings forth a rumble of objections. Several attendees challenge the chairperson, saying they don't believe middle managers are empowered to affect the rest of the business process in companies of any size. A few seem to want to relate personal anecdotes to illustrate that premise, but time is running short. Amidst the din of overlapping voices, the same point keeps coming through to you: moving a company from baseline to entitlement requires active support and a forcing function from the very top on down. You hope your division manager knew whereof he spoke when he said top brass was committed to a new way of life.

You have a plane to catch. Outside the Bermuda House, dreading the inevitable rattle-and-jolt ride to LaGuardia, you're not sure exactly what to do when you get back to your office. You watch your counterparts as they emerge through the hotel's revolving door and scatter for parts unknown. How many of them, you wonder, are in the same boat—people with a goal but no roadmap to guide them?

2
Life
at the Interface

A Case in Point:
Purchasing and Its Interaction
With a Key Vendor

The Bermuda House doorman flagged down a cab, and Larry Coile climbed in, dragging his bulky suitcase and a tote bag full of souvenir T-shirts behind him. He had plenty of time to reach LaGuardia, but a long, broken flight to John Wayne Airport lay beyond that. His overcaffeinated body was still operating on West Coast time, so he felt wide awake despite the fact that the conference had been on the dreary side.

It had been—up until the end, that is. That was when, annoyed at the small return he seemed to be getting for his money, he had spoken up, telling the bigshot experts that they had underestimated the problems middle managers face when trying to "interface" (Larry hated words like that) with their superiors. For almost two days, the VIPs had preached short-cycle-time management to the converted—who else would have dragged themselves to such a conference?—as though everybody present had to be coaxed into improving performance. What they hadn't done, alas, was offer any practical workshops on just where and how to start. How was he going to justify the conference expense to the Godfather?

he wondered. Probably by going through the usual motions: he'd call a meeting, play the conference tapes, and comment philosophically on the generalities. That might satisfy the Godfather, but it frustrated the hell out of Larry Coile. Larry was so frustrated by the time he reached LaGuardia that, when he bolted from the taxi, he left his tote bag behind on the cab's back seat.

Middle Management at Retrospace: A Success Story?

At the age of 31, Lawrence Coile was the best of several purchasing managers at Retrospace Industries, a big-ticket, high-tech defense contractor that occupied a parklike industrial campus in Orange County, California. In another area of the company's operations, Larry would have been a "fair-haired boy" on the fast track to the top, but in Purchasing, things were different. His immediate superior, 10 years his senior, held down the top purchasing slot at Retrospace. Since that was probably as far as a purchasing guy was likely to get in the engineering-based culture of Retrospace, Larry might well be stuck where he was indefinitely. Larry didn't worry about that. He liked his work, at least until lately, and never regretted having switched out of engineering eight years back.

Larry had grown up in Greene County, Tennessee, and had graduated from the University of Texas with an engineering degree. His parents, meanwhile, had retired to Southern California, and while visiting them right after graduation, Larry and his bride, Nancy, had decided to settle down in the Golden State. Larry started at Retrospace as a specifications analyst but soon tired of the job, even though it almost certainly was a stepping stone to better things in Engineering (all of Retrospace's top management had come up by that route). Instead, he envied the human contact and wheeler-dealer activity enjoyed by his counterparts in Purchasing, so when a spot opened up there, he took it.

His buddies told him he'd made a major career mistake, but Larry was one of those even-tempered extroverts who don't take themselves or their careers too seriously. Being a purchasing agent was as much fun as he'd hoped, and his engineering savvy served him in good stead. He did his job well and never looked back. Unlike a lot of purchasing agents, Larry was unofficious and winsome, and he never forgot favors. Three years later, he was made a purchasing manager, and he now had eight buyers reporting to him.

Not that everything was perfect. There were a few problems: Larry's boss, for instance. Around the office and among Retrospace's vendors, the boss was known as the Godfather because he never forgot the few favors he had done for others and had extracted his professional pound of flesh from each one many times over. In addition, he was one of those who gave the profession a bad name, self-importantly lording over his miniempire and forever thinking up new hoops for anxious vendors to jump through before an order was signed. Larry couldn't imagine why. To him, the art of negotiation was pure pleasure, and the soft touch worked every time. He had had to use that soft touch now and then, in fact, to undo some of the Godfather's damage. On the other hand, the Godfather was no office tyrant and seemed content to leave competent subordinates to their own initiative. Although they couldn't have been more different, Larry got on well enough with his boss and, being an optimist, expected eventually to replace him.

The other flaw was that things beyond Larry's control were changing and he seemed powerless to react. Orange County was filling up, and after Kerry and Kim were born, the Coile house, located in deep suburbia 11 miles inland from the plant, no longer seemed big enough. Anything larger, however, was simply unaffordable. Like other young couples in their neighborhood, Larry and Nancy pursued their image of the good life which, in Southern California, meant that they lived at the limit of their means, although their only extravagances were a small cellar of wines they had "discovered" on trips to the Napa Valley and a bottom-of-the-line

BMW Larry used for commuting. Last year, in fact, Nancy had taken a job as a teacher's aide to help ease the financial burden. Occasionally, stopped in traffic and staring at brown hills, Larry would almost ache for the sight of the blue-green Smoky Mountains and wonder what he and his family had to look forward to. The market price of their little California "patio home" would buy them a luxury spread in Tennessee. Then he'd arrive at his office, the phone would ring, and everything would snap happily back into place. Larry's job satisfaction was more vital to him than he realized because it made up for those big problems he wanted to fix but couldn't.

Crisis Control: Is This Management?

Lately, however, Larry's job satisfaction had been eroding. He noticed that he was spending more and more phone time correcting foul-ups with vendors, trying to keep the supply lines open and running to schedule. That was part of the job to be sure, but he was beginning to feel more like a crisis control expert than a purchasing manager.

Virtually all of Retrospace's business was with the government, supplying a variety of frightfully expensive, ultra-complex systems for military aircraft and vehicles. Competition was cutthroat, and the Pentagon was getting increasingly irritable about quality and on-time delivery. Larry, whose specialty was a rapidly changing line of vibration monitors (VMs), knew that when Retrospace failed to meet its contractual supply schedules, which was by no means unusual, the company could count on personal visits from no less than generals and admirals, all of whom reminded Retrospace that there were other, possibly more responsive, vendors eager for the business. Occasionally, these flaps had made the papers and local TV. When demanding better service, or mix, or quality, or whatever, such VIPs did not hesitate to wrap themselves in the flag, insinuating that Retrospace's poor performance threatened the nation's security. If

Retrospace was a patriotic corporate citizen, why did it not keep its promises? That sort of thing.

Although nobody asked him, Larry of course had thought up replies to such questions. In the first place, the government's specifications were so needlessly picayune that just getting new models designed could take years. Then, after production had commenced, the military would often change some minor specification, which caused major tie-ups. The result, he knew, was that by the time many systems reached the field, they were technologically obsolete. If the Pentagon cared about national security, Larry wondered, why did it prolong developmental cycle times? And why did it diddle with so many minute specs, thereby stopping supply dead in its tracks? But that didn't cover all of Retrospace's problems. There was no denying that the company was having more and more difficulty getting even unchanged, mature products out the door as promised.

Notwithstanding the complexity of the systems it supplied, Retrospace was to a large extent a designer and assembler, subcontracting with dozens of vendors for hundreds of specialized components, putting the pieces together, testing the assembled products, and shipping them out. Accordingly, the company's ability to respond to orders was an elaborate act of logistics, balance, and coordination. And that is why Larry Coile, tucked away in a windowless office out of sight of Retrospace and Pentagon brass alike, was a crucial arbiter of his company's performance and, if the Pentagon pundits were on the level, national security. Larry located, bought, and approved the stuff it took to assemble the systems that kept Retrospace in the black and the Free World safe.

None of that occurred to Larry, and he would have laughed if it had. He was, however, getting alarmed about Retrospace's increasing inability to turn on the government's dime. At the very least, he was convinced, the fun would soon be gone unless Purchasing found ways to head off the constant snafus that waylaid schedules right and left. He was stumped, however, about what to do because, being a small cog in the wheels of industry, he lacked a sense of the company's overall modus operandi. From where he sat it looked highly automated and ultrasophisticated, a data-heavy system that logged and tracked processes from beginning to end.

His own piece of that operation was indeed high-tech. He and his buyers worked from a vast computerized inventory of components and the suppliers thereof. When Retrospace received an order for VMs and authorized production, his buyers divided the task of purchasing the requisite components, negotiated price with vendors, and entered the pertinent data into the computerized control system. Any order over $1000 a copy or $250,000 overall was Larry's personal responsibility. He also managed changes in orders, selected vendors, and coordinated all purchases with the company's master production schedule. His software was so elaborate that often, after spending hours on the phone with a vendor and checking the attendant paperwork, Larry could set things in motion by striking a single key on his PC and then typing a two- or three-digit code. The elegance of that instant never ceased to amaze him, but bringing matters to such a point was another thing altogether.

Larry knew he was the company's best purchasing manager because people in that division from the Godfather down were evaluated primarily on the cost reductions they achieved through purchase price variance. Purchase price variance was a system that compared the price Retrospace paid for selected items with a standard price established by the company for such items. The idea was to keep buyers on their toes and satisfy sharp-penciled watchers at the Pentagon that Retrospace was careful with taxpayers' money. Larry's variance to standard was the most favorable in the division.

Big Bucks for Fast Turnaround

His status was most favorable, that is, except for the last quarter, when an emergency had arisen. The specs for an avionic

VM had just changed, necessitating a last-minute switch to a
new microclock design. The heat was on. Larry quickly
shopped around and got the best price from Slumbertech:
$19 a shot, which was a dollar a unit favorable to standard.
Larry took it even though Slumbertech's promised delivery
schedule was dangerously long. Slumbertech was usually as
good as its word on delivery, but twice before, its long delivery times caused idleness on the assembly lines and sleepless
nights in Purchasing. That was the last thing Retrospace
needed at this point. The new VMs were a vital order, and
the longer they took, the more change orders, idleness, and
foul-ups were likely to occur.

When Slumbertech's earliest guaranteed delivery date fell
beyond Retrospace's hurried schedule, Larry decided the
company couldn't afford Slumbertech at any price. He canceled the order and called Neptune, a company that always
delivered on schedule and charged accordingly. The microclocks arrived right away—at $24 a copy—and there was
scarcely a blip in the Retrospace schedule.

Making the switch to Neptune, Larry figured, had saved
his company millions, to say nothing of future contracts. He
was feeling especially good about his timely action when a
memo arrived from the Godfather. Higher-ups, it read, had
noted the change in purchase orders and the premium now
being paid to Neptune: an unfavorable variance to standard
of almost $4 per microclock. On the order in question, the
switch to Neptune was going to cost Retrospace a cool
$20,000. Larry was admonished to reexamine the issue and
try to get his variation favorable again. Larry Coile, no longer
the merit leader in Purchasing, wrote "NO GOOD DEED
GOES UNPUNISHED" across the memo and sent it back
through the interoffice mail.

Under the circumstances, he was probably lucky that the
Godfather okayed his attendance at the New York management conference two weeks later. The idea to go was Larry's,
and was inspired by a few intriguing references to cycle time
management he'd run across in the *Wall Street Journal*. Everybody seemed to be talking about that subject but not ex-

plaining it. He wasn't sure how much of Retrospace's time problems lay in Purchasing, but what could he lose?

In his office a few days after his return, he went over his conference notes and was surprised at how they had gelled. When, at the conference, discussion had turned to the responsibilities of middle managers to come up with innovative ways of shortening cycle times and to share those ideas with receptive superiors, the remarks struck a nerve. Larry was still smarting from the Slumbertech-Neptune flap and not in the mood for platitudes. But the participants had also stressed the need for proper measurements, which sounded like a generalization until he thought over what was bugging him about Slumbertech-Neptune. It was this: at Retrospace, the measurement of purchase price variance stank. It could make a penny-pinching buyer into a departmental hero while holding up the whole company or sending lower-quality items down the line to cause a major hemorrhage in somebody else's department. Suddenly the comment about viewing business as a process, which had sounded like gobbledegook in New York, made practical sense. But what, after all, did he know about Retrospace's process before and after it came through Purchasing?

Starters: A Casual Measure of WIP

He stood up, looked out his door, and listened to the muffled clatter emanating from each cubicle. He strolled down one carpeted aisle and peered into the work spaces. On every buyer's desk was an in-basket stacked with paper: work in process, things to buy. Last year, during a crunch, the stacks in those baskets had grown to well over 6 inches in height. He had calculated that it took most people a day to get through an inch, which was too long, because his section usually ran on a five-day cycle time per order. That had been enough evidence to successfully apply for another buyer. Now, looking again at the baskets, he noted that the stacks were at least 6 inches high, even though business had been flat for months. How long had this been going on? His department had more manpower, state-of-the-art equipment, and dedicated staff, yet its cycle time was obviously getting longer. There had to be some way to smooth out the flow or simplify the task short of hiring another buyer. Because misery loves company, he walked through the other sections of Purchasing with grim satisfaction: every buyer seemed be talking on the telephone, squinting at paper, pecking at a PC, or all of those things at once. That got him to thinking about where the paper came from.

Charting the Flow: Where Does It Go?

Returning to his desk, he tore a blank sheet from a pad and began to doodle a kind of flowchart. He understood the process up front pretty well, and he hastily jotted it down: The military determined what it needed and when, and let a contract. At Retrospace, planners forecasted what demands would be made on plant and resources and generated a requirement for the necessary people, equipment, and components. The component requirement went through a planning system and eventually emerged on the screens and desks of Purchasing. All of those steps, he realized, drawing on his conference experience, could be analyzed as discrete cycles. How long would it take for each? he wondered.

What happened in the process after Purchasing negotiated and placed an order? Obviously, the vendor would then have to process it, plan, schedule, make the product, and ship it to Retrospace. Then what? Larry wasn't sure, so he decided to walk himself through the process.

That little walk, it turned out, took hours. His first stop was across the campus at the receiving dock. Trucks there were unloading cargo under the nervous eye of a supervisor who, Larry learned, was doing his best to fit the activity into a precise, preplanned time sequence in which the purchased materials would supposedly arrive at the assembly point exactly when they were needed, not too soon or too late. Not every vendor played ball, the supervisor told him. Some—who knows why?—delivered early and complicated the problems of storage and inventory; more often, orders arrived late, with damage already done to the production schedule.

Charting the Flow: Cycles Within Cycles

Despite the undeniable sophistication of the receiving operation, there were more steps to it than Larry could have imagined. Once unloaded, incoming goods were immediately bar-coded for Retrospace's receiving system, which checked the count and confirmed the purchase order. Larry noticed that one recent order, apparently bypassed by the process, was sitting on a rack off to one side. The rest, however, were moving on roller conveyers from the dock into a room which, despite its size, was dominated by two monstrous, rumbling carousels consisting of vertical columns of assorted metal storage bins. The stacked bins moved around a closed loop of track and were stopped by electrical command at the loading point much the way Larry's dry cleaning rolled to the pickup counter.

The carousel closest to the dock received unloaded and bar-coded material, each lot of which was duly stashed in one of the coded, predesignated bins and sent on its way to an inspection point by the push of a button. Larry followed one such lot through its inspection and watched another batch of indeterminate objects enter an oven...for how long? Nearby was a gross of gizmos tagged for tomorrow's electrical test. After inspection, all the lots went to the second carousel, whose attendants eventually dispatched them to their respective plants for immediate assembly or, more likely, warehousing.

The cumulative effect of this interlocking, synchronized hubub dizzied him. As he recrossed the campus to his own cubbyhole, he realized he was more confused than ever. He had to remind himself about the reasons for his little fact-finding exercise: he was hunting for a way to test the principles he'd learned in New York. He was also becoming painfully aware of the folly of rating people on a purchase price–variance criterion and was suddenly determined to find more realistic measurements than that.

Then there was the big picture. Today's observations suggested to him that Retrospace was systematized to the teeth but losing ground just the same. (Those piles of paper in the departmental in-baskets haunted him.) If that were true, the whole company was on a downward slide. For his own good at least, he wanted to do something about it. But what?

Pushing Enlightenment Up the Ladder

Bright and early the next day, he popped into the Godfather's office. "What did you find out in New York?" asked his boss before Larry could pronounce one word.

"More than I realized at the time, I guess," he replied. "Listen, that conference stirred up a lot of anxieties I've been having about the department and, for that matter, the whole company. Two months ago, when I got nailed for spending twenty grand to save Retrospace several million, I could see that something is very wrong with the way people are measured around here. The New York conference confirmed that. You may not agree with me about purchase price variance as a standard, but we both know that Purchasing is running harder and harder to stay in place. I'll bet that's one reason you let me sneak off to New York.

"The conference also scared the hell out of me about time management. Retrospace ought to be doing something about it, but we aren't even at the discussion stage. One of the speakers in New York showed how it was possible to reduce white-collar cycle times by removing barriers to performance improvement and instituting proper measurements. I think that's what we need to do. Not to jerk your chain too much, but the price-variance standard, which I'm convinced is a lousy measurement, may be the tip of an iceberg. Retrospace could be wearing itself out measuring the wrong things! Yesterday, when I looked around, I saw procedures used from here to the assembly lines and back that don't result in the type of performance they're designed to, and that includes my department. This whole outfit has got to get leaner, meaner, and more responsive before Uncle Sam takes his business somewhere else. *That's* what I learned in New York."

Empowerment: Expertise Is Cheaper Than Anarchy

Larry then thought of two other lessons: "We talked about empowerment and expertise. Who has the *power* to make things change in a big company? Aside from my own area, which is pretty small, I don't see how I could transfer any insights I might have to other spots in Purchasing or up and down the line, or somehow bootstrap a new kind of culture into Retrospace from where I sit. Then there's the matter of expertise. I can probably identify a few barriers in my own operation; but I have the feeling that our accepted practices, procedures, and attitudes are blinding us to a lot of other problems. Those kinds of barriers may need to be identified by an outside objective observer. What are Purchasing's chances of getting somebody from outside who can at least start us off? I bet it wouldn't cost as much as my price variance on the Neptune purchase."

This brought a smile to the Godfather's face. "Maybe not," he said, "but there are rules around here about hiring consultants. If you're that fired up, and if you can practice being a little calmer, I'll arrange for us to go upstairs tomorrow and ask for some money. I know we'll get it, and not just because you're persuasive. Last week, there was another pow-wow on competitiveness in the boardroom and the CEO has since put pressure on all division managers to submit their 'competitiveness improvement plans' without delay. This division really has no plan, so your rationale is just what it needs to fill that bill and at least keep up appearances. It'll fly. In the meantime, get the address of the guy who removes barriers."

Larry got the address, and Purchasing got the money.

"This is your baby," the Godfather told Larry on the way back downstairs. "Purchasing needs someone to interface with the cycle time experts, with me, and with anyone upstairs who you think might help us. You're the interface." There was that word again. Did he have the time? the expertise? Larry wondered if he had unleashed a hurricane. As he turned into his office, where his fancy phone was lit up and winking like a jukebox, the boss proffered a final word of counsel: "Make sure the rescue squad understands our business, then give them the information and whatever else they need. *Don't* give them the upper hand."

Larry called Dallas and, on the first try, got through to the cycle time speaker he'd heard in New York, who gave him a ballpark figure and promised to send someone out in 10 days. "Meanwhile," he told Larry, "try to identify the major pieces of your purchasing cycle. As you do, you may well uncover barriers that were right under your nose. As I said at the conference, you should have no trouble identifying subject matter barriers that lie within your area of expertise. The others — business process and cultural — may be a little more subtle. Oh — this is important in a purchasing context — think about your vendors' cycle times. They're a big part of your problem!"

Coping With Outside Cycles

The vendors' cycles times sure were a big part of the problem; for example, Slumbertech was unable to deliver microclocks to suit Retrospace's quickening schedule. Then there were the boys at Neptune, who could make poor Retrospace pay through the nose because their cycle times allowed them to respond quickly. Out of curiosity and, perhaps, the hope that someone else was to blame for Purchasing's problems, Larry called Bob Landon, his contact at Slumbertech. The two had never met, but years of telephone conversations had made Larry and Bob friends of sorts. Based on Bob's grunts and tics and the sound of his voice, Larry imagined Bob to be an overweight, jumpy guy about his own age. (He was wrong on all counts.) What he wanted from Bob was a rundown of how Slumbertech went about filling Retrospace orders.

Bob Landon was not in the best of moods since Retrospace's cancellation: "I'll tell you what we do, Larry. We spend a lot of time talking to your buyers because the specs on your orders are usually incomplete. That takes time. Since most of our work is commercial, we turn over government work to a single specialist with, let's see, at least 20 years of experience, poor guy. He sometimes gets overwhelmed, but he absolutely refuses to make a move on a government job until all the details are in. Maybe those details are clear to you guys, so you don't bother to fill in the blanks, but we've learned the hard way to stand pat until we have every *i* dotted and *t* crossed. Then we have to convert the specs on your all-purpose form — which, by the way, is almost incomprehensible — to a format meaningful to our system.

"*That* takes time. After that, the matter is out of my hands. But why do you need to know all this?"

"Just asking, Bob, just asking. Thanks." *Click.*

Wow! It was clear that Larry's section was responsible for at least part of Slumbertech's long cycle time. Larry checked the file on the late, lamented microclock transaction; sure enough, once he had placed the order, Slumbertech people had had to get back to Retrospace buyers twice to check specs. Here was a barrier he could attend to right away. But Retrospace's order only took a week to straighten out. The rest of the delay was the vendor's problem, right? That was one of many questions he'd have to take up with the cycle time specialist next week.

Barrier Removal: An Outside Perspective

Equipped with a Texas accent, a laptop computer, and a business card bearing his photograph ("Now when you see the name, you'll remember the face"), Marv Allen arrived at Retrospace in a rented Taurus. He was champing at the bit to talk to Larry and his superior, and after he had done so for the better part of an hour, he, Larry, and the Godfather were all using the same lingo: baseline, entitlement, Cycles of Learning, and the like. When they were alone again, Marv had Larry take him on a tour of the same spots Larry had lately visited so that he might get a feel for the general business process.

The view from Retrospace's loading dock revealed the same impressive array of systematized discipline, but Marv was soon taking notes, asking questions, and pointing out to Larry some glitches in the system. Take, for instance, the pile of components still sitting forlornly in the holding area more than a week after it had first attracted Larry's attention. Marv asked the supervisor about the pile. "It couldn't be matched to any known purchase order," the supervisor replied, "so it's an orphan until somebody rectifies the situation. It's probably just a numerical mistake in the purchase order. But since we operate on a just-in-time basis, we don't refuse to unload stuff that comes to the dock. It could be something delivered to the wrong address. Time will tell."

"How much of your incoming material gets put on hold this way?" asked Marv.

"About 2 percent. Eighty percent of that gets off hold and on its way eventually. The rest, only about half a percent of our total incoming material, turns out to have been incorrectly shipped. The system isn't perfect, but it is really fast overall. Our dock-to-stock cycle time is only 14 days."

The Cross-Training Barrier

Marv and Larry proceeded past the first huge carousel to the inspection area and beheld another orphaned batch of inventory. Larry asked a nearby inspection specialist about it.

"It's our job to remove items from carousel number one, make sure their specifications match those on a microfiche we've been issued, and then rout them out of here to carousel number two," answered the inspector. "But we don't have a microfiche to match with this stuff. We're awaiting a replacement. As soon as we locate a specialist who can make a new one and send it over, I'll get busy again. Last time this happened, it took several days. Meanwhile, I pretty much twiddle my thumbs."

At other inspection points, however, people seemed to be hard pressed indeed. "Lack of cross-training," said Marv to Larry as he made another note. "If more of these inspectors shared skills, the flow of material through the process would be a lot smoother — and faster."

The Inventory Barrier

At one end of the inspection area, near carousel number two, was what looked like a miniwarehouse of miscellaneous crated and shelved material. This was the reject area. Material here awaited a decision as to whether it was to be shipped back to the vendor or used with an engineering waiver at Retrospace. But there was so much of it! Looking for the person in charge, Larry and Marv approached the door to the service area only to be confronted by a hand-lettered sign: "OPEN FROM 11:00 to 1:00 DAILY."

"I've seen this sort of thing before," Marv said to Larry. "And I'll bet that even as an outsider, you've spotted a few business process barriers that the guys around here haven't noticed or are willing to tolerate." Larry nodded. "This operation has spent a lot of resources upgrading their methods. They're awash in equipment and systems but they're also ankle-deep in barriers, some of which are caused by the very systems that are supposed to streamline the process."

At Marv's request, Larry, the dock supervisor, and the idle inspection specialist did a rough estimate of the value of the inert lots of items in the area. Retrospace was taking delivery of about half a million dollars' worth of material a day but, at any one time, it had $10 million tied up in material that was

going nowhere fast. "That's pretty poor resource management, and I can see that the first-pass yield is likewise poor,"
observed Marv. As for the 14-day cycle time we heard about,
I estimate it's more like 20 if all the items on hold are
counted. And of course they're nowhere near entitlement.
On the basis of what I've seen today, I'd bet that their entitlement is about 4 days, not 14. That makes me wonder if,
culturally speaking, Retrospace is a company that is kidding
itself about the efficiency of its systems."

"And its measurements," Larry added.

Business Processes: An Outsider Looks Inside

When the two had returned to Larry's office, Marv went over
Larry's makeshift flowcharts. "I can already see that Purchasing operates in a bimodal pattern," he told Larry after a run-
through of the chart. "Orders over $250,000 have to run
through a series of senior sign-offs that prolong the process.
That loop costs you several days before the computers are allowed to take over. So we've really got two separate processes
to examine."

For the next two days, Larry gave Marv the use of one of
his section clerks, who pulled together step-by-step data on
the last 200 completed orders, from the initiation date of the
purchase request through the actual date the order reached
the vendor. The resulting curve revealed that the average for
low-dollar orders was 4 days; at the high end it was 12.

Finding a Scenario for Realistic Cycle Times

With the individual steps isolated, Marv could compute
Purchasing's theoretical cycle time: the back-to-back process
time needed for a single order to undergo every stage of the
process without waiting, slippage, or time lost due to error.
The theoretical cycle time for low-dollar orders was an hour

and a half; for high-dollar orders it was half a day. Theoretical cycle time provided a basis from which to compute a practical entitlement cycle time, which Marv's observations, data, and previous case experience convinced him was eight hours at the low end and two days at the high.

When, the next morning, Larry saw those entitlement numbers, he was incredulous: "Eight hours? That's faster than the fastest time we achieved on a top-priority, emergency basis!"

"That doesn't surprise me," replied Marv. "You see, operating at baseline, your fastest performance was obstructed by a lot of barriers that won't exist at entitlement. For example, your first-pass yield should be a lot better. Do you know what percentage of orders go through without a hitch on the first try?"

"No," Larry admitted, "but I know our spec form is sometimes hard for vendors to make sense of. It overdoses them with irrelevant details and expresses the essentials in a format they have to translate to their own system. I've already begun to put that matter right. Meanwhile, however, my buyers complain constantly that they have to call back on almost every purchase request to find out exactly what's being requested, because they really don't know enough to tell the supplier. A lot of those orders are put on hold awaiting a technical reply."

The Myopia Barrier

"That sort of thing is apt to get worse with time," said Marv. "Remember Cycles of Learning? You and your people should be using feedback from the everyday process to eliminate future foul-ups of the same type. The need is to solve the *business process* problem that causes these subject matter—related delays. Why hasn't anyone addressed the business process before?"

"Probably because there's no management incentive to do it. Purchasing doesn't keep tabs on first-pass yield. Buyers are measured on the number of orders placed per month but are not penalized for entered orders that get stalled somewhere else in the pipeline. And of course the standard for orders per month is based on historical performance, so it is probably self-serving. For instance, the general assumption around here is that it *should* take longer to place a big order than a small one, because big ones are likely to be more complicated. Ouch! I see what you're probably driving at: Purchasing's criteria *invite* low first-pass yield. We accept in advance the notion that things will take a lot of ironing out."

The Paperwork Barrier

Over the next few days, Marv and Larry uncovered other business process and cultural barriers that had hitherto gone unnoticed. One of these surfaced while Marv was questioning a buyer whose chief responsibility was executing low-dollar purchase requests for a custom VM built at Retrospace's Fort Worth plant. (Retrospace staff referred to the company's manufacturing plants near and far as "the projects.") Before Retrospace's automated purchasing system was installed, standard procedure had been for buyers to forward hard copies of all orders to the projects initiating the requests. In theory, that practice had been dropped after computerization, but because of distance and an innate distrust of electronic data systems, Fort Worth's project manager still insisted on those hard copies. Accordingly, Larry's buyer was duly feeding the new system while still printing out and mailing paper orders to Fort Worth for review before commitment, an activity which waylaid even the smallest transaction by at least five days. Marv suggested that Larry wean the Fort Worth manager slowly by switching first from paper to electronic mail. When the bugaboo of computerization had gone away, Purchasing could then bring the Fort Worth project in line with its other transactions.

Cross-Training Revisited: Attacking Backlog

For several days, Marv had been hoping to interview Dick Hyman, Larry's senior buyer, because he assumed that Hyman's years of experience would be revealing. Hyman, however, was out with a case of the flu. On the third day of his absence, Marv peered into Hyman's cubicle and noted that the pile of unattended paper was now as thick as *Webster's Unabridged Dictionary*. "Why not have somebody cover some of Hyman's work?" asked Marv.

"None of the other buyers have enough expertise to handle it," Larry answered. "Dick's a real technical specialist."

"Judging by the size of that pile of paper and the rate of work, I'd say it could be weeks before Dick will be able to whittle that backlog down to size. What do you do when Dick goes on vacation?"

"Same as now, only Dick tries to clear his desk before he takes off."

"What if Dick leaves the company?"

"The truth is, Dick is about to take early retirement. I just found out about it last month, and I haven't had time to face the issue. I get your point: we need to cross-train our people. But all of our buyers are flat-out with daily work, so..."

"Does everybody go on vacation at the same time?"

"No. Purchasing uses a rolling vacations policy so we always have buyers on hand to place orders."

"Okay, but by the same token, there's always a backlog of unattended orders piling up somewhere on a vacationer's desk. That explains a lot about the gyrating cycle times on the curve we plotted. I'd say that cross-training should be part of a more general cycle time training program. There's no getting around the fact that such a program will require your buyers to put in long hours for a while. But in the long run, they'll recover the time they invested with dividends.

"Now, as you eliminate the barriers we've uncovered, your people will certainly cut their response times. Typically, as they arrive at a plateau of improved performance, they'll encounter a new set of barriers that must be identified and eliminated. Short cycle times require constant attentiveness, use of Cycles of Learning, and the institutionalization of a new culture that measures and rewards the right criteria. It'll be an uphill battle, especially if Purchasing is the only part of Retrospace to make the effort. Good luck!"

Marv's data-collecting task was now completed, so that was his last pep talk. As agreed, he would return on a monthly basis—he called it a "pulse program"—to help break logjams and identify and remove barriers. Just before his departure, however, he reminded Larry that Purchasing's response time was partly a function of vendor response times and not to let sluggish vendors off the hook because they were theoretically out of range.

Who Is the Customer?

Marv's visit to retrospace had opened Larry's eyes to operational obstructions he couldn't see for looking. It had given him some disturbingly dramatic figures on just how much better Purchasing might operate. It had also brought to life the principle Larry had heard bandied about in New York: that the name of the game was quick response time, from the initiation of a customer's need until the satisfaction of that need. (Larry's "customers" were the guys in the projects.) By shortening its response time a day or an hour at a clip, Purchasing could streamline the cluttered processes that were making Retrospace lose ground. If only the whole division would get involved. If only it weren't a whole month before Marv's next visit.

Time for Implementation

After Marv's departure, Larry got the Godfather's okay to schedule twice-weekly cross-training sessions in which each specialist was responsible for presentations to two others in the section. He also instituted weekly classes in short cycle times, a program that Marv had customized to fit Retrospace's needs. He personally interceded with Mr. Paperwork in Fort Worth, guaranteeing him that E-mail was as good as the Postal Service only faster, and promising to look after all orders until the project was satisfied. He began to track his buyers' progress by dividing their orders in process by orders placed. He then analyzed their highest and lowest cycle times—a simple approach to Cycles of Learning—and the average response time for both low-dollar and high-dollar orders began to come down. On the strength of that, he persuaded the Godfather to let him institute two new criteria for evaluating his people: first-pass yield and cycle time. Amazed by Larry's figures on the delay caused by the requirement for multiple signatures up the line, the Godfather volunteered to take the sign-off matter upstairs.

New Barriers for Old

Over the next few weeks, remembering what Marv had told him about the second layer of barriers, Larry kept his eyes and his office door open. No news was good news until one morning a letter arrived on his desk (typed and posted, not E-mailed) from Fort Worth. The gist of this uncomplimentary missive was that several crucial order requests sent from Fort Worth to Purchasing more than three weeks earlier had sunk like stones. Somehow, Larry knew by these tidings that the second barrier layer had been reached.

There was a simple explanation: now that his buyers were being measured on first-pass yield and cycle time, they tended to give immediate attention to uncomplicated orders, moving difficult ones to the back of the line. Fort Worth's was one of the toughest—it should have gone to Dick Hyman—so the buyer responsible was irresistibly putting off the moment when he would have to cope with it. Hyman got the job of unscrambling the mess, and Mr. Paperwork got a full E-mailed explanation from Larry.

The lost Fort Worth order was, of course, but one of many. All Larry could think of to crack that barrier was to take his slowest, most methodical buyer off the line and assign her the task of unscrambling the complicated on-hold orders. That worked so well that Larry routed all similar orders to that desk in the future. Perhaps this was the person, he thought, to replace Dick Hyman.

In his absorption with his section's cycle times, Larry had almost forgotten that Marv's assessment and upcoming pulse program had been funded as a piece of corporate eyewash to persuade Retrospace's CEO that the division had a program to improve competitiveness. But Marv's first visit had gotten results: Larry's orders moved through the pipeline faster. After each subsequent pulse, they moved faster still.

Barrier Removal: The Domino Effect

As his section began to remove barriers and cut its response times, the other section managers began asking pointed questions and talking among themselves as if they were missing out on something important. Meanwhile, the Godfather had decided to enlarge the experiment. His first move in that direction was to call a meeting of Larry's peers, during which, contrary to his stereotype, he decreed that all of Purchasing was to add Larry's new performance measurements. He had Larry itemize the barriers he'd encountered thus far and assigned him yet another "interface" responsibility: developing an orientation course for his fellow managers. At the meeting, Larry at first hoped that instituting first-pass yield and cycle time as departmental measurements would mean the end of the hated purchase price–variance criterion. He was mistaken. Neither his peers nor the Godfather were willing to eliminate the practice, so adding two new measurements to the bureaucratic list struck Larry as a mixed blessing and his peers as a surcharge on their busy schedules. The Godfather's unwillingness to budge on this point was a surprise.

There was another surprise at the meeting: The Godfather had division vice president Vince Moore in tow. It was Moore who had broken loose enough cash for Marv's help. After listening to Larry's account of spotting barriers from vendor relations through dock-to-stock, Moore became almost manic about applying the techniques in a wider context.

"Would Marv Allen be interested in putting a broader cycle time program in place for the entire division?" he asked Larry as the meeting was about to fold.

"I'll bet he would," said Larry. "During his initial assessment, he continually stressed that better performance meant understanding the entire business process. I know what he means. Over these last months, I've felt like David against Goliath, and all I wanted to do was ease the crunch in my own department. But Marv would also tell you that getting and keeping entitlement is not a program. It's a fundamental change in corporate culture; a commitment to a new lifestyle. It's harder to keep that commitment than to make it, or even to implement the process."

"Get me that guy," said Moore. "And be in my office tomorrow at three. I need a cram course in how to talk his lingo."

The Ego and Turf Barriers

At this point, Larry, if he were interested in such things, would have realized that he was a master at interfacing. Despite, or because of, his distaste for office politics, he had leveraged an irksome departmental problem into what just might be a major opportunity for Retrospace. Meanwhile, his job was interesting again, although he knew he would not be able to relax for months at least. He was beginning to look forward to the next year at Retrospace.

Larry cared enough about office politics to worry about his superior's reaction; they didn't call him the Godfather for nothing. Had he upstaged his boss? In any case, if Vince

Moore became a convert to short cycle time, it was going to mean a lot more work than people in Purchasing realized. What was all that effort going to cost?

Larry decided to test the waters the next morning, when he spotted the Godfather in the parking lot. "I don't know how you feel about Vince Moore's reaction yesterday," he began as the two fell in step, "but I'm pretty excited. I hope to hell he's serious. The last thing we need is another flash-in-the-pan program. Anyway, I appreciate the leg-up you gave me when I started all this awhile back. I guess that's one I owe you."

There was no response for a few seconds, then this: "Actually, that's one I owe *you*. Now sell the concept to Moore and I'll make sure Purchasing delivers. With you interfacing with the rest of the departments, of course." Larry knew right then that he would never understand office politics.

External Barriers: Whose Business?

That very day, between talking with the Godfather and pitching to Vince Moore, Larry tripped over another departmental barrier. Why, he asked a buyer, were a few straightforward orders taking four days too many to transact? "It's simple," he was told. "Slumbertech's defense specialist is set in his ways and will only deal with this kind of material on Fridays. The orders were in on a Monday, but we knew nothing would happen at the other end for four days." All of which got Larry to thinking about his flowcharts again. There was a time when he would have minded his own business once Purchasing was off the hook of accountability. But why should Retrospace's cycle times be hamstrung because a vendor couldn't or wouldn't keep up?

Later that day, another tangle was plopped on Larry's desk: a change order from the projects. The microclock order for Retrospace's long-term "Big Green" VM had been cut again, and he was going to have to hash out the changes with Slumbertech.

Suddenly, a light bulb clicked on in Larry's head, illuminating the link between vendor response time and the number of annoying change orders. He asked Dick Hyman to analyze this matter. "I'll get you the data," said Hyman, "but I can tell you here and now that the longer the vendor takes, the farther into the future the projects have to forecast. The truth is that they're not too good at long-range forecasting, so they cover themselves with a general order and correct it later when reality is clearer and closer to hand. It happens all the time. The best way to cut down on change orders is to cut the time between request and delivery."

Within five minutes, Larry was on the phone to Bob Landon. "Bob," he began, "remember three years back, when Retrospace was deep into its quality program and Slumbertech agreed to conform to our quality specs?"

"How could I forget?" said Bob. "After all, accomplishing that task amounted to a quality program for Slumbertech. In case you're interested, our ability to deliver your kind of quality at low price is still the best in the business. That's why I was so disappointed when you canceled an order a few months back."

"Then I don't think that what I'm about say will make your day, Bob. The problem isn't quality. Yours *is* the best. But our cycle times are way too long. We're working on various ways to eliminate the hassles that prolong those cycle times. For instance, I'm willing to devise an order format that meshes with your own internal systems. But what Retrospace needs are vendors who can respond to our orders fast. Faster than before. Faster than what sounds reasonable. Faster tomorrow than today. Retrospace hasn't much choice, and I'll bet Slumbertech hasn't either."

"How fast is 'faster than sounds reasonable'?" asked Bob before Larry took permanent possession of the soapbox.

"Well, in VMs, you seem comfortable with a 12-week delivery cycle," replied Larry. "Those days are over, I'm afraid.

Off the top of my head, I'd say 4 weeks would do the trick."
Larry paused to get Bob's response, but there was none.
"Anyway," Larry continued, "I'm about to go upstairs and
sell a short-cycle-time program to the divisional VP. If he
asks me for ideas, and he will, I'm going to tell him that
Retrospace must insist on short, shorter, shortest response
times from its vendors. Whatever the VP says, this part of
Retrospace Purchasing is going to make short cycle time part
of its requirements for vendor contracts."

"Thanks. I really needed that."

"Sorry, Bob," said Larry. "Gotta go upstairs. I'll talk to you
again soon, of course."

Larry replaced the receiver and gathered his flowcharts
and notes. He was so eager to see what the next step would
be that he ignored the red light on his telephone signaling an
incoming call. It'll keep, he thought as he headed for the
stairs with big things on his mind.

Interfacing Solution:
The Crossfunctional Team

Some important news awaited Larry upstairs. After mulling
over his talk with Larry and conferring with Marv Allen,
Vince Moore had decided to create a "divisional interface
team," made up of middle managers from each department.
The team's purpose was to identify and overcome barriers
which in themselves might be small, but whose consequences
for the company as a whole were quite large. The team's
long-range objective was to refine a single process within the
division and a single-process culture in which employees at
all levels would forsake their parochial mindset for the
greater good. Hearing this announcement in Vince Moore's
office, Larry was struggling with its textbookish vocabulary
when the VP looked him straight in the eye.

"Since we have in our midst one manager who's gotten a leg

up on this kind of thinking," said Moore, "it's logical to make that person the head of the new team. Larry, stand up."

Bridging the Midmanagement Power Gap at Retrospace: Three Lessons

The incoming call that Larry had decided to ignore as he left for his meeting was from Jack Betters in New York. Jack, an editor at a major business publishing house, had met Larry during the recent management conference.

Like other attendees, Jack had discovered how important cycle time thinking had become for middle management, and ever since, he had been assembling notes for a book on that subject. Shopping around for possible sources at that conference, during which you, he, and the executive from Atlanta had dined out together, Jack had taken an instant liking to Larry because of his outspoken comments and obvious sense of frustration. Here, he thought, was an unfolding case history with real instructional potential.

With Larry's okay, Jack had decided to track the young purchasing manager's attempts to identify problems and implement change at Retrospace. Like most of Jack's contacts, Larry doubted that his example was of any importance, but he was admittedly pleased by such professional attention. The plan was for Jack to call Orange County every few months for an update. He seldom got through, however, because Larry was usually buried by his responsibilities as divisional interface team leader. Jack bided his time, kept notes, and waited for results.

Although he kept dutifully abreast of the business press, Jack noted no mention of big changes at Retrospace over ensuing months. But at last, in a lengthy conversation with Larry, he got an earful. During the customary telephone preliminaries, Jack could tell from his tone that Larry's sense of discovery was alive and well despite the extra burden he'd shouldered.

Jack, of course, had his eye on future book sales. "What I'd like to know," he said to Larry after a few minutes' chat, "is whether you or your team have acquired any important practical insights since you attacked cycle times in Retrospace."

Larry had been expecting such a question, of course. "I can give you three lessons I've learned that ought to be chiseled in stone over the doorway," he said.

"The first is that to manage time effectively, a company has to adopt the proper mindset.

"The second is that *every employee* has got to look at the company's overall activities as one single, seamless business process within which she or he has a role to play, not a bunch of disconnected subprocesses.

"The third is that implementing the right remedial steps is a crossfunctional process which requires a handpicked team with members from various disciplines."

"Details, please."

The Importance of Cultural Commitment

"Well," said Larry, "as to mindset: It's clear that living by short cycle times is a major change for most people. Within any company, therefore, the change should occur on as large a scale as possible. But it can't be expected to sweep through a company without a lot of commitment and direction from above. Looking back, I realize that my efforts in Purchasing grabbed the attention of my superior, who grabbed the attention of his superior, and so on up to the top. If that hadn't happened, Retrospace would probably have seen no more than a few improvements in my own section.

Adopting the Business Process View

"Now to that second point: looking at everything we do as business processes. Although I wondered what was wrong with my department, I'd never seriously considered the way my people were subloops of a larger activity. That truth is so obvious that few managers think about it on the job, much less apply it. Once I started to consider what happened before or after my department performed its task, I realized I couldn't operate in a departmental vacuum. Each business process in this company is interconnected from the moment a customer expresses a need until we satisfy that need by delivering the end product.

"To get this point across to my people in Purchasing, I distributed a chart which contrasted our outdated method of looking at the business as a series of disjointed organizational *functions*—marketing, manufacturing, engineering, and so forth—with a new method in which the business was expressed as a series of connected, sequential processes—order entry, scheduling, materials obtained (our own baliwick), production, and delivery [*as shown below*].

"Like most companies, Retrospace is organized functionally, with each step in the process headed by a competent specialist. But if those specialists have not approached the business as a single process, there are bound to be walls between functions—high walls. I pointed out that we didn't have to

AN OUTDATED METHOD: DISJOINTED ORGANIZATION FUNCTIONS

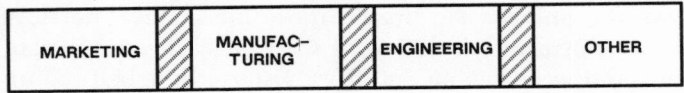

THE NEW METHOD: INTERCONNECTED BUSINESS PROCESSES

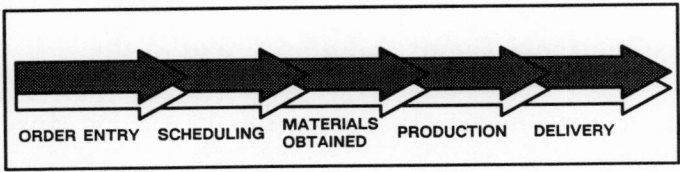

Business as a process.

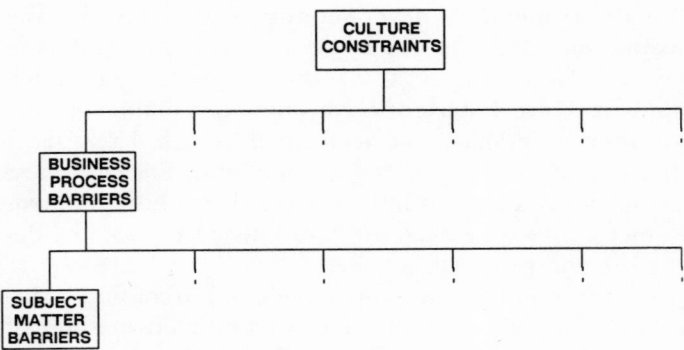

Understanding hierarchical barrier relationships.

change the organizational structure, only the business processes and the interfaces between them, so that we function
as a seamless team.

"Another thing I made sure that my people understood
was the hierarchical nature of barriers [*as shown above*]. At
our level, we were faced with a number of obstacles that were
endemic to our specialty. Above those, but related to them,
of course, were barriers that existed as part of the company's
general business process. Those, in turn, were part of an
overall cultural viewpoint that could only be altered by top-
down effort.

"Now, the only way to breach those hierarchical barriers
was to set up teams to deal with them at each appropriate
level within the make/market effort. I started the ball rolling
in Purchasing, and the thing just grew from there."

Crossfunctional Teams: Empowerment at the Midmanagerial Level

"I take it, then, that that is where your third point, crossfunctional action, comes in," prompted Jack.

"Absolutely right!" answered Larry. "By identifying the
barriers in my own bailiwick, I saw that my actions had a

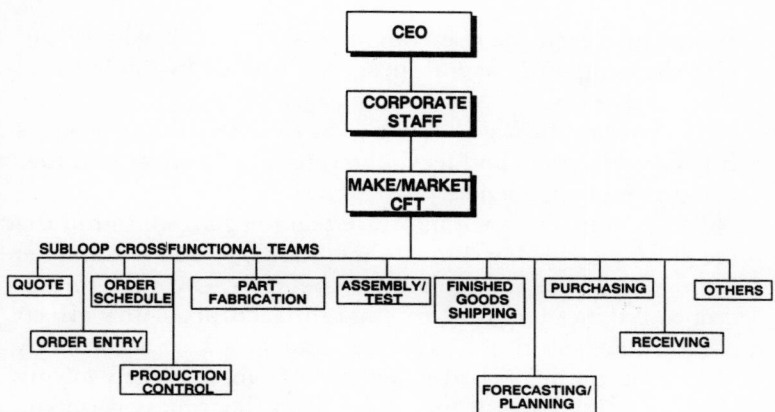

Typical make/market teams.

whopping impact on other areas of the company such as manufacturing, shipping, and inventory control, but I realized that as a middle manager I was not empowered to carry improvements to their logical conclusion. Neither was my counterpart in some other division — design, for instance — whose decisions could impact *my* effectiveness. If Retrospace was to deal with problems as part of a single business process, it obviously needed interdisciplinary teams [*as shown above*] that would sit down and discuss barriers in terms of their broad impact. That's exactly what it got."

Making a Crossfunctional Team Work

"How does a company put together a crossfunctional team like yours?" asked Jack. "I can appreciate the concept in principle, but in the real world, every member of your team must have had his or her own departmental axe to grind."

"Well, it wasn't easy," Larry admitted. "I should know, because I was the unlucky individual who had to interface with the various departments and make the team work. There's no trade secret formula for choosing the right participants except that each member ought to see the necessity of putting the company's overall process ahead of his or her individual concerns.

"After that, the big challenge was to isolate the truly cross-functional barriers and leave the rest to be dealt with in their respective departments.

"When our divisional interface team began, we found that the spirit was willing, but the methodology was weak. Then Marv Allen—I've mentioned him before—sent me a formatting tool that allowed us to diagram each problem's effects, causes, and substitute processes and attack it accordingly. With that, the team had a *methodology* for problem solving. I'll send you a copy of the cause-effect diagram if you like."

"I like. Thanks."

"Here's how it worked: We identified an unacceptable effect—our long dock-to-stock cycle times, for example. Then we asked ourselves, 'What are the major causes of that effect?' We noted two biggies: In Receiving, orders were stopped and parts were being rejected. Why? We worked back from there and found a slew of causes. Aha!

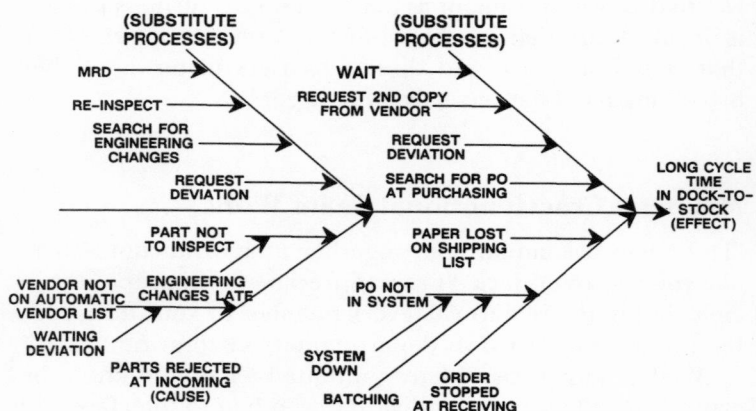

Cause-effect diagram.

"Once we had isolated causes of the problem, it was essential to characterize them: Which were crossfuntional problems, and which were better dealt with inside a single department? We also defined the substitute process being applied as subject matter "aspirin," to compensate for the causes versus solving the fundamental business problem.

"Our team adopted a guideline for individual managers that said, 'When you hit a barrier, could you remove it if your job depended on it?' If the answer to that question was yes, the barrier wasn't crossfunctional. If the answer was no, the team knew the problem was our baby. I'll send you a copy of the procedure we established for our teams.

BARRIER CHARACTERIZATION PROCESS: CHARACTERIZE BARRIERS & ASSIGN OWNERSHIP

- Anyone can bring barrier to team for characterization.

- Classify barriers as subject matter, business process, or culture to put them in perspective.

- Use cause-effect diagram or other methods to determine relationship of barrier to process.
  - Cause-effect relationships
  - Substitute processes

- Stop cause-effect analysis at the generic business process barriers.

- Quantify impact of barrier: first, on cycle time; then, if easily accomplished, of first-pass yield, cost, revenue, and resources.

- Determine if barrier can be handled internally to crossfunctional team by asking the question: "If your job depended on it, could you resolve the barrier?" If yes, then rank-assign ownership, and enter resolution stage. If no, escalate the barrier solution task.

- Each crossfunctional team should have the right to assign ownership outside team to peers and their reports.

- If external, take to total make/market crossfunctional team for ranking and ownership assignment.

"Now remember," Larry continued, "all this team effort and methodology would have been for nothing if upper management had not empowered us to act. The team acquired the *skills* to solve problems, but without the *responsibility* to act, which we got from upper management, we'd have gone nowhere. It wasn't easy for the Godfather—oops! I mean my boss—to hand over that kind of authority to a team consisting mostly of outsiders for the good of the general cause."

Crossfunctional Problem Solving: An Example

"You sound pretty enthusiastic," observed Jack. "Give me an example of your team's accomplishments."

"I'll give you my personal favorite," replied Larry. "You recall how frustrated I got about being measured on purchase price variance—frustrated enough to try to get that criterion junked altogether. No dice. But our team *has* gotten purchase price variance into perspective. It's still in place, but it's only one of several measurements in Purchasing.

"The team talked to people from Manufacturing who demonstrated how a 'good buy' in Purchasing could rupture the process in their area. Because Retrospace now looked at a problem as part of the overall business process, we could implement measurements in one division that helped the process in another. In Purchasing, we added new criteria for the selection of vendors: responsiveness measured in days, quality measured in parts per million. It was our way of making vendors conform to our standards, not their own. We resolved to quit doing business altogether with unresponsive vendors, no matter how good their prices were. By the same token, our new criteria allow us to use some very pricey vendors if their speed and quality justify the cost.

"What is interesting is that the consequences of our new mindset have spread to our vendors, whether they like it or not. And they have gotten results. Have you been talking with Bob Landon in Slumbertech about that, as I suggested?"

"Ever since you gave me the tip several months ago," said Jack. "But tell me, Larry, what has this crossfunctional odyssey done for you personally?"

Larry laughed. "Well," he said, "I can now use words like *interface* and *mindset* without wincing. But seriously, when I first challenged Retrospace's purchasing practices, it was because I smelled smoke somewhere in our company and I didn't want my own butt to get burned. I never suspected it was my mission to do anything more than make Purchasing a more sensible, fun place to work. My original reason for switching out of Engineering was that Purchasing was more fun; that's still my key measurement of a job.

"When I suddenly found myself heading up the company interface team, I was uneasy about the career consequences for Larry Coile. The team experience has been challenging, but I missed Purchasing and wondered if I'd ever get back to my old duties."

"Did you?"

"Not exactly, because our divisional team has been a rousing success. Our vice president, Vince Moore, who is no fool, saw to it that it caught the eye of Retrospace's top management. There's a plan afoot in the boardroom to fan out the sort of results we got into companywide crossfunctional teams so that every warm body in Retrospace's make/market function will operate by that seamless business process mentality I told you about. ('seamless business process' has lately become the in-phrase around here.) Since I was the guy who'd 'started all this'—those were Moore's words—I'm gonna get offered the new team leader slot.

"Whoa! I thought. Starting all this has indeed made me interested in the broader view, but I do have Larry Coile's future to consider. What will I do after the team reaches its objective? To make a long story short, I'm willing to accept the new task on the condition that when the work is done, I can return to my desk in Purchasing. It should be more fun than ever there, now that we don't operate in a vacuum. As for the future, I doubt if my crossfunctional work has hurt my chances as a possible VP of Purchasing, to put it mildly. But that's a daydream I'd like you to keep off the record, Jack."

"Okay, Larry. I'll keep mum in exchange for your cause-effect diagram and the team rules you promised. You may be seeing that in my book someday. Thanks. And good luck!

"Now I've got to get an update from Bob Landon."

"Do that," said Larry with a chuckle. "But don't say I sent you. I don't know if we're still friends or not!"

Jack's Checklist:
Key Barriers Encountered by Larry Coile

1. Not perceiving business as a process, resulting in significant barriers between elements of the organization.

2. Attempting to solve problems without the use of cross-functional teams.

3. Cultural barriers: incorrect measurements and controls, in particular purchase price variance as an overriding measure of purchasing effectiveness.

4. Preoccupation with subject matter issues versus business processes and cultural issues.

3

PTS Meets PDQ

Responsiveness Versus Performance to Schedule

There was never a moment when Bob Landon and Larry Coile were not friendly, although their professional relationship had had its ups and downs lately. It reached its lowest point several months back when, after canceling an important microclock order, Larry had added insult to injury by insisting that Slumbertech respond to orders more rapidly or risk losing all of its business with Retrospace.

After that unpleasant telephone conversation, it sounded to Bob as though Larry "Short, Shorter, Shortest" Coile was on a corporate crusade. That, however, didn't entitle him to preach to infidels outside Retrospace. Furthermore, Larry's news couldn't have come at a worse time. Slumbertech was cleaning up after the big quake and Bob Landon had quite a few personal pieces to put back together.

Bob Landon was Slumbertech's western regional sales manager. His office was in downtown San Francisco, and he lived nearby in the Marina District in a small attached house he'd had the foresight to buy before prices went out of sight. Forty-four years old, a confirmed bachelor, physically fit, glib, and something of a ladies' man, he enjoyed a lifestyle that—until the earthquake, at any rate—was the envy of

Slumbertech's other sales managers. Elements of that lifestyle included *Cosmic*, a 28-foot Cape Dory berthed a few blocks from his house, and a red Porsche 944 Turbo tucked away in the garage below his living room. Bob had three nonplatonic "meaningful relationships" going to complement his interests in sailing, sports cars, and jazz.

The week of the quake, Bob had been spending evenings sorting his collection of vintage jazz records, which were neatly and lovingly stacked on the living room floor. When the earth began to move and Bob rushed home from work to assess the damage, he had to heave his front door open against a pile of Bluebird 78's which had migrated in a heap to the front hallway. The sight he beheld when he forced his way in was appalling: records and fragments thereof were everywhere, along with sundry scattered elements of the household. Ten days later, with the last aftershock come and gone, Bob was still crunching pieces of his shattered collection underfoot; he hadn't the heart to inventory the damage. There were plaster cracks everywhere, but his insurance would cover that sort of thing. Somehow, aside from a layer of stucco dust, the Porsche had emerged unscathed, but *Cosmic*, hauled out for repairs the week before, was a total loss.

Which is a long way of saying that at the time of Larry Coile's short, shorter, shortest call, Bob was about at his lowest point, psychologically speaking, in 19 years of selling for Slumbertech, although his worries were mostly nonprofessional.

Bob was an extrovert whose ability to chat people up made strangers treat him like an old friend after just a few minutes' acquaintance. But he seldom discussed his pre-Slumbertech background, about which he was very self-conscious, with anyone. If pressed, he would say that he had never finished college, but the truth was he had never attended at all. He had been drafted toward the end of the Vietnam war, and his service training had familiarized him with basic electronics and maintenance of high-tech equipment. A native of the Bay Area with no wish to move elsewhere, Bob had made a marriage of convenience when, after his discharge, he joined Slumbertech.

That move had worked out very well indeed. From the start, Bob was entirely comfortable with the vast line of electronic and electromechanical timers, fuses, meters, and test equipment that Slumbertech supplied to aerospace and commercial manufacturers. He also very quickly mastered the art of office politics and, best of all, proved entirely self-reliant, which was exactly what a regional sales manager had to be at Slumbertech. His sense of humor was a bit small for a sales manager. His ego, though, was characteristically big, but unlike so many of his similarly equipped peers, he felt perfectly secure about his abilities. Bob knew what other Slumbertekkies thought about him, and he agreed entirely: his job situation was just about ideal.

Precision: A Strategy for Success?

Slumbertech, headquartered in Chicago, did about a billion dollars' worth of business a year. The company was profitable, though its yearly growth rate, at 8 percent, was about two points behind competitors of similar size and seven behind the market's rate of expansion. Seven years earlier, the company's top management had developed a strategy for success that turned on high quality and reliable customer service. The objective was nothing less than the promise to supply products precisely as scheduled with a miss rate of no more than 2 percent. (At the time, Slumbertech, like most of its competitors, had poor process control and poorer predictability of delivery, and customers simply resigned themselves to such service as the cost of doing business.)

Raising the quality of Slumbertech's performance had been an arduous and expensive task involving wall-to-wall consultants, programs, and forced marches. But the goal eventually was reached, so when Bob told grousers like Larry Coile that Slumbertech's performance to schedule (PTS) was the best in the business, he wasn't kidding. And that applied across the entire product line. Furthermore, Slumbertech's prices were at or below their sloppier competitors'.

When On Time Is Not Enough

Growing up in a business whose watchwords were *confusion* and *complication*, Bob Landon had become adroit at managing his customers. As PTS improved at Slumbertech, he found he had a powerful new sales tool. Along with his regional counterparts in Chicago and New York, he capitalized on the company's improving PTS, telling customers that Slumbertech alone could restore some much-needed order and predictability to the industry. Because Slumbertech kept its promises to customers, Bob had been able to grow his business where predictability was more than a convenience: microclocks for example. Accordingly, he had successfully cultivated a large-scale relationship with Retrospace Industries, and although he'd been put through the wringer by its purchasing head at first, Bob had for five years accurately predicted and delivered an increasing volume of business with that customer.

And now look what's happened, he thought the morning after Larry Coile had lowered the boom. Good old disorganized Retrospace is reading us the riot act about the future, as though our low price, high quality, and precise delivery are things to be taken for granted. It particularly galled Bob to be outmaneuvered by a smaller outfit like Neptune, which had parlayed its smallness and speed into competitive clout. Right or wrong, Slumbertech had lost a nice chunk of business to a company with shamelessly high prices but quick response times. But Bob knew he really didn't have a convincing comeback. Did Larry say Neptune could deliver VM microclocks in 4 weeks? Slumbertech's schedule for that product was 12 weeks. If Neptune could do the job in a third of the time, perhaps the benefits to Retrospace were worth $4 a clock.

The Quick-Response Challenge

If Retrospace's gripe had been the only one of its kind, Bob could have rationalized it to himself and, in the next sales review, to his boss in Chicago. The trouble was that his top salesperson had lately lost two smaller commercial orders over the issue of quick response. One customer even wanted the contractual right to change the mix of the order within two weeks of delivery!

Learning of those setbacks, Bob had shrugged them off because the accounts were small potatoes and, anyway, commercial customers were forever making unreasonable demands because their markets changed so fast. But Retrospace was a 600-pound gorilla; a ponderous contractor not famous for quick turnaround, to put it mildly. When a 600-pound gorilla called for speed, even at a higher price, it sounded like the beginning of a major trend. Suddenly, Bob Landon had butterflies in his stomach. He told his secretary to hold all his calls and spent the rest of the day in conference with himself.

Isolating the Problem—Whose Problem?

Himself was all he had. Bob's boss, Vice President of Marketing Hal Burns, who lived in the ivory tower at "Ground Zero," Slumbertech's Chicago headquarters, believed that regional sales managers should be seen occasionally and heard only when they had something good to report. Such a policy looked okay on paper because it allowed his three regional subordinates to run their own show most of the time, but it cut both ways. Anyone in trouble had better not darken Burns's doorstep or cloud up a sales meeting unless she or he already had the solution to the problem.

Bob knew this from recent experience: during the last sales meeting, held in New York, he had reported the loss of the Retrospace microclock order. Burns had broken the awkward silence that followed, not with a question about what had caused the cancellation, but with this: "What are you doing to get that business back, Bob?" For once, Bob had been at a loss for words, and he knew his peers weren't going to come to his rescue. Burns let Bob twist in the wind for what seemed like an hour before changing the subject. Now, faced with two small cancellations over delivery times and Larry Coile's virtual ultimatum, he was really in the hot seat; but he knew better than to broach his misgivings about eroding orders until he had a positive plan for restoring the business.

First he had to isolate the problem. Sitting alone in his office late on Friday afternoon (the silence of the telephone was positively creepy at first), Bob got to the crux of the matter with surprising ease. The good news was that Marketing was not to blame for the erosion of orders. The bad news was that both the problem and its solution were beyond Marketing's range of effective action.

As Bob saw it, Slumbertech's single biggest weakness was its single greatest source of pride: performance to schedule.

The Myopia Barrier

In the seven years since consultants had made it the cornerstone of the company's survival strategy, PTS had acquired a reverential mystique at Slumbertech rivaled only by the laws of supply and demand and, possibly, the Ten Commandments. Top brass came by such reverence honestly. There was nothing shallow or trivial about the concept of delivering goods of superior quality at competitive prices, and indeed, the five-year ordeal of pulling the company out of the doldrums and up to that standard had burned out quite a few middle and upper managers: designers, marketers, manufacturing types, planners, the lot. But the company's secret weapon, and the thing that seemed most elusive during those years of struggle, was the issue of predictability. Slumbertech's goal was to be able to deliver as promised *precisely on schedule*.

During the struggle to achieve that standard, Bob and other salespeople had often found themselves out on a limb, having guaranteed a customer a delivery date only to be told by Manufacturing (which had determined the date in the first place) that there would be delays. Taking the heat for a few missed deliveries was among Bob's most unpleasant memories. But meanwhile, Slumbertekkies from the CEO on down were determined to make PTS work. If Manufacturing couldn't be reasoned with, Burns or the CEO would designate a lagging order an emergency and pull whatever strings it took to get it out the door as promised. For a few horrendous months at Slumbertech, emergencies outnumbered ordinary business.

Eventually, as the bugs were worked out of the system and the company accumulated inventory as a hedge against unexpected orders, Slumbertech's production control people learned the art of accurate prediction. Give them the specs for a potential order and they could predict with astonishing precision how long it would take to deliver it at tip-top quality and a competitive price. For the last two years, Marketing had been exploiting the sexiness of that combination and Bob had been able to kiss his late-night headaches good-bye.

Being the Best of the Worst

There was a catch, of course. Effective performance to schedule required Slumbertech salespeople to manage their customers. (*Massage* was the word Bob used, but not to their faces). The trick was to persuade customers that Slumbertech's self-determined production cycle time was acceptable for all concerned. Bob could usually sell that concept. Production and delivery cycles throughout the business were either chaotic or interminable, and the very ability to keep delivery promises packed a wallop—until lately; until guys like Larry Coile began to intimate that high quality, low price, and precise delivery had lost their sex appeal.

By the time Bob had put this much together, it was getting dark. He now badly wanted to make a couple of calls, but they'd have to wait until Monday.

That weekend, he took his mind off the disappearing orders by sweeping up three plastic bags worth of shattered 78-rpm records for the rubbish ("It could've been worse"), picking up several compact disc reissues of some of the lost music ("no more 78s!"), driving his 944 very fast out to Half Moon Bay to check out an advertised 14-foot day sailer ("I can afford to lose a boat like this"), and taking a significant other to hear Nancy Wilson at the Venetian Room ("Life goes on"). All in all, it was a very satisfying weekend. As things turned out, this was the last such weekend Bob would enjoy for quite a while.

Bright and early Monday morning, Bob began to ask questions. He was punching Larry Coile's telephone number when something made him hang up before the call could go through. Why should he voluntarily play into Retrospaces' hands by abjectly asking Larry for more details? He could imagine the conversation well enough: He would repeat Slumbertech's desire to continue its good relationship with Retrospace and once again point out his company's stellar performance to schedule. Larry would reply that the key word was *schedule*: the delivery dates were set by the supplier, not the customer. If the opposite were the case, could Slumbertech still offer competitive prices and high quality? Could Slumbertech cut its delivery time by two-thirds? No? Then there was a problem....

Quick Response: Is It That Important?

Bob decided it was probably a wise move not to talk to Larry. Maybe Retrospace's sudden infatuation with lightning response was a one-shot deal. That prompted him to spend the rest of the morning telephoning the purchasing directors of Slumbertech's five other top customers, asking in the name of customer satisfaction if they foresaw any future problems with Slumbertech's PTS. No problems, said three. But the other two, both defense contractors, responded differently. Both explained that they were implementing just-in-time programs and accordingly were under pressure to minimize inventories and liberate the cash tied up therein. "When we try to do that," said one, "we'll surely make mistakes in our planning and we're going to have to backfill quickly. So yes, speedy response will be more and more essential to us. I hope Slumbertech will be able to move with the times. God knows *we're* trying!"

By the end of the morning, the message had come through loud and clear: Slumbertech had a problem that went far beyond Retrospace. Without a doubt, the company would soon be in trouble with other key customers unless it could respond faster. Bob spent his lunch hour trying to figure out the next step. There was no next step, he decided, at least so far as Marketing was concerned.

Foraging Across Divisional Lines

Putting Marketing out of his mind for a while, Bob put in a call to Richard Hicks, Slumbertech's production control manager in Chicago. Inevitably, Richard (who never went by Rich, Rick, Dick, or any other diminutive) was on another line, but within the hour he returned Bob's call: "What can your humble servants in Manufacturing do for you?" Richard's opener made Bob feel as though he were talking to the front lines.

"A few things have come up lately that look like trouble," Bob began, "and I want to get your input before developing a plan of attack."

"Shouldn't you go through marketing channels? I doubt if anything I could say would be helpful."

Bob was suddenly reminded of what a klutz Richard was at the art of politics. He hadn't even heard the question and he was already backing away. Nothing to do but state the case. "I think you might be exactly the person I want," Bob persisted.

"But I just realized this is something to discuss in person. I'll be in your office at 8 a.m. tomorrow, if that's okay."

"Now you've made me really curious! Right. See you tomorrow. But make it, uh, 8:35." Nothing like being precise, thought Bob.

The Mindset Barrier

Bob kept his appointment. To him, the worst part was that the date took place at "Ground Zero." Even without the red-eye flights and long limo rides that were a part of every visit, Bob wouldn't have worked in the Windy City for twice his salary. He was careful, however, to keep this sentiment to himself lest it influence the choice of Slumbertech's next Marketing VP. The company was not legendary for the creature comforts and decor it provided its employees, and Bob had never realized how many shades of grey there were until his first visit to Ground Zero.

Richard Hicks, who looked like Woody Allen with a crewcut, got off the phone promptly at 8:35 and waved Bob inside his office. The room reminded Bob of most others in the company: scuffed, institutional furniture, stark, uncurtained venetian blinds, and the obligatory glass ashtray bearing the company logo. The surface of Richards' desk was ringed with the circular stains of a hundred coffee cups. His ashtray had apparently not been emptied since the Carter administration and the entire office reeked of stale cigarette smoke, a touch that Bob, as a fitness freak, found almost claustrophobic.

For his part, Richard Hicks had absolutely no inkling about what might prompt a regional sales manager to fly halfway across America to talk, so Bob outlined how his office had lost two commercial contracts and had had a third canceled by the embattled Retrospace because Slumbertech could not respond quickly enough. He also reviewed the disturbing phone conversations he'd had of late. "Neptune was able to supply Retrospace in four weeks—a third of our quoted time. I'm sure this kind of thing is going to get worse unless we can deliver faster. Since I have no control over production schedules, I thought I'd better talk to you."

Richard kept a poker face. "Well, let's start at the beginning. Do you have a copy of the canceled contract with Retrospace?" Bob did, and he handed it over. After scanning it a couple of minutes, Richard looked up again. "It's a very easy matter to understand," he said. "You said Neptune could turn out these gizmos in 4 weeks against our 12? Well, I don't have any data, but I'll guarantee you Neptune's quality standards aren't in our ballpark. No one's are, actually. They're faster, but our overall reliability is better—and cheaper. Retrospace knows that. We chose not to sacrifice price and quality for raw speed. There's more than one way to be competitive in this business."

"You said it," answered Bob. "And Neptune just outcompeted us, despite our quality and price advantage. They define PTS differently than we do. They move faster, with a higher reject rate I guess, and they charge more. Their PTS is certainly lower than ours, but their short delivery times are vital to some customers, and all the signs point to a trend here. But wait a minute. Did you just imply that Slumbertech is potentially as fast as Neptune?"

"Not potentially. As fast, right now, if we wanted to be. We don't, though, because our PTS would drop. We can't afford that."

The back of Bob's neck was getting very warm, but his voice remained calm: "Since I have to sell our stuff, I know just how important price, quality, and predictability are in landing contracts. We've pursued PTS with a passion for years, and it's paid off. But we've been so smug about our PTS that we've missed the signals from the marketplace. What Retrospace and the rest of these guys are saying is that speed counts as a measurement. What good is it to be able to deliver 100 percent on time, if the deadline we prescribe is eight weeks longer than our customer's deadline? And anyway, does it make sense to have cycle times three times as long as Neptune's if our PTS is only, say, 10 percent higher than theirs?"

"Look: I know something about cycle time management." said Richard. He rooted in an overstuffed shelf adjacent to his desk, pulled out a book, and handed it to Bob. "Take that with you. It makes a strong case for shortening cycle times. If quick turnaround were the only consideration, we could out-Neptune Neptune. But that's *not* the only consideration at Slumbertech. We've rebuilt our whole manufacturing rationale around PTS. It's the key element in our culture. Your boss measures it. *My* boss measures it. *Their* bosses measure it. Should we chuck it because we can't be all things to all customers? There's not one warm body in senior management who thinks so, not one. Anybody at our level who rocks the boat — and I have a feeling you're looking to do that — will get exactly nowhere. Except maybe out of Slumbertech. Better you than me."

"Before I've even asked, you're saying you won't help shorten Manufacturing's cycle times because it wouldn't look good. What about saving some of the business that'll go somewhere else? What about getting new contracts because we can match Neptune's speed? Wouldn't that look good, even to the people on top?"

"It might do you some good, I don't know," admitted Richard. "In the short run, reducing our turnaround time will make me look very bad, PTS-wise, and that's the measurement that counts here."

Bob was up against a stone wall. "Before I go, one last question," he said. "What constitutes the difference between Neptune's 4-week response time and our 12 weeks?"

Bob got the answer he expected: "The time and effort it takes to ensure the highest possible quality. We don't make promises we can't keep, like some others in the business. If we say 12 weeks, we are certain we can deliver virtually the entire order as promised."

"Gotta run, Richard. Thanks for listening." Out in the hallway, Bob headed not for the main entrance, but for the manufacturing floor. There he hunted out Ernie Page, Director of Manufacturing, and made a date to meet him for lunch in the cafeteria.

More Foraging for Cycle Time Barriers

When the two met in the cafeteria, Ernie chose today's special: beef burritos; Bob settled for a fruit salad. After the two had sat down and exchanged a few pleasantries, Bob got to the point: "Listen, I'm hitting a few marketing snags because we can't get stuff to customers fast enough to meet their schedules. So I gotta ask you how come it takes 12 weeks to manufacture microclocks?"

Ernie's eyes widened. He gasped and gulped a mouthful of water. The burrito's red-hot chilis and Bob's question had both taken him off guard. "What do you mean 12 weeks?" he finally asked, fanning the air in front of his face. "We build microclocks in 10 days! You think we're incompetent or something?"

"Then how come I have to quote 12 weeks to my customers?"

"Oh, I see what you're getting at. Well, the business process runs 12 weeks, I guess. For instance, it takes about a week to enter an order. That's not bad, but Production Control only gives us the schedule once a month, so on average, 2 weeks are tied up there. The actual manufacturing runs only 10 working days, which translates to 2 weeks. It probably takes a week to inspect and another week to pack and ship."

Bob had been taking notes. "That's 7 weeks maximum, not 12," he said.

"Well jeez, the rest is, you know, pad."

"Pad?"

"Padding. A little extra time in the schedule for us to correct unexpected mistakes or unusual stoppages. Because we guarantee delivery by a certain date, we have to be prepared to overcome unforeseen setbacks and still make the deadline."

"You call 5 or 6 weeks of pad 'a little'?"

"Well, a little here and a little there. For instance, the quality-control guys have some elbow room in the schedule. So do the people in shipping. So do I."

"A little here and a little there adds up to a very long response time to customers."

"But that's the only way we have to guarantee PTS. Hey, I just work here. I gave you a straight answer about how long the actual manufacturing takes. You have to be realistic about the whole process."

After Ernie had polished off his volatile lunch and returned to Manufacturing, Bob lingered over a second cup of coffee. Mindset, he thought. During Slumbertech's quality drive, *mindset* had been a positive term denoting the cultural dedication and consensus by which Slumbertekkies would put themselves back on top. Now, it seemed, the PTS mindset looked more like indoctrination: it had blinded middle and upper managers to its drawbacks and apparently numbed their fear of the competition. After half a day at headquarters, Bob still felt those butterflies in his stomach.

Returning to the Bay Area, he had the better part of a month to think about what, if anything, a sales manager was supposed to do about all this. He was scheduled to return to Chicago for Slumbertech's next sales meeting, which would also be attended by his regional counterparts and the Marketing VP. At the very least, he thought, he would have to say something at that meeting about his disturbing encounter with Retrospace. But his last meeting, at which the cool Hal Burns had waited for ideas that never came, had made Bob chary about sticking his neck out.

Strength in Numbers: A Makeshift Support System

Ten days before the meeting, Bob called the regional sales managers in Chicago and New York, inviting them to meet with him a day early. If neither of those guys had any anxiety about shortening cycle times, he'd pick up the dinner tab, get a good night's sleep, and do nothing to disturb Slumbertech's complacency.

Nine days later, Bob took his two peers to dinner at La Français in Wheeling, his favorite dining spot in the Chicago area. There, looking across the dinner table, Bob remembered that the regional managers were known by company salespeople as the Marx Brothers, and he had to admit there was something to the name. George Finlay, out of New York, made a good Groucho: he had black bushy eyebrows, wisecracked constantly, and favored huge, expensive cigars that were as much a prop as a vice. By way of contrast, Ted Mara, his Chicago counterpart, was a reflective, fair-haired guy whose sweet, almost shy disposition charmed clients: Harpo. Bob's irreverence and way with the ladies let him pass for a Chico. But appearances aside, these three were, like their original namesakes, an energetic, competitive, and formidable team. They had one other thing in common: as salespeople, they identified with their customers almost as much as with dear old Slumbertech, so they were not reticent about going to bat for their favorite accounts.

Barrier Removal: Old Tricks of the Trade

When the wisecracks and trade talk had died down, Bob related his misgivings about changes in the market and asked George and Ted if they had run into problems like his own. "Just one," answered Ted. "I lost an order because the customer needed quicker response than I could promise. I didn't think much about it at the time, although I'm not looking forward to tomorrow's meeting."

"No problems at my end," said George. "I've heard that Neptune is picking up market share here and there, although it hasn't affected me. But there is one thing.... Okay, I'll tell you both, but this is off the record. I had an order two months back that required 6 weeks' response instead of our customary 12."

"What did you do?" asked Bob.

"I filled the order."

"You can't do that."

"I did it on a one-time-only basis. I took the order and immediately acted as if it was an emergency. I went into Production Control, waved my cigar under Richard Hicks' nose, and said that our future relationship with the customer depended on expediting this particular order. It was a great performance. Then I also pulled in a few markers in Manufacturing, where they agreed to expedite the entire order and run it through on a red-tag priority basis. And listen to this: I needed six weeks. Those bastards got it out in five!"

"But how did you get around the PTS mindset?"

"This is the part that's confidential. I backdated the order form by 6 weeks so it looked like a regular 12-week order that had gotten into trouble. That way nobody up above would question the hot-lotting. Everybody from Production Control through Manufacturing was covered. It's a weird system when you've gotta camouflage the fact that you're fast. It *has* made me think, Bob, but what are we supposed to do? I can't play the emergency game again; I used up all my favors on that one account."

"Well," said Bob, "we've got a strategy meeting staring us in the face tomorrow morning. Should we start something we can't finish? You know Burns' old routine: 'Don't bring me your problems without your solutions.' The solution to all this is for Marketing to use whatever muscle it has to break the PTS mindset at Slumbertech. I'll make the pitch, but you guys have to back me up. Now I guess I'd better switch from brandy to coffee."

Bob picked up the tab, but the good night's sleep he'd been hoping for was out of the question.

Taking a Stand: Speed-to-Market Versus Status Quo

The next morning's meeting was the first in which, contrary to custom, he stressed the dire impact of bad news rather than soft-pedaling it. When Hal Burns, growing restless, asked the inevitable question, Bob firmly declined to produce a "solution" until George and Ted had given their reports. When it was George's turn, Bob was astonished to hear him tell the entire hot-lot story, even the part about the fudged paperwork.

Then Bob spoke for the group: "We wouldn't have made an issue of the market's acceleration without thinking the matter through and deciding what needs to be done. The answer here is that Slumbertech must develop a new brand of PTS in which our schedule is determined by the customer's requirements, not our own comfort levels. In the case of aerospace products like microclocks, we have to get our PTS from 12 weeks to 4. As you can see from George's hot-lot story, it probably could be done.

"My own informal survey indicates that our 12-week response time is more than 40 percent pad. Without the pad, we could probably deliver 85 percent of every microclock order inside seven weeks. I can tell you with full confidence that companies like Retrospace, who have their own tie-ups and back-filling to do on any project, would rather have us deliver 85 percent in a hurry than 100 percent in twice the time. At the moment, we're not meeting Retrospace even half way because we keep chasing the Holy Grail of perfect PTS. The world is not perfect, especially in the aerospace industry. My guess is that the day we reach 100 percent PTS is the day we'll turn out the lights at Slumbertech for the last time. The answer? The three of us have talked about that. We hate to say so, but Marketing has got to force the rest of Slumbertech to come to its senses and revise its PTS measurements."

Pushing Change Upward

Burns swiveled back in his armchair and looked successively at each of his regional managers, then clipped the gold-filled pencil he always used into a pocket of his attaché case before speaking in measured tones: "You guys outnumber me, and you've prepared your ambush very well. But as to the 'answer' you're prescribing, you've done nothing more than redefine the problem in order to get off your respective hooks. Let's say you're right about PTS. The 'answer' is the method by which Slumbertech successfully changes its PTS. These pads you talk about are in Operations, not Marketing. Vince Harris got to be Operations VP by championing the current PTS system when it was unpopular. He and the CEO have complete faith in it.

"As for what to do about the matter: You know me well enough to realize that it's not my style to be dictatorial, so I'm certainly not going to cross swords with Vince Harris about the way his people may be ruining Slumbertech. Your only choice at this point is to work out informally some changes inside Operations with guys like Hicks; it looks to me as though Production Control is the open sesame to the whole scheduling issue.

"Here's what I'll do: If you get Operations to change its PTS in the name of winning more business—and if you actually win more business—I'll take the heat in the front office. Make no mistake, there will be plenty of heat. If business goes up and PTS drops, Marketing will look good but Operations will look bad. You can hardly blame people over there for objecting. I'll cover for you at the top because, in the final analysis, the CEO won't object to more business. But the effort is up to you. Now the CEO and I have got to catch a plane for Boston. Sorry." Burns snapped the clasps of his attaché case and rose.

Breaking Divisional Barriers

When the conference room door had whooshed shut behind him, the Marx Brothers began to feel a bit reckless. "What the hell are we supposed to do now?" snapped George as he poured the dregs of the coffee into his cup. "Overwhelm Production Control?"

"Exactly," replied Bob. "There are three of us and only one of him." George and Bob both decided to put in one more day at Ground Zero.

By 10:00 the next morning, Vince Harris was becoming downright sore at his inability to get Richard Hicks on the phone. He knew his production control manager was around; he had said "hello" first thing this morning while passing his office. Since then, however, Hicks's door had been closed and he was apparently not acknowledging Harris's telephone callback request. Harris needed a printout from Hicks for a presentation he intended to make that evening. By 11:15, having lost all his patience, Harris decided to take matters into his own hands.

He noticed that the production control secretary made herself scarce as he approached Hicks's office. From behind the closed door came the sound of angry voices; two or three loudly declaiming at once. As a career manufacturing manager, Harris was hardly straitlaced, but there was no excuse for such commotion in Ground Zero's white-collar sanctuary. Then he heard a thud. Had someone kicked something— Hicks, perhaps? Without hesitating, Harris opened the door and barged in on the melee. The noise level dropped almost to zero the instant he crossed the threshold. Hicks, seated behind his cluttered desk, and Slumbertech's three regional sales managers, standing in various attitudes of agitation, all froze as they recognized the Operations VP. An in-flight wastebasket someone had booted bounced off a side wall and rolled against his feet.

"What is the meaning of this?" demanded Harris. "Or am I interrupting a private chat?"

There are times in everyone's life when a great deal hangs by a chance remark or an accident of timing. Looking back, Bob Landon would recognize that Harris's interruption of the shouting match in Hicks's office was one of those moments. And, priding himself on his ability to massage managers and customers alike, Bob would wonder if a sixth sense had directed his response. That would be hindsight. At the time the door flew open, Bob was simply embarrassed by the sudden, incriminating silence and knew from his army training that the best defense was an attack.

"The three of us are here on our own behalf," Bob said to Harris. "Nobody sent us. Each of us is losing orders because Slumbertech is simply too slow. Tried and true customers are turning to other, faster vendors. It's getting serious and it's going to get worse.

"George, Ted, and I have been twisting Richard's arm—not literally, you understand—to eliminate the fail-safe pads built into Operations. They help you meet your PTS goals, but they're killing our business. Richard says planning is none of our affair, and technically speaking, he's right. He also refuses to cater to marketing guys in any way that will make Manufacturing look bad.

"We were trying to get Richard to cut cycle times in one area, microclocks, to prove to the company that we can get more business by cutting response time even at the expense of high PTS. The bottom line is business, after all, not PTS ratings. Or is it?"

Vince Harris had had many occasions to thank his lucky stars he was not a marketeer, and this was one of them. Hotshot salespeople always blamed everyone else for their lapses, and their big egos made them disrespectful of the work of others. He decided to take charge of this fiasco: "Let me straighten you out on turnaround time. Manufacturing is three times—*three times*—as quick today as it was five years ago. We've cut our production cycle from a month to 10 days. Blame somebody else if you can't sell our products."

"Mr. Harris," replied Bob, taking a formal tack, "over the last five years, the turnaround times I've been given by Production Control have hardly dropped at all; 10 percent, maybe. We've been trading on quality and punctuality. But punctuality is not speed. That strategy has been getting weaker by the year. Marketing now has to be able to quote a delivery time that's proportional to your two-thirds reduction in manufacturing time. We're not empowered to do that because Production Control dictates the schedule, and it's usually longer than the competition's so that Slumbertech can reach its PTS objective. In other words, the schedule is as long as it takes to ensure that nothing will screw up the PTS.

"If you can build microclocks in 10 days, why do we have to quote 12 weeks? Neptune, which delivers in 4 weeks, is clobbering us!" (Bob had decided to use the most dramatic numbers he could and let Harris figure out how much of the processing time was pad.)

"Neptune is quoting 4 weeks?" replied Harris, astounded. "Let's get out of Richard's office. All of you meet me in mine at 2:30. I need to think."

The Marx Brothers used their brief respite from Harris to hit the men's room, grab lunch (cheeseburgers all around), and walk off a little tension. Killing time in the lobby at 2 p.m., George lit one of his nasty cigars and tried to rationalize: "Maybe it isn't any of our business, Bob. Why should Richard Hicks have to take a dive for Marketing?"

"Ask yourself this: Why should we take a dive for Manufacturing?"

Barrier Removal: An Experimental Attack

When the five reassembled in Harris's office, the Operations VP came to the point immediately: "This situation needs a dose of first aid. PTS is a great standard for a company like ours, and it put us back on the map. I have no intention of torpedoing that standard, and neither has the CEO. But if we're up against cycle times like Neptune's, it stands to reason that there's room for improvement inside Slumbertech.

"The crisis you guys have described forces our hand in Operations. Before we lose more microclock business, I'm going to authorize a pilot program to revise the microclock PTS. Instead of prescribing a fail-safe PTS for those customers, I'm willing to let Retrospace or anybody else tell *us* when to deliver and try to meet that goal. That's a change that'll require some hard selling by you marketing guys. The microclock experiment will be a trial run on how we might shorten our manufacturing cycles across the board and, eventually, align the shortened cycle times with our traditional PTS."

"Meanwhile, our PTS *will* go to hell, Vince," ventured Hicks. "I guarantee it."

"Sure it will, for a while, because you are going to systematically eliminate all the time benefits you've allowed Operations to build into the microclock schedule," said Harris. "But it'll come back up again—I guarantee that—just as it did five years ago. And as it does, we'll take what we've learned and apply the techniques across the board. That means we'll have to reimplement our old practice of regularly reviewing and applying the lessons we've learned. Meanwhile, in the interest of consensus, I will exempt the microclock business from Operations' overall PTS evaluations. There is thus no reason for Production Control to tolerate padding in the name of the overall PTS. But understand me clearly, Richard: The pad has got to come out of microclock operations starting yesterday. Landon, what are you doing tomorrow at, say, 7:00?"

"I was planning to be at my desk in San Francisco, but if—"

"Right. Please see me here instead. Should I thank you guys? Maybe another time. You'll be hearing from us. Until tomorrow then, Landon." Without missing a beat, Harris picked up his phone and told his secretary to get Hal Burns on the line.

"We'll always remember you fondly, Bob," said Ted as he and George made their getaway. Bob spent the rest of the day rearranging his schedule, perfecting verbal comebacks for all manner of tomorrow's scenarios, and catching three lively sets of Dave Frishberg at the London House before passing yet another uneasy night. And it rained.

The Divisional Turf Battle Continues

"What are you, some kind of masochist?" asked Vince Harris as Bob diffidently entered his office. Although Bob's private life had familiarized him with the term, he was uncomfortable with such lingo and didn't understand the reference. "Either that or you're foolhardy. Haven't you heard of going through channels? I'm not used to having my butt kicked by nonoperations people."

Or even by operations people, thought Bob, although he of course kept his peace. Sometimes, he knew, the best way to massage his way out of trouble was to remain silent; but Harris waited him out, so he had to come up with something. He tried this: "George, Ted, and I had no intention of kicking your, uh, butt. Remember, we were talking to Production Control when you walked in, and we were only trying to break a logjam at the lowest possible level. In Marketing, we're taught—forced, even—to fight our own battles."

"I'm aware of Marketing's management style; in fact I've just had a long conversation with Hal Burns. He agreed with my suggestion that the customer response problem transcended divisions at Slumbertech. With a little more encouragement from me, he also agreed that we should establish a crossfunctional team to ensure that Marketing and Operations work together starting right now on how to realign PTS to market realities. Burns and I will have no trouble getting the CEO's authorization to start the program with microclocks. Are you following me?"

Bob was, and he knew what was coming next. "Since it was you who brought the PTS problem to light in both divisions," Harris continued, "Hal Burns and I have decided to appoint you—no, *anoint* you—coordinator of the Slumbertech Crossfunctional Competitiveness Committee. Your team will include key people from both divisions, including your pal Hicks and of course Ernie Page, and will report to Burns and me regularly—and equally, in case you're wondering. Burns and I have a lot of details to work out, but I wanted to be the first to give you the good news."

So deadpan was Harris's demeanor that Bob was unable to detect even the slightest trace of humor. He decided to play it straight, too: "This is a great idea, but it's a big responsibility for the team leader. Inasmuch as most of the changes are going to come from Manufacturing, are you sure you want me to head it up?"

"I'm sure, for two reasons. The objective is to produce companywide improvements. Accordingly, getting this program to work is going to require inspired salesmanship inside Slumbertech. In the second place—and don't kid yourself about this—Marketing has as many bad habits to overcome as Manufacturing. Under the circumstances, you're the guy to head the team. Plan on seeing Burns and me three weeks from now here at Ground Zero. Meanwhile, you've got some preparation to do. Start with this."

Harris handed Bob a black-covered book on cycle time reduction, the same title Hicks had given him two days before. Maybe Hicks will be wanting his old copy back, thought Bob.

On the way out, while leaving his phone and fax number with Harris's elegant secretary, Bob made just enough eye contact to feel better about the prospect of frequent visits to Chicago. On the plane to San Francisco, he resolved to call Larry Coile first thing tomorrow and give him the good news about Slumbertech. Whether such news was good for Bob Landon was not at all certain. One thing was sure, however: he had a lot of boning up to do. He wouldn't be needing another boat for some time, and he'd be too busy to attend to the repairs on his house personally. After takeoff, he resisted the temptation to watch the in-flight movie and opened the book on short cycle times.

Orienting on Customer Needs

In his years as a business writer and editor, Jack Betters had become a master at networking from contact to contact. Thanks to a tip from Larry Coile, Jack had zeroed in on Bob Landon as another manager whose struggles might be worth watching. His instincts proved right. Over the next few months, during which they conversed several times, the two never met face-to-face, but Jack found Bob's nonchalance (which was more apparent than real) and the obvious enjoyment he got out of holding forth very winsome. Jack, meanwhile, had been making slow progress on his book, which he was moonlighting in addition to other work.

At 35, Jack had made a name for himself as a competent editor of how-to business books. Consultants, CEOs, and business school professors seeking to get their words of wisdom into print had all winced at his unblinking editorial comments but, by and large, they found his criticisms salutary. Although as a salaried editor at a major publishing house he realized no public recognition or financial surges from his daily work, he drew considerable satisfaction from a fat file of letters in which top dogs of North American industry thanked and praised him for his assistance. He had no track record as a businessperson himself, and in his Harris tweed jackets and turtlenecks, he cut an unbusinesslike figure. But such things actually worked in his favor when he interacted with business types. He listened, asked the right questions, kept an open mind, and argued if necessary without having to face dire career consequences. He soaked up information like a sponge.

He had been soaking up information about Slumbertech from Bob Landon ever since Bob had been assigned to his company's crossfunctional committee. Jack could see that the way in which the Slumbertech and Retrospace stories meshed, with Bob and Larry as protagonists, had real possibilities for his book project.

Jack, who checked in with Bob every so often, knew that Bob was at first uncomfortable with his committee assignment because he feared his own background did not equip him to go head-to-head with Slumbertech's hardnosed manufacturing types. Enough time had passed since their last conversation for Bob's committee to have made headway, so Jack telephoned Bob for an update.

True to his calling, Bob always indulged in several minutes of telephone pleasantries before Jack could get down to business, and today was no exception. When the right moment presented itself, Jack got Bob started with a very general question.

"Bob, what were the most important things you and your committee discovered in the last three months?"

Bob had expected a question or two of this sort. Because his image-consciousness caused him to worry about making a fool of himself for the record, he had jotted down some notes from which he now read (although it did not sound so over the telephone). He also had a set of letter-sized diagrams on his desk ready for use.

Treating Corporate Myopia

"There were three major discoveries," he said. "One was that a company with good intentions and high skill levels can become unbelievably myopic. The kind of effort it makes to compete may have almost nothing to do with the real world unless the customer's needs are considered first and foremost.

"The second follows from the first: The way a company measures itself must be meaningful to the customer, not just to some internal set of values.

"The final one is that companies like Slumbertech must develop a balanced sense of urgency."

Jack of course asked for details.

Corporate Myopia Is Come by Honestly

"The myopia part is easy to explain," answered Bob. "A few years ago, when we boot-strapped ourselves to high quality and world-class performance to schedule, we thought we had a secret weapon which would give us the edge on the competition. There was something to that, of course. But we spent the next several years patting ourselves on the back for our predictability and reliability without really checking with our customers to see if that's all they needed — or wanted.

Corporate Myopia Has an Internal Logic

"As to proper measurements: We were hypnotized by our ability to ship good products precisely on schedule and we rated our performance according to those capabilities. Such measurements were useful up to a point, but that point had been passed and the marketplace had changed in favor of high quality and fast customer response. Meanwhile, we kept kidding ourselves about giving the customers what they really wanted. As we did, inventory was building up to offset our lack of responsiveness, and our scheduling got more and more conservative to keep our high performance to schedule from slipping. Despite all that, our internally driven criteria told us we were 'Tops in the Industry'!"

"I was just talking with Larry Coile," said Jack. "At Retrospace, Larry found that the barriers to responsiveness came in three tiers [*as shown on the following page*]. All around him were subject matter issues that could be dealt with expeditiously. But looking up, he saw business process barriers and, beyond those, the cultural atmosphere that allowed all of these things to flourish."

"Larry is right," Bob replied. "Cultural barriers are like a great umbrella that shields the inner workings of a company from the light of day. They come in many forms — measurements, controls, incentives, strategy, structure, accountability — and they define a company's approach to the world. Business processes reflect the culture's overall way of doing things, while the steps in these processes reflect the application of our subject matter expertise.

"You know, Jack, one important point Larry made to me was that the average executive spends more than 90 percent of his time working on subject matter issues, with almost no time spent on the business process within which he is applying his subject matter expertise — a sobering thought!"

TYPICAL BARRIERS		
Subject matter	Business process	Culture
• Chemical process	• Redundant business process steps	• Measurements, controls, incentives
• Material hardness	• Prevention versus inspection	• Cultural blindness
• Plastic strength	• Value-added versus non-value-added	• Denial
• Soldering process	• Controlling inputs	• Organization structure
• Pricing	• Communications/ geography	• Accountability
	• Lot/work package size	• Designing with undeveloped technology

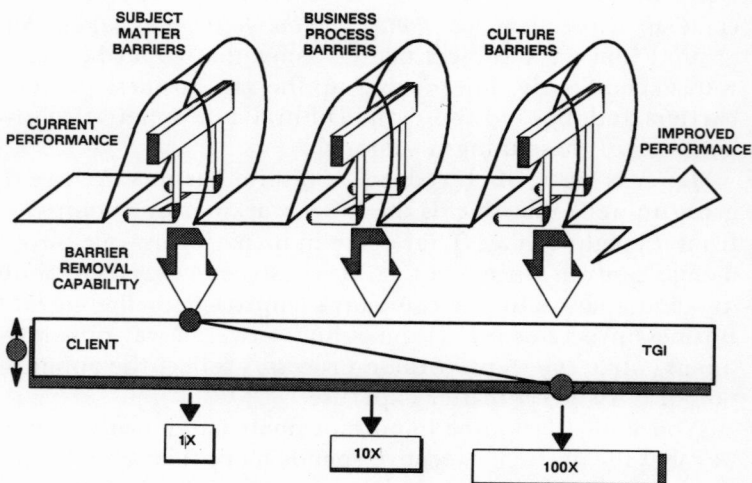

The three categories of barriers.

"And, speaking of Larry, it often takes an outside force to shed light inside the company. Larry was that outside force here.

"When Retrospace blew the whistle, my marketing instincts made it easy for me to see that we had more than a sales problem on our hands. By hook and crook, I and my Marketing buddies got the attention of people outside our division. That led to the creation of our crossfunctional competitiveness committee, which has led to some some impressive repairs to the system around here.

"As you know, the team consisted of managers from Operations and Marketing. One of the smartest things Slumbertech did, if I do say so, was putting a marketing guy — me — in charge of the committee. Make no mistake: I hated the appointment, but I'm the one person on the team who has dealt face-to-face with customers, and in an argument I always take the *customer's* part. I think I've kept the other members of the committee honest."

New Measurements for Old

"What did your committee accomplish?" asked Jack.

"We started by purging Operations of the individual measurements that contributed to overall myopia. There were plenty; in Operations, almost 80 percent of the performance measurements were internally directed, self-serving, totally irrelevant to marketplace realities.

"It's been a helluva task to convince Slumbertekkies who owe their careers to 99 percent performance to schedule that such a high percentage is harmful because it's been making us too slow. Try persuading a production control guy or a line supervisor that it's better for the company to lower its PTS percentage and win more business!

"Meanwhile, we've had to adopt new measurements which track our responsiveness: short cycle times, for instance, and proper Cycles of Learning. You have no idea what long cycle times Slumbertech's Production Control tolerated in order to protect itself against pressure and bad surprises."

Mindset: A "Balanced Sense of Urgency"

Having talked with Bob on previous occasions, Jack did in fact have a pretty good idea of those long cycle times, which were now falling in both Manufacturing and Marketing. But the last of Bob's three lessons was still unclear to him. "Could you explain what you meant about the need for a 'balanced sense of urgency'?" he asked.

"Yeah," answered Bob, "but I want to fax you a diagram that'll help me over the philosophical part." Bob took Jack's fax number and, sure enough, a diagram began to roll out of Jack's fax machine even as the two talked.

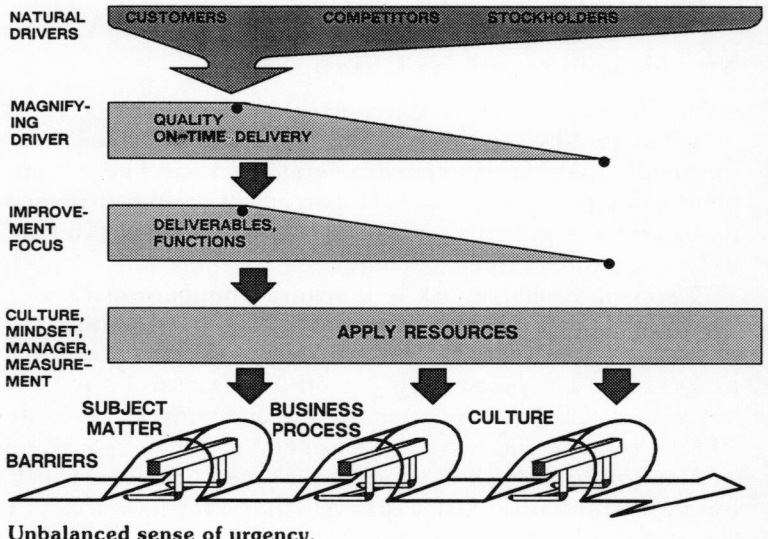

Unbalanced sense of urgency.

Bob continued: "A company's decisions are driven by the priorities of customers, competitors, and stockholders. But such drives can get narrowly focused within a company. At Slumbertech, those priorities had driven us to focus on improving the subject matter level of our business: upgrading quality and performance to schedule. But we failed to take into account the business process and culture as a whole.

"Nonetheless, Slumbertech prided itself on its problem-solving capability. If a problem arose, we'd jump through whatever hoops we had to to fix it. The trouble was that for us to act, a problem had to *appear*. Say that Slumbertech got a complaint. Somebody would isolate the spot where the trouble occurred, assign a specialist to fix it, and then life would go on.

"It wasn't until Retrospace's cancellation that we made an institutional breakthrough. It was suddenly obvious to me that while I could possibly expedite a quick order and then try to seduce Retrospace back into the fold, that sort of stuff couldn't work forever. We had to start seeing the big picture: getting at the root cause of recurring problems, analyzing them in terms of their effect on the company, and making a massive effort to correct once and for all the process and the cultural attitude that was causing them."

As his fax machine miraculously disgorged another diagram [*as shown on the following page*], Jack realized he was getting a smooth, mixed-media tutorial by a master of the high-tech sales pitch.

"A company with a balanced sense of urgency," said Bob, who was obviously enjoying all this, "focuses primarily on barrier removal, period. The fundamental drivers are the same, but internally there is a refocusing to include business process and cultural issues.

"In such an environment, middle managers balance their subject matter specialities with a sense of how their specialized approach to problem solving will impact the rest of the business process. We have a training program in place for that purpose."

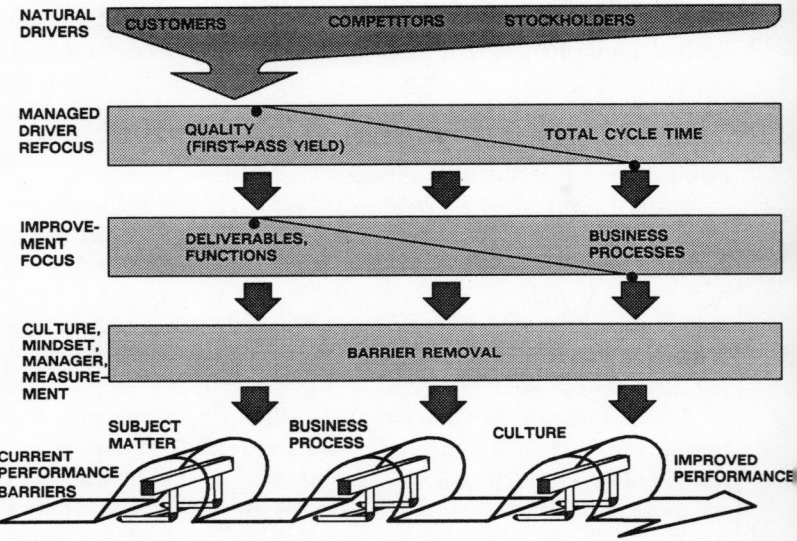

Achieving a balanced sense of urgency.

Extending the Crossfunctional Approach

"The committee provided a platform for that kind of balanced thinking," said Bob. "As you know, we were only assigned to rescue the microclock business, but within a few weeks it was obvious that what had happened in microclocks would happen everywhere else unless we revamped our entire business process. Microclocks were the tip of an iceberg, and I guess all of us here should be glad Retrospace brought us to our senses in the nick of time.

"What the committee did was develop a new, more pertinent, more complete set of performance measurements. We had a systematic method for accomplishing this. First, we listed all the existing measurements in our area of responsibility. Then we categorized them as primary and secondary, secondary being measurements that were a function of pri-

maries. Next, we noted whatever desirable measurements
were missing—in our case it was first-pass yield and cycle
time—and then rank-ordered and evaluated every primary
measurement, new and old, according to its effect on customer service. Wait a minute, I'll show you." Jack's fax machine began again to whistle and beep, and out came the following list:

MEASUREMENT METHODOLOGY
1. List current measurements used in company.
2. Categorize them as primary and secondary. A secondary is a subset of a primary.
3. Identify missing measurements, e.g., first-pass yield, make/ market cycle time.
4. Test each primary with the questions, "Will improving this measurement improve performance in the customers' eyes"? Will it drive one of the Three R's of competitiveness?"
5. Rank-order primaries, including any new primaries.
6. Try to reduce to 10.
7. Use this set to form the top of the hierarchical set of measurements for the operation under review.

That list is one for my book, Jack thought to himself.
"That list is one for your book," said Bob. "Anyway, the
committee is now applying its method to the rest of Operations and Manufacturing. We've got a long way to go, but at
least we've got our priorities in order, and we're measuring
ourselves according to what's best for the customer rather
than by our old internal system."
"Personally speaking, Bob, where do you go from here?"
asked Jack.
"Nowhere, I hope! This committee stuff has been eye-
opening, but I'm not a committee type at heart. I want to stay

in San Francisco, which is my territory, and pick up where I left off. I cut a deal with my VP that committee duties should rotate around Marketing so that as many managers as possible can benefit from the experience. Come next month; it's George Finlay's turn. Better George than me. I want to have a little fun selling the new Slumbertech to our old customers. Larry Coile won't know what hit him!"

Jack's Checklist:
Key Barriers Encountered by Bob Landon

1. Meaningless internal measurements, contributing to poor response to customer.

2. Imbalance in the sense of urgency within the company, leading to throwing resources at problems instead of addressing the underlying business process.

4

A Touch of Glass

An Acquisition Scenario: Imparting Cycle Time Standards Across Cultural Boundaries

Free of its usual string of hopper cars, the powerful, shiny Pacific 4-6-2 climbed the long grade without losing momentum and disappeared into the mountain tunnel. Tyrell watched as the locomotive emerged from the other side and accelerated as it started down the grade. He had planned carefully. This is it, he thought; just a few seconds more. The locomotive gathered momentum as it approached the dangerous switchback that lay ahead. At the last instant—too late—Tyrell realized that the engine was not going to make it: another disaster. Reaching the curve, the Pacific hurtled straight ahead, jumped the rails, and plunged over the edge. Tyrell broke the fall with his left foot, but the engine's coal tender took a nasty bounce off his tool box.

The accident hurt R. D. Tyrell's pride more than his foot. He had been fussing with this model railroad layout for almost three months but still could not engineer a switchback that his expensive Japanese-made locomotive could negotiate at more a crawl. Well, back to the drawing board. R. D.'s new hobby, intended as a relaxing diversion, was becoming a pain in the neck.

He had inherited the railroad idea from his son, R. L., who as a boy scout had assembled a few kit boxcars and promptly lost interest just as the old man was warming to the hobby. R. L. had since grown up and left for the University of North Texas, leaving his boxcars behind for Dad to play with.

The generous size of R. D.'s house allowed him to conceive a veritable mini-empire. Real estate had gone begging lately in the Dallas–Fort Worth "Metroplex," so he and his wife Angie had traded up to a spacious, maintenance-free, sandy-colored brick ranch home with a narrow yard of raked gravel on Shady Creek Lane in Carrollton, just north of Dallas. It included a recreation room where R. D. could expand his hobby out of Angie's sight. If only he could get the damn thing to run.

The reason R. D.'s train couldn't handle his homemade mountains was that they were preposterous peaks through which no self-respecting railroad, HO gauge or otherwise, should ever have been constructed. Their designer was at a disadvantage because, as a sedentary lifelong Dallasite, he had never seen a mountain up close. Looking over his layout last week, Angie, a Coloradan, had frankly told her hopeful spouse that his peaks looked like Disneyland. "Stick with what you know," she advised him. "Flatten it out." But then it would look like Carrollton, he thought.

All this might someday seem funny. Meanwhile, R. D. Tyrell was not getting the off-hours fun he craved. Until lately, the Tyrells had cruised their 18-foot Starcraft on Lake Dallas, a brown artificial lake just a short drive from Shady Creek Lane. But with R. L. gone and the pressure of his job increasing, R. D. just wasn't up to the effort, so the Starcraft had been sitting like a beached whale in their driveway for months while its owner tinkered with his trains and tried to forget his job.

For the first time in his 23 years at Keller Window Corporation, R. D. was really under the gun. Keller had lately been taken over by Fasglass, Inc., an Atlanta-based glass manufacturer whose VP of operations was determined to change everything. As Keller's plant manager, R. D. was taking all the heat.

Alan Cullen, R. D.'s new boss in Atlanta, seemed to know a lot about business in general, but almost nothing about window manufacturing. R. D. Tyrell knew a great deal about window manufacturing but little else. He had never had a business course in his life, having started at Keller right out of high school. Back then, the business was family-owned. Its founder, Mervin Keller, was a member of a local country club at which R. D. caddied during his senior year. Mervin and R. D. had become friendly and, upon graduation, R. D. had a job waiting for him. He had stayed at Keller ever since, learning the window business from the ground up and advancing accordingly. He had made plant manager when Joe Keller, Mervin's son, retired.

Anatomy of a Comfortable Baseline

Keller Window's stock in trade was a line of aluminum-framed windows manufactured at its plant in Carrollton. The technology had changed little in the 30-odd years since Mervin Keller had set up shop to take advantage of the post-war prefab building boom. It had grown, however, but had topped out at about $45 million in business a year, with net profits of about $900,000 and no reasonable expectation of an increase. The plant was situated off Route I-35E, part of an interminable industrial strip which, like so much of the Metroplex's urban sprawl, was a mishmash of dull structures and parking lots hastily assembled without concern for esthetics or durability. Keller occupied several large, high-ceilinged, metal buildings, hot in summer and cold in winter, located between the interstate and a railroad siding. The plant took in raw materials, mostly glass, aluminum ingots, and insulation stripping by truck and rail (some of R. D.'s model freight cars were exact copies of the ones that delivered such material to a siding behind the plant), and shipped out plate-glass windows of all sizes in prepainted aluminum frames. Like most such companies, its business was regional, based upon established relationships with distributors, contractors, and developers, and undisturbed by foreign competition.

Over the years, R. D. had established and cultivated tight relationships with the right customers and suppliers. He grew intimately familiar with Keller's manufacturing processes and slowly evolving product line. His office, part of a crowded warren of cubicles just inside the main plant's front entrance, was distinguished from the others by its imitation-walnut paneling. It had, ironically, no window, but sported a large collage of Tyrell family snapshots glazed and framed to resemble one of the company's bread-and-butter products. In one of his friskier moods, R. D. had hung on an opposite wall a complimentary calendar sent him by a glass supplier on which, month by month, shapely cuties smiled out through shiny picture windows. Those touches and a fax machine were the only new additions; otherwise, the office was unchanged since the days of his predecessor. In adjoining cubicles were R. D.'s support staff: his secretary, a production control manager and assistant (called "planner" and "assistant planner" at Keller), an engineering manager, and three manufacturing managers, one each in charge of aluminum frame construction, glass cutting, and assembly. There was also a small accounting department which reported directly to a financial officer in Atlanta. The rest of the lofty, drafty main building was given over to those three manufacturing segments and storage of work-in-process inventory. Other buildings handled packing and shipping and the storage of raw materials.

Short Cycle Time: New Tricks for an Old Dog

It was in that unpretentious office, six weeks earlier, that R. D.'s new boss had lowered the boom on him. He should have seen it coming. Months had passed since Fasglass ac-

quired Keller, and he himself had made no move to acknowl-
edge the change beyond writing Alan Cullen to say that he
looked forward to being part of the Fasglass team, which was
a lie. R. D. had been perfectly happy running his own show
for the snoozing Kellers and was understandably in no mood
to deal with strangers. What did they want with Keller, anyway? Fasglass's forte was custom-tempered and insulated
plate glass, nothing else. Its four plants, located in Atlanta,
Sioux Falls, Provo, and Oklahoma City, were legendary for
their response to customers: 48 hours from receipt of an order to shipment. That kind of speed entitled Fasglass to
charge the highest prices in the business, and every one of its
regional factories was highly profitable. None of these specialized plants, however, did business with Keller.

Acquisition of the latter by the former was a decision by
the Fasglass directors to diversify, not vertically integrate.
From that, R. D. had deduced that he might still remain au-
tonomous so long as he kept Keller's business on its even
keel. It was not to be. Without warning, Keller's small marketing department had been moved to Atlanta under the
shadow of its new parent. The marketing guys now reported
to the home office, not Keller. For the last three months,
R. D. and his manufacturing people had been coping with
forecasts made a thousand miles away and subject to rapid-
fire faxed revisions. If this kept up, Keller's manufacturing
operation would be tied in knots within a year. When he
heard about Cullen's intended visit to Carrollton, R. D. rehearsed the most forceful way he could dream up to protest
the removal of Keller's marketers and the nicest way he could
dream up to tell Cullen to butt out.

Close Encounter of the Worst Kind

Suddenly, there was the stranger from Atlanta sitting in his
grubby office: young, impeccably suited, the very picture of a
well-schooled M.B.A. who had never gotten glass shards in
his fingertips. After they had shaken hands, R. D. sat down at

his desk and was about to segue into his agenda of complaints and recommendations when, without warning, he was ambushed by the worst confrontation of his life. Cullen shot from the hip, and a lot of his shots went by in a blur. The collective impact, however was unforgettable. In essence, said Cullen, R. D. was going to have to "align Keller's corporate values to those of Fasglass."

Since acquiring Keller, Cullen said, the entire corporation took in about $90 million, half of which was the gross from Keller. But the profit from the glass factories was almost 25 percent pretax against Keller's "barely marginal" profitability. "If the price of aluminum weren't low, you wouldn't be making any profit at all," said Cullen, adding insult to injury. "What Keller must do is adopt the same kind of short cycle times as the parent factories. Maybe not 48-hour customer service, but something close to it.

"Right now, your cycle time from order entry to delivery averages four weeks. That's no good.

"And you're swimming in inventory. Our glass factories have about 3 percent of sales tied up in inventory; you have 22 percent. Flush it. Fasglass doesn't believe in inventory."

Denial: The "Volume" Argument Against Low Inventory

R. D. could see that Cullen was absolutely serious about all this, so he somehow kept his rising anger under control. "My first reaction," he replied at last, "is to tell you in all respect that you don't know enough about aluminum windows to issue such orders. Aside from the fact that both our products use glass, Fasglass and Keller are not at all alike. All of Fasglass's orders are custom, so it's natural for you to emphasize fast turnaround; you're not manufacturing standardized items in large volume. I can well understand that Fasglass doesn't believe in inventory, as you say, because custom work is inventory-proof.

"At Keller it's another matter altogether. We make a lot of

catalog products in a lot of sizes and colors. We manufacture according to our marketing forecasts — which ought to be plotted here at the plant, by the way, not in Atlanta — and we have to respond to unexpected orders for odd sizes or colors. We keep inventory around for that purpose. Keller can't simply conjure up a tall stack of 50-by-30 combos in desert brown frames anytime a customer decides that's what he wants. So I can't in conscience accept your directive to flush our inventory. If you check around, you'll find that we're as good or better as the regional competition. I think you need to let Keller operate in the tried and true manner."

"Sorry, but no," said Cullen. "The tried and true manner is only marginally profitable."

Recognizing a Cycle Time Opportunity

"Since you brought up your competitors," Cullen continued, "I'll let you in on a secret: Fasglass bought Keller because the performance in the window industry is so uniformly poor we were sure we could grab a bigger and more profitable share of it. If you're convinced you can't cut Keller's cycle times and inventory, you'd better be prepared to step aside, preferably within 60 days, so I can get somebody in here who will accomplish our objective. We are determined that inventories *will* be reduced, profitability *will* be raised, and return on assets brought to Fasglass's level."

The room was by this time swimming around in R. D.'s field of vision. Could this be happening? "Nobody with any experience in the window business would take on those objectives," he stammered. "They just don't fit."

Facing Facts and Finding Help

Cullen stayed cool, but firm: "Then Fasglass will have to settle for someone from outside the window business." Then, coming down off the high horse which he had obviously found uncomfortable, Cullen thawed a little. "In the time we have, I can't convert you to the merits of shorter cycle times, aside from assuring you that your profitability and volume will increase as your assets are reduced. I especially can't convince you that your present operation is more complicated than it needs to be, or that if you got rid of the needless complications, you could slash your cycle times. What I will do is bring you and Clyde Farwell together. Clyde runs the Fasglass plant in Oklahoma City, and what he doesn't know about short cycle times isn't worth bothering with. I'm on my way to see him tonight. Fax me your decision via Clyde's office tomorrow morning. If you're willing to take on the new assignment, I'll bring Clyde into the loop and he'll be down here in a jiffy to help you get started. Otherwise, Clyde will have to put off his visit to Keller until we find somebody else. I hope that won't be necessary."

"I need more time to give you my answer," said R. D. "We're talking about me possibly chucking 23 years of service to Keller."

"If by that you're implying that maybe I need some time to come to my senses, the answer is no. Time is the most precious thing Keller has going for it at this point. We can't fritter any more of it away. Fax me tomorrow.

"One parting piece of advice: Since you now know Atlanta is absolutely intent on revamping Keller, you ought to pass along the urgency to your subordinates. No need for you to take all the heat. And you're going to need everyone on your side from now on. Might as well put the fear of God in them, too.

"R. D., I know you can do this job, and I think you'll find it exciting. Stay with us."

It was positively amazing, thought R. D. through his haze, how Cullen could manipulate the conversation to a point where he sounded conciliatory. There was nothing more to say until tomorrow. Cullen clicked on his automatic smile, rose, and left for Oklahoma City. R. D. crumpled the paper on which he had written his abortive agenda, rose, and left for a double Jack Daniel's.

Facing Facts and Accepting Help

During the sleepless night that followed, R. D. got almost none of the sympathy he craved from Angie. After he had reviewed the conversation with Cullen for the third time, Angie had had enough. "Look, R. D., the guy didn't can you. He didn't attack your manhood. He's asking you to do things a new way or else, I grant, but he obviously thinks you're the guy for the job. You're not seriously considering spitting in his eye, are you? We can't afford a heroic gesture like that. Talk to the man from Oklahoma and give it a try. Meanwhile, keep your options open. But don't walk the plank tomorrow morning. Now, go to sleep!"

The next morning, R. D. did not walk the plank. Instead, he faxed a message to Cullen:

OKAY.

SEND ME CLYDE FARWELL.

R. D. T.

Within five minutes, the phone rang. It was Clyde Farwell. R. D. and he arranged to meet at the Keller plant in two days. Obviously, Clyde practiced what Cullen preached about short cycle times.

A Quick Cycle Time Analysis

Because he had no office window to watch from, R. D. awaited Clyde Farwell's arrival at the glass-and-aluminum front doors of the Keller plant. Five minutes before the appointed time, a Silverado pickup exactly like R. D.'s but wearing Oklahoma plates pulled into the parking lot.

R. D. had been prepared as a matter of principle to dislike Clyde, but that proved impossible. Clyde was a droll, middle-aged Sooner, lanky but not laid back, with a nervous appetite for work and food. He was, in R. D.'s words, a walkin' around guy like himself. But he'd better not start throwing his weight around. Clyde didn't. He immediately put R. D. at ease by admitting he was not an expert in the window business and asking to have a look around.

After Clyde had stopped at a vending machine to secure a pack of M&Ms, he and R. D. walked through the three stages of Keller's manufacturing process. The first of these, called the Extrusion Department, fascinated him although it was old hat to his host. Keller had three extruders: machines resembling oversize lathes that converted 2-foot aluminum ingots called bullets into flanged moldings for window frames. A preheated bullet was rolled into position on the extruder before a die containing three apertures. Then a hydraulic ramp forced the bullet against the die. Out the other side of the dies, at a rate of about a yard a second came three ever-lengthening strips of window frames; at least 60 feet per bullet. Clyde actually laughed at the speed and apparent ease with which fat ingots were transformed into extruded frames.

The shiny, silvery extrusions were then cut into shorter lengths and hung like sides of beef along an overhead moving track that bore them into spray chambers for painting. Today's color was pumpkin gold. Once painted, the extrusions were tracked to a drying area. Dry extrusions were then cut to desired lengths.

In the next production step, they were united with glass cut to measure and assembled into the finished product. Today's windows were two-layer types, so the process involved fitting an insulating spacer between the grooves on the extruded frames into which the glass panes slid. "There you are," said R. D. with some pride. "Add a little rubber sealer around the edges, and you have a window. Our line includes tempered and untempered, tinted and untinted. We aim to please. A lot of our output is standardized to general building specifications. All in all, we build 32 different models, each in several sizes. We can also do custom orders, of course, and I pick up some loose change knocking out specialty glass products like fanlights for front doors and lighting fixtures."

Clyde had taken a packet of salted peanuts from his pocket and was popping them one at a time into his mouth. "Let's go back to your office and talk about this," he suggested.

Charting the Flow: The Inventory Mindset

In the office, Clyde stepped to the chalkboard and roughed out a flowchart depicting the manufacturing steps from extrusion through assembly. "This helps me understand the operation better," he explained, standing back and scrutinizing the series of boxes and arrows. "My old boss at Fasglass used to say that outperforming the competition was a matter of simplifying production, getting rid of every unnecessary step in the process. He was right, and the difference between Fasglass's profit margin and the poor competition is that we've chucked those steps and they haven't. If, as you say, Keller is on a par with its competitors, you and they both probably tolerate the same sort of complicated steps. If you find those and chuck 'em before your competitors do, you've got it made.

"Meanwhile," Clyde continued, "I'm keeping in mind your need to reduce your inventory. Look: you've got five points where there is always work in process: stuff moving through the Extrusion or the Glass departments that meets at the end of the line. There's an *awful lot* of stuff moving through those departments. I couldn't help noticing all the inventory piled up at various points on the line, not just at the end of the manufacturing process. For example, when the extrusion boys finish extruding, cutting, and painting, those frames accumulate. Over in the Glass Department, the cut pieces likewise build up in numbers, waiting for the assembly step. All in all, your work-in-process inventory looks very high, higher than it needs to be. I'd say that you could shorten your customer response time if you trimmed production to the exact quantity needed to fill the order. That would also cut down on your finished goods inventory, of course.

Rationalizing Capacity: A Major Barrier

"A minute ago," Clyde continued, "I was talking about barrier removal. One of your barriers might be the lack of coordination between the departments. Another seems to be the time, space, and expense you use up making and servicing overproduction. Can those areas be improved? Perhaps if the three production sectors coordinated more precisely...."

"I'm not sure they should be improved," R. D. answered, a little defensively. "In the first place, we're comfortable with the process as is; it's the way we've always done things. But, to be more specific, I doubt if it's a good thing to cut inventory in a business like ours. You saw all that expensive equipment, especially the extruders. We feel we should optimize the capacity of our machinery. Making windows isn't exactly high-tech, but it's pretty complicated work. It's also hard to forecast. So when we get an order for a standard product, we try to estimate what additional demand there will be for the same item. Then we do as large a run as possible, ship what was ordered, and hold the rest in inventory. The objective, of course, is to keep setups at a minimum and the efficiencies of the machines at a maximum. That's pretty standard in the window business. Another thing: because our storage space is limited, we like to build our best sellers in the largest lots possible. Those uniform batches stack easily, and when a big order comes through, we won't get caught with our pants down.

"We don't do our own forecasting anymore, dammit. Those people have been moved to Atlanta and we get our instructions from corporate headquarters. We schedule production four weeks in advance. My two planners are pretty good at determining just how much we can get done in that time. They don't use computers or anything like that. They block out time sectors on a wall-size scheduling board so everyone can track the work."

Time-Related Loss of Business

Clyde withdrew a Baby Ruth bar from his windbreaker pocket and studied it closely before peeling back its wrapper banana-style. "Have I got this right?" he asked. "You plan your output a month in advance and you can't change the mix within that time?"

"Yes," said R. D. "In fact, since the planners are scheduling a month ahead of the output, we're locked in for upwards of two months into the future."

"So, if you got, say, an order for 500 two-layer windows in battleship gray that had to be delivered in three weeks, you'd turn it down."

"We'd have to. It happens now and then."

"I admit my business is different," said Clyde, "but it's been years since I let a big machine tell me what I should produce and how much. I see why you—what did you call it?—optimize the capacity of those machines. But if Atlanta wants you to cut your inventories, going to smaller lot sizes will do the trick.

More Barriers: Setups, Line Balance, Lack of Cross-Training

"Why don't you consider making only as many items as are actually ordered?" Clyde asked.

"Two reasons," said R. D. "The first is that we have the production capacity and ought to exploit it, I think. The second is that it takes close to four hours to set up an extruder every time we use a different die. That's one hell of an interruption. If we changed dies every time an order came in, we'd quickly fall behind."

"Unless you figured out a faster way to change the dies," Clyde said with his mouth full. He crumpled up the candy wrapper and dropped it in R. D.'s overflowing wastebasket. "Let me ask you this: does the work flow through the lines evenly?"

"Predictably, but not evenly. It tends to move comfortably at the beginning of a four-week cycle and bunch up uncomfortably at the end."

Evening Out the Work Flow

"That might be another barrier you need to look at," said Clyde. "The reason I asked is that when we were out on the floor, I saw one group doing very little while the rest of the work force was pushing pretty hard."

"Those were probably members of the Engineering Department. They work their butts off when we have to do something like change a die. When they go into action, it's the line workers' chance to relax." Then R. D. added what Clyde must have been thinking; "Looks pretty stupid, doesn't it?"

"Well," replied Clyde, smiling, "I wouldn't want good ol' Alan Cullen to notice something like that when he's in one of his moods. But I wonder if your engineering and manufacturing people could be cross-trained. When the engineering people have to change a die, why couldn't the idled line workers pitch in and get the job done faster? You see what I'm getting at? If, say, you could cut your setup times in half, you could go to smaller lot sizes, cut your inventory, and get products out the door quicker."

R. D. had no answer at all to that one. While he was trying to come up with one, Clyde spoke again: "How long did you say it took to change dies in an extruder?"

"On a good day, three and a half to four hours. There's some heavy work involved, moving the jigs around."

"What if you could do it in a half an hour?"

The guy's a kook, thought R. D. Just when I was beginning to believe him....

"You think I'm crazy, don't you?" asked Clyde. "But those damned setups are a major problem for you, and they'll *really* be a headache if you follow through on your orders. You ought to give the matter some thought as soon as you can."

R. D. decided that Clyde wasn't crazy. His oddball slant on things Keller took for granted was, well, fascinating. He began to feel a glimmer of hope that he could please Atlanta without selling his soul.

Calculating Cycle Time, Step One: The Historical Approach

"Now," said Clyde, "I'm gonna give you a quickie on how to figure what your potential cycle time could be. First thing is to determine your actual performance per lot. Here at Keller, your lot size and run size are the same thing, and you probably have job tickets that will give you the information you need."

R. D. did indeed have that information. Clyde suggested that they zero in on one part of the operation, so R. D. provided the last two years' job tickets from the Extrusion Department. Clyde quickly drew on the chalkboard a crude chart. Its vertical scale represented frequency of occurrence, and its horizontal scale measured cycle time in days. On this he and R. D. plotted Extrusion's performance. In most cases, the time was about 12 days from bullets to frames; but R. D. was surprised to note the wide spread: a low of 7 days and a high of 20.

Calculating Cycle Time, Step 2: Theoretical Cycle Time

"Okay," said Clyde, admiring their work. "That's your historical performance. Now you need to compare it with your theoretical cycle time. Theoretical is the minimal time it would take to run a lot size of one through Extrusion without any setups, mistakes, stops, or delays. Computing that is an exacting process, but for the moment, let's rough out an estimate." The two segregated every production step in Extrusion and added up the cycle time: nine hours!

R. D. was surprised but unconvinced. "But that's purely a theoretical figure," he protested.

Calculating Cycle Time, Step 3:
Finding Entitlement

"Yeah," said Clyde, "but listen to this. Generally speaking, an operation that performs at its entitled cycle time achieves a level of *two to three times theoretical*. You can see, however, that Keller's best performance is a lot longer than that. The rule in such cases is to take the multiple of theoretical as your guide. That's where the room for improvement lies. I'm certain that when you do more precise measurements, they'll corroborate these estimates."

Clyde then drew a diagram on the chalkboard that used the multiple of theoretical to show graphically the difference between baseline and entitlement performance. It looked like this:

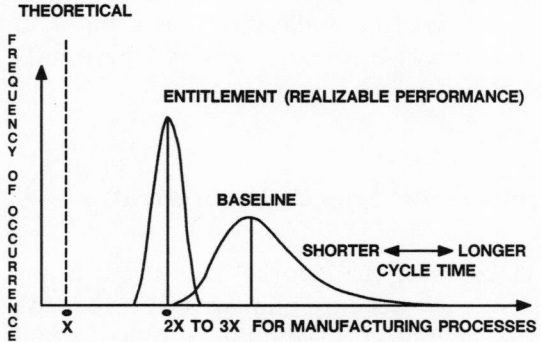

Typical performance distributions.

"This chart shows you something important about performance distribution. It demonstrates the impact of entitlement performance on your responsiveness to customers and the predictability of your output. At baseline, there's a wide performance spread between your fastest and slowest response. That gap narrows dramatically when you reach or exceed entitlement. In fact, as you can see, at entitlement your typical response time is *faster* than your fastest baseline. Moreover — and this is important — your predictability of output and delivery is vastly improved. Your customers are gonna love that.

"R. D.," said Clyde, tossing his piece of chalk in the air and snatching it as though it were a flipped coin, "even with your one-shift operation, a four-day total cycle time is achievable in this plant."

"Easier said than done. I seriously doubt if anything like that is possible."

"Oh, it's possible all right. Probable. Virtually certain. When Fasglass bought the plant in Sioux Falls, they moved me up there to bring cycle times down to the level I'd achieved at Oklahoma City. It took me 18 months. I never doubted for a moment that I could beat down the cycle times, but it didn't happen overnight.

"But you're right, it is easier said than done. You've got your work cut out for you. My guess, based on experience and my quick look around, is that you'll be a year, maybe 14 months, getting from four weeks to four days. And you won't make it unless you get everyone behind you. But that four-day entitlement is out there, believe it. The process is like skinning an onion: You peel away the obvious barriers, and the cycle times drop. Then they stall, because another layer of barriers appears that wasn't noticeable at first. It's not easy, but it pays off.

Short Cycle Times Improve Return on Assets

"Now here's the other payoff," Clyde continued. "As your cycle times come down and you can respond to customers more quickly, you don't need to carry much inventory. Hell, with cycle times of less than a week, your work-in-process and finished goods inventory ought to be negligible. That'll do wonders for your return on assets and make the big boys in Atlanta think you're a hero. Speaking of Atlanta, I hope you see that Alan Cullen's ultimatum did have a few points in its favor."

"Right now, I'm still trying to convince myself that you're pep talk has a few points in its favor, so let's put Alan Cullen on hold. Are you hungry?"

Clyde patted his pockets, feeling for a possibly forgotten candy bar. He was all out. "Yep, I'm hungry," he said. The two drove in R. D.'s Silverado through stifling night heat to a real Texas-style joint in Ponder where the specialty of the house was steaks jumping on a sizzling platter, hash browns, and, of course, Lone Star beer. It was just what the doctor ordered, and it was the first time R. D. had seen anyone go around twice on those T-bones and still have room for lemon pie.

Dealing With Denial and Resistance

Despite the noisy restaurant chitchat and a blaring jukebox, the two kept talking. R. D. asked how readily workers and managers took to the new system. "That depends on the company." Clyde answered. "Yours is set in its ways and your people don't know any other way of doing things, so there's bound to be resistance. Employees who have performed their tasks in good conscience don't enjoy hearing that they're way below their entitlement. They'll probably howl when you tell them the cycle time has got to shrink by 75 percent.

"Another thing: people love to see inventory lying around. It's physical proof that the company will have something to do tomorrow. Mark my words: as your backlog of extrusions, glass sheets, and finished windows gets low, a lot of workers are gonna feel threatened."

"What do I do?' asked R. D.

"Well, you wait them out. As they get used to the new culture, they'll outgrow that attitude. But that's not enough. After your goals are in place and you're tracking toward lower cycle times, start evaluating your people according to their performance in the new context: short cycle time and low inventory. That'll mean setting up new criteria right down the line.

"But look, R. D. I see you're still doubtful yourself. You have to believe in all this before you begin to change the process. Tell you what: I'm staying with my daughter in Denison tonight and she has plenty of room. Ride with me back to Fasglass and see some of this for yourself. You can get a plane back to Dallas. It'll be time well spent, I guarantee."

What the hell, thought R. D.

Seeing Is Believing: No Backlog, No Inventory

During the long ride from Denison to Oklahoma City, Clyde kept fueling himself from a pocketful of vending machine delights, and R. D. kept telling himself there was nothing in common between Fasglass and Keller. But from the minute Clyde's Silverado pulled into the Fasglass parking lot and he beheld the woebegone, jerry-built plant, he began to doubt this. Even Clyde's office looked like home, right down to its eye-high partitions and plastic imitation-wood paneling.

"C'mon, I'll give you a quick tour," said Clyde. They proceeded to the Customer Service Department, which consisted of one young woman who at the moment was taking a telephone order. She nodded and smiled as she filled in the telephoned specs on a multiple-copy form: size, quantity, tinting, tempering. After hanging up, she entered some information of her own, tore off one sheet to use as an invoice and, reaching through a portal in her office partition, dropped the form in an in-basket. "The form that Judy just deposited is the lot traveler for the order," explained Clyde. "Let's follow it."

Clyde headed for the manufacturing floor. "Shouldn't we look first at your order-entry section?" asked R. D.

"You just saw order entry. It's Judy."

"Well, where do you enter the order onto a computer? Production control must have something to work with. Who tracks your backlog?"

"There's no production control and no backlog," Clyde answered. "Judy's form goes straight to the floor. We work on a lot size of one order, and we ship every order within two days. Why would I want to keep a backlog?"

The manufacturing manager who had picked up Judy's order form did have a PC, into which he entered the customer's specs for the new order. The computer, he said, would provide optimal patterns for setting up the cutting table. "In an hour, that order will be on the cut," said Clyde, who then pointed to some sheets of cut glass moving on a roller conveyer into a large furnace which dominated stage center in the plant. "Those are going in for tempering. Notice that the order form stays with each lot as it moves down the line."

On the other side of the furnace, gloved workers were carefully removing tempered glass which, although it had been cooled by blowers, was still hot. The glass was then taken directly to a dock at the rear of the building where several company trucks were loading. Each of these trucks, said Clyde, had regular delivery routes. A glance at the directions Judy had entered onto the lot's traveling order form told loaders which truck was to take the glass. As the latest order went onto the truck, R. D. leaned over the edge of the loading dock and touched it. It was still warm.

"Now, about inventory," said Clyde, anticipating R. D.'s next comment. "There isn't any, at least as far as finished goods are concerned. We have a stockpile of assorted glass at the front end of the plant near the cutting table. Our other computer tracks that and keeps us one week ahead of anticipated orders. Out total inventory is 3 percent of sales."

Short Cycle Time: A Culture, Not a Program

Pausing, Clyde tapped the last few Sno-Caps out of their box and gobbled them one at a time as he talked. "It wasn't easy to iron out the process. It began out of necessity. Our founder, the late Owen Fassenden, started on a shoestring. He could only get enough bank financing for the tempering furnace, so he decided then and there to operate the plant without inventory. You know how necessity is the mother of invention. The original employees were never taught the joys of inventory, so they were perfectly comfortable without it. A lot of those people are still here and they've passed that attitude along to the newcomers."

Defying Economies of Scale

"But Clyde," countered R. D. "aren't you afraid of running out of inventory now and then? And wouldn't your yield be better if you waited for enough orders to optimize the cutting and tempering schedule?"

"Sure it would. In fact, that's what my competitors do. They sit around for weeks waiting for the order to use up that last piece of glass. When they're through, they stack it and restack it as they try to match finished glass to order. And as you well know, each time you move a piece of glass, you raise the probability of breaking it."

Fitting Labor to Demand, Not Vice Versa

Clyde continued: "At Fasglass, the whole operation works on a flex-hours system. We deal with the load of the day, and our maximum tolerable backlog is two days. That means that every employee is paid on a base plus. Everyone is compensated for at least two thousand hours a year, although that means they have to move with the flow of orders. Some months they may work only 120 hours, in which case they're free to go after, say, four o'clock in the afternoon. Other months it's 180 hours and everybody stays on the job till the load of the day is out the door."

R. D.'s resistance was weakening, but he still had to reconcile Clyde's operation with his own experience. "You must get repeat orders for the same product, right?" he asked. Clyde nodded. "Well, why not prebuild those and stack them neatly at the end of the line? You'd be balancing your work load and better utilizing the tempering furnace."

"R. D.," answered Clyde, "Fasglass can turn out any order in eight hours as is. If I built up my inventory, I'd have to pay for it, count it, move it. And I might break it. The 1 or 2 percent I'd save would be more than offset by the cost of carrying the inventory. Nope, you can't change my mind on this subject. I'm supposed to change yours. And I will!"

He had, actually. Although R. D. couldn't stretch his imagination far enough at the moment to consider such innovations as flex time, he had to admit that the Fasglass system had much to teach him. "To tell the truth," he said, "I'm sort of excited about making a few changes at Keller. The trick will be to get my people to go along. They haven't seen Fasglass."

"It won't be easy But of course they have no more choice in the matter than you. Make sure they understand that shortening cycle times and cutting inventory is here to stay. I'll give you all the advice I can. Cullen means what he says about having me as your advisor and I intend to keep in close touch. Let's plan to meet in Carrollton in a month for a review.

"You haven't been given an impossible task. Trust me: you can slash those times drastically. You know, I envy you the challenge you're faced with and the results you're gonna get."

By the time he got on the plane for Dallas, R. D. believed everything but that last statement. When Angie met him at the airport, he told her there was an outside chance they could hold onto their new house and not have to pull R. L. out of college. "I figured," she said.

Getting Started: Looking at the Business Process

The next morning, the hype had worn off and things looked the same as they did every other day at Keller, so R. D. had to force himself to sit still and plot his next move. He spent all of that day and the next defining the various production steps and estimating the time it took to complete each one. When his own figures on theoretical cycle time fitted Clyde's preliminary estimate, his last shred of denial fell away.

Getting Started: Pushing Involvement From the Top Down

Now to get the ball rolling. R. D. knew he was a poor tactician, but a lot was riding on how he started the drive to lower cycle times. What about barriers? One of the biggest might be the people themselves. Where should he start? He decided to let his managers and planners in on the new requirements and worry about the next step after they'd gotten the news. Just before the group crowded into his office, he remembered Alan Cullen's parting advice that he should spread the heat around. He couldn't. His own anger had dissipated with Clyde's gentle assurances. And why take it out on subordinates, most of whom had been around Keller as long as he? Doing so would make him look like more of a jerk than he felt right now.

What he did do was state as calmly as possible that Atlanta had decreed an entirely new manufacturing philosophy for Keller to which the company had to convert without delay. He then outlined the rationale for the new philosophy and assured them that Keller had the resources and talent to make the cultural leap successfully. Because time was short, he then concentrated on immediate steps to implement the changes. Keller was going to go to smaller lot sizes, he told them. Keller was going to learn how to even out its production and reduce the time it took to change mix. Keller was going to flush its inventory and not replace it. And the planners were going to stop scheduling by the month. Then he hit them with his objective: Keller had to be operating on a four-day cycle time in about a year.

"Now, I realize that this is a profound change we're undertaking," he admitted to his incredulous staff. "Up to now, our performance has been based on 60-day ironclad scheduling and excess inventory. Both of those methods are now down the tubes. Scary, huh? We'll start the changeover by winding down lot sizes and using up our inventory while we devise alternative methods. From now on, we go to weekly planning."

The manufacturing managers took the news surprisingly well. Not so the planner, who insisted that shorter cycle times implied bigger, not smaller, inventories: "If the guys have to assemble windows in a hurry, we'll need to have all shapes and colors of extrusions on hand to speed up the process. Shouldn't we increase our inventory?"

R. D. stood firm. "Absolutely not. If you want me to get as nasty about it as Cullen was to me, I will. If you don't understand the rationale, do it anyway. From now on we produce only what's been ordered, to weekly schedule."

"You're the boss," said the planner, "but it doesn't make sense to me and it won't to the people on the line, either. When they see our inventory shrinking, they'll resist."

The Right Measurements: Cycle Time and First-Pass Yield

They did resist, which was why Clyde was a sight for sore eyes three weeks later when he appeared at Keller. "The staff is unconvinced and I'm floundering," R. D. began. "I obviously need some help on devising the proper measurements and controls. How about it?"

"That's easy," said Clyde. "Well, fairly easy. You need to measure two fundamental areas very precisely: first-pass yield and cycle time. The way to get your folks to take the new measurements seriously is to make it clear that they're being evaluated accordingly. And make sure that mindset goes right down the line."

Measuring First-Pass Yield

"Our first-pass yield is damn good," said R. D. "Ninety-two percent." He was surprised by Clyde's reaction.

"Whoa! That doesn't seem possible in view of your other figures. Are we talking about the same thing: the percentage of work completed perfectly the first time?"

"Yes."

"What about rework, scrap, and stuff on hold?"

"Well, it's the 8 percent that's not perfect."

"Uh-uh," said Clyde, heading for the chalkboard. "The basic formula for determining your yield is to divide output by input."

"That's what I do."

"That's what most people do. And they're kidding themselves about their yields because it's not that simple. During manufacturing, you inevitably have some things that need to be reworked: badly painted extrusions, for example, don't you?" R. D. nodded in agreement. "Boo-boos like those must be factored into your computations even though they don't show up as scrap at the end of the line. Then there's material that's stopped for quality checks or on hold for some other reason. That stuff is likewise a factor that impacts first-pass yield.

"In other words, first-pass yield is output divided by input, multiplied by the percentage of product that does not require rework, multiplied by the percentage of work that is not held up. If you compute those three categories — I'll show you the formula — you'll see that your actual first-pass yield rate is a lot lower than you think."

Clyde and R. D. got down to actual cases. Records showed that the window-making process involved eight rework points which averaged 4 percent per point. There were also three hold points with 20 percent of the parts held for some reason at each point. Like a schoolmaster, Clyde noted all this down on the board. He then wrote out the formula for first-pass yield, and he and R. D. computed. When they were finished, the board's display read:

FIRST-PASS YIELD

The percent that are completed perfectly the first time.

$$\frac{\text{First-Pass Yield}}{100} = \frac{\text{Measured Yield}}{1} \text{ (Typ. Reported)}$$

$$\times \left(\frac{100 - \text{Rework \% per Step}}{100}\right)^n$$

$$\times \left(\frac{100 - \text{On Hold \% per Step}}{100}\right)^m$$

n = Number of Rework Points in the Manufacturing Process
m = Number of Hold Points in the Manufacturing Process

For example,

Measured Yield

$$= \frac{\text{Number That Reach End of Process}}{\text{Number that Entered Process, Regardless of Time}} = 92\%$$

$n = 8$ (−8 Rework Points With 4% Rework)
$m = 3$ (−3 Hold Points With 20% Held for Some Reason at Each Point)

First-Pass Yield $= .92 \times .96^8 \times .8^3 = .92 \times .72 \times .51 = 34\%$

R. D. was aghast: "A first-pass yield of 34 percent!" he exclaimed. "Bad news!"

Measuring Cycle Time

"The news is not good," Clyde agreed. "There is a lot of room for improvement. Your people will figure out how to get some of it if you measure them on first-pass yield, but you also need Cycles of Learning that come from cycle time reduction. Now, you also have to make sure everyone uses the real measurement for cycle time. Most people know the basic formula: work in process divided by speed. But they conveniently ignore things that are sidetracked for quality checks or put on hold by Production Control or whatever when they compute work in process. If those are included, the cycle time figure will be much higher than your people imagine.

"Be sure that you measure first-pass yield and cycle time the right way. Otherwise, the numbers will lull you into a false sense of security."

Improving Morale With Incentives

After Clyde's departure, R. D. lost no time establishing the new indices of measurement. All his managers seemed to get the point. Moreover, they claimed to be implanting the same criteria down the line. But because the new regime's philosophy was precisely the opposite of the one they were used to, the inertia was tremendous. Setup times, for example, remained at four hours despite the fact that their increased frequency should have made the Engineering Department faster at the job. Then there was the matter of the forgotten order, a small-potatoes account that apparently didn't fit conveniently into weekly schedules and so slipped through the cracks. R. D. found out about that via an irate phone call.

One morning in early fall, while seeking refuge in his office from the confusion on the manufacturing floor, R. D. answered a call from Paul Bigard. Bigard owned and operated Bayou Beacon, a manufacturer of electric traffic barriers and signals, located in, of all places, St. Francisville, Louisiana. Bayou's business was an example of Keller's "loose change" sidelines. Keller produced the special dome lights Bayou needed for the assembly of its products. The quantities ordered seldom exceeded a hundred at a crack and were therefore almost a nuisance to Keller. As Bayou's sole supplier, R. D. had run off several hundred dome lights last year and stockpiled them for the sake of convenience; but this year, Bayou had redesigned its products and changed its order. Needless to say, the new order was ascribed a low priority and in recent weeks nobody had given it a thought. Not surprisingly, Bigard's call was to find out when he was going to receive his "hundred goddam dome lights."

"My best delivery is six weeks," R. D. told Paul Bigard. "We've got some major manufacturing problems here. Could you settle for last year's model? Immediate delivery."

"No way, Sonny, and I can't live with six weeks. I'll be there tomorrow to talk about this."

Sure enough, Paul Bigard strode through the door at noon the next day, wanting to know what the problem was. R. D. gave him the complete earful: short cycle times, flushed inventory, confusion and low morale, the works. "Hell, Sonny," said Bigard when the litany was finished, "your new requirements are nothin' but a pain in the butt to these people! You need to do what I did: build in some new incentives to go with the new requirements. Then you might have a chance at winnin' the hearts and minds of those folks."

"What kind of new incentives?" asked R. D.

"Incentives that are tied to your monthly operating profit. Here's how we do it at Bayou: Every human being in my company is part of a point system based on our monthly profit. How much each person earns per point depends on his or her wage scale. In addition to wages, the system gives everyone a bonus paid by separate check and based on the multiple of the profit points times the dollars per point. Its goal is to establish a direct connection between each individual and the company's performance. The better Bayou does, the higher everyone's bonus per month. It works both ways, of course; if we lose money, the loss comes out of future bonuses.

"The point system's immediate effect was to get people very interested in improving performance and willing to share their ideas. That encouraged us to find ways to listen to and implement those ideas. At every level in the operation, people started to talk about last month's performance and discuss ways to improve it. In other words, we have a companywide Cycle of Learning every 30 days. We're getting better and better, learning more every month, and a piece of that improvement goes directly into everybody's pockets. End of morale problems, and the potential for improving performance is unlimited. By the way, I'm breathing down your neck because if Keller screws up our schedules, it will impact every employee at Bayou, including me.

"I'll tell you what, R. D. If you stop whatever you're doing and rush that little bitty dome light order through like a nice guy, I'll send you the entire point-system formula for your consideration. An even trade." That was an offer R. D. couldn't refuse.

Linking Rewards to Cycles of Learning

After reviewing the Bayou point system and adapting it to Keller, R. D. called Clyde to test the water. Clyde was enthusiastic: "It's a great idea. Your friend Bigard understands how important Cycles of Learning are in a short-cycle-time environment. Keller has been operating for years with little, if any, attempt to learn from its experience and improve accordingly. Think of the opportunities that were lost. Well, no more, *if* you make the earned bonus points one of your required measurements, and *if* you can get Atlanta to go along."

It took R. D. two days to accept the fact that if Atlanta said no, he'd have to scrap the point-system idea. When his call went through to Alan Cullen, however, the latter did most of the talking: "I was contacted yesterday by Clyde Farwell," Cullen began. "He outlined the monthly point-reward idea you explained to him and said he thought it was super. He wants to put it in place in Oklahoma City, which means I'm considering implementing it across the board."

"Does across the board include Keller?" asked R. D.

"You bet. It's a great idea. After all, if we expect you to conform to our criteria, we should at least give you every chance to do it right. Nice going."

Well, what do you know? thought R. D. as he hung up the phone. Maybe that's another one I owe Clyde. In any case, how sweet it will be to match the new regime's demands and measurements with a little reward for the troops.

And how sweet it was.

The next several months provided two occasions for R. D. to address Keller's entire work force head on. The first of these came just after he got the go-ahead on the point-reward system. With that okay (and with his own spirits accordingly revitalized), R. D. gave advance notice to his managers that something important was up; then he personally addressed the assembled workers and supervisors of each shift.

He had no way of estimating how convincing his arguments were for abandoning the old methods, but the good news about the point system gave him what he needed to end with a bang. If the work force identified the new system with new rewards, he thought, the changeover could overcome the initial confusion and resistance. He proved absolutely correct about that.

Cycles of Learning and the Setup Barrier

In the month that followed, Keller flushed enough inventory to increase sales and show a respectable profit, which meant that everyone's monthly wage was supplemented by a bonus. There was perceptible excitement as the first-shift workers left the building, talking animatedly about getting a fatter check next time. The following Monday morning, the departmental managers noticed how much informal feedback was going on between employees about how they had contributed to the bonus and the lessons they'd learned that could further improve this month's take-home pay. On Tuesday, they arrived for their scheduled meeting with R. D. with a great deal to discuss.

"Everybody in my department is hell-bent to raise profits," said Rich Ellis of Extrusion. "I've got a proposal from the Extrusion Department that is so crazy it might work. Yesterday, we hashed through a mess of problems, real and imaginary, about cutting cycle times. As you know, going to weekly schedules has put pressure on us and the engineering people as well. Anyway, it wasn't too long before we identified the long setup times for the extruders as the major barrier to better performance."

"Amen," said R. D. "Everybody from Planning through Engineering orbits around those times. They're the main reason Keller started scheduling production by the month and optimizing the machinery."

"Well, we decided it doesn't make sense for us to stand around watching while a couple of engineering people struggle to reset an extruder for three or four hours. That's taking money out of our pockets! And there are a lot more setups necessary now that we're onto weekly schedules. We were wondering if we couldn't somehow lend a hand in order to cut the downtime."

"Damn!" said Ben D'Amato of Engineering. "My guys suggested that they be trained to work in Manufacturing when work piled up there. What do you say, R. D.?"

Wow, thought R. D. This is the sort of crazy stuff Clyde suggested we try. "We're really talking cross-training here," he replied. "Tentatively, I say okay. But the first priority is to cut the time it takes to change extruder dies. Doing that is more than a matter of labor. We'd have to train and practice on the machines themselves, and they're in operation five and a half days a week. What about Sundays?"

R. D. suddenly saw his Sundays slipping through his fingers for weeks to come. So what? What else would he be doing? Tinkering with his boat? Flattening the right-of-way in the rec room? Shortening setup time was a job he could probably do well. But he could see reluctance on the others' faces. "Okay," he said. "What about Sundays at time and a half until practice makes perfect?" Faces brightened.

"I think we could sell that to our people," said Rich with a grin. Ben nodded.

"One condition," said R. D., remembering Clyde's kooky hyperbole. "Perfect means we change dies in a half an hour."

"No way!" answered Ben. "That would take a platoon of people dancing around each other like a ballet troupe. And a *lot* of Sundays."

"We've got 'em. Then it's settled. Get together, pick out the platoon members, and we'll all start a week from Sunday."

Removing a Barrier: A Case Study

A week from Sunday, it was just as Ben D'Amato had described, but not before a two-hour bull session in which Ben orchestrated and diagrammed an exercise that looked like an extended football play. Most of the afternoon was taken up with officious instruction by engineering people determined to reveal all the secrets of die exchange at one fell swoop. Late in the afternoon, the newly organized teams gave it a go.

The results were disappointing. It took the expanded crews almost as long to do the job as two engineering people working under the old system, and by the time all were finished, it was too late in the day to try again. Next Sunday, however, R. D. decided to use Clyde's device of a flowchart. With everyone gathered in a circle, he diagrammed the process. Unlike Ben D'Amato's drawing of the previous week, this diagram was readable by all parties. R. D. had copies run off for each team member to take home for study. Then the teams got busy. Their first attempt cut 15 minutes off the old time. Not bad. Another try and the teams achieved just over three hours. After each run-through, everyone gathered in a circle and critiqued the previous performance, uncovering blunders, identifying improvements, and making appropriate choreographic changes. There was enough enthusiasm to try a third time, which ran well under three hours.

At the last review, D'Amato made a breakthrough: "We're losing a lot of time because we're working with only one forklift," he said. "The lift is loaded with the old die, drives it to the storage area, unloads it, loads the new one, and brings it back here. If we had a second lift to fetch the new die while the first was returning the old one, we could probably save close to half an hour just like that. R. D., there's a forklift in the other building that's used to stack finished inventory. It's idle most of the time. Could we sort of borrow that truck when we needed to?"

"I'll see to it," R. D. promised. "There's the matter of producing a jig to fit onto the lift, but I'll get that taken care of also before next Sunday. Wow. I'll bet two lifts will really make a difference. See you next Sunday." R. D. had never seen so convincing a demonstration of the value of learning cycles.

Seven days later, the Dallas area was in the grip of a winter storm — a "blue norther" — that turned the roads into sheets of glare ice, and R. D. expected attendance to be way down. It wasn't. That afternoon, using the two forklifts, the teams did the setups in 80 minutes, and everyone was ecstatic. On Monday morning, word had spread throughout the plant, and the change in morale was palpable. R. D. okayed one last Sunday's practice, in which the teams broke an hour. That was close enough to allow them to perfect the technique during working shifts. Within another two weeks, one team had actually switched extruder dies in 27 minutes. Now manufacturing people were scheduled to cross-train their engineering counterparts. Meanwhile, another review session had produced a proposal for a similar approach to speed up color changes in the paint section. As soon as the weather improved, R. D., giddy with success, treated all the teams to a catered Sunday barbecue in the company parking lot.

Removing the extruder barrier proved exponential in reducing the overall manufacturing cycle time and, in the process, exposing other time-honored practices as useless. It also eliminated the compulsion to optimize capacity and accumulate inventory.

The entire manufacturing dynamic was thus altered within a few weeks. The planners, who had stopped chewing their nails over weekly scheduling, now sought ways to make the work move evenly day to day.

Reflection and Evaluation

This happy period spanned Christmas, making that season one of the merriest in R. D.'s memory. Home from college for the holidays, R. L. gave his dad a scale model kit of a trackside factory that with a little customizing could look like a miniature Keller; but R. D. wasn't sure whether he'd have the time or the need to wrestle with his trains for some time to come. R. D. sent Clyde a gross of Mallo Cups to help him through the season.

That prompted a call from Oklahoma City just before the New Year. "By the way," said Clyde during that call, "I hope you're proud of the results you're getting, because they're not going unnoticed. I got word of them from none other than Alan Cullen. He's tickled with your results, partly because it reflects damn well on his leadership."

"Leadership comes in strange packages," replied R. D. He then recited the extruder story, adding that "when the idea came up to cross-train people, I threw your wacko figure of a half an hour at them. I knew you hadn't meant for me to take that number seriously, but what the hell. And they went for it!"

"What makes you think I wasn't serious?" said Clyde. "Anyway, you're not out of the woods yet, so keep up your momentum."

A New Barrier: Adjusting Production to Demand

In a way, R. D.'s momentum began to turn on him. As Keller's cycle times declined, its productivity increased commensurately. Not one to hide his light under a bushel, R. D. made sure higher-ups in Marketing took notice of Keller's new responsiveness, which now hovered at two weeks, and waited for more business. It didn't come; orders remained flat and Keller's improved production overtook them. Urgent calls to Atlanta revealed that Marketing doubted Keller's claims of short delivery time and thus had played it safe by not selling that capability.

If faced with such a problem last year, which would have been unlikely, Keller would have used the lull to create more finished goods inventory. This year, however, that was out of the question. Suddenly, R. D. Tyrell was looking at a major layoff. Before panicking, he telephoned Oklahoma City. "Clyde," he said, "I feel betrayed, and I'm afraid the rest of Keller will too. We've been playing the game like real soldiers. We've driven down cycle time and inventory to a point where it looks like we'll meet Atlanta's objectives on schedule. And now, *because* we've played the game, we're gonna get socked with a layoff. How am I supposed to face my people?"

Seeking Alternatives to Layoffs and Repairing Broken Morale

Clyde's words were interspersed with earsplitting crunching sounds. R. D. figured it was probably a Twix bar. "Calm down, R. D.," he said. "The problem's a short-term one, and laying people off is not a sensible option. All your shifts have got to stay in the saddle and stay on track, and you can't afford to lose anybody at this point. You'd better put every shift on a shortened workweek. And get some support from Atlanta."

Getting High-Level Support

It was very hard to do so, but R. D. called Alan Cullen and explained the situation. "I feel as though my credibility is on the line," he told Cullen. "I've been pushing these guys for months and now I've got to tell them to bear the brunt of the slump."

"What do you want from me?" asked Cullen.

"Three things. First, have it out with Marketing and get me a clear picture about how soon they'll utilize our greater productivity. And while you're at it, I wish you'd reconsider moving the window marketers back to Carrollton. If they'd been here to see the changes, we wouldn't be sucking air right now."

"That's two things. What's the third?"

"This: I'd like you to come out here and show the flag next week when I tell the shifts they're going to a four-day week. It'll boost my credibility, possibly head off some embarrassing situations, and safeguard the integrity of short-cycle-time thinking."

"What do you have in mind?"

"I'll give 'em the bad news. It's my job; and anyway, the rumors are already flying, so it won't come as a surprise.

"*I'll* tell them that the shortened week is to spread the hardship evenly and keep the cycle times on their downward path. *You* tell them — all three shifts — that they've done a helluva job, which is the truth, that they've exceeded corporate expectations, which I suspect is the truth, and that you'll do whatever is necessary to get us up to full steam in a hurry, which is a must."

To R. D.'s excruciating pleasure and relief, Cullen agreed readily. And he kept his word. By the time the reduced workweek was officially announced, the departmental managers had made sure their subordinates and labor understood what had caused it and, more important, what had not. And because that month's profits were high, everyone at Keller received a sizable bonus that offset the anticipated hardship.

Restructuring: The Final Breakthrough to Entitlement

Although it was his recent track record that gave him the necessary clout with Cullen, R. D. was uncertain about how to take Keller from its present eight-day cycle time down to four. Cullen, meanwhile, was unwilling to concede that the marketers should return to Carrollton. But during his visit, the VP rendered an important service to Keller. After attending a weekly review, he waited until he and R. D. were alone, then said, "Don't you think you should accelerate your learning?"

R. D. was mystified by this because ever since the Sunday team practices he had made sure every department tracked its progress, discussed it, and made salutary changes on a weekly basis. He said as much to Cullen.

"Yes, but look," replied Cullen, "you're organization isn't unified. You've got three department managers pulling separately, working like hell to hone their sectors."

"And they're getting damn good at using their Cycles of Learning," R. D. replied.

"Granted. But it's too decentralized. You've reached the point where it's probably more effective to have one manager covering the whole manufacturing process. Keller needs to be able to analyze its total output and results, yield, and re-work, and coordinate all that throughout the operation. In other words, I'm suggesting a reorganization to create another level for the entire business process. If managed conscientiously, it would virtually guarantee your four-day goal."

Once again, R. D. felt threatened by the gratuitous advice of his boss. How could he defuse this idea politely? "I see the benefits of feedback around the whole process," he replied. "But, practically speaking, we're doing pretty well with the structure we've got. And I can't afford to add more people, experts, managers, or otherwise."

"You'll get no argument from me there," said Cullen. "And in view of what you've told me, you don't want to antagonize your various managers by bringing in an outsider just as they're mastering the new culture."

Score one for me, thought R. D. But Cullen wasn't finished. "What you *could* do...," he said, gazing at the ceiling.

R. D. waited for the other shoe to drop.

"What you *could* do," repeated Cullen, "is give new jobs to your extrusion and glass managers at the same pay and perks. You just said those two were becoming sharp at refining the process. They'd make great analysts if they were specifically responsible for exploiting Cycles of Learning in the areas of their specialties. The entire manufacturing operation, I think, ought to be under one person. Logically, that person would be your assembly manager, who's always been responsible for coordinating the products of Extrusion and Glass into finished items."

Was this an order? wondered R. D. He decided to treat it as a request. "I'll give that one a lot of thought," he said, bringing a smile to the face of Alan Cullen.

As Cullen probably knew, R. D.'s favorite way of giving thought to something was to contact Clyde. He did just that the minute Cullen's rental car left the parking lot.

After hearing Cullen's suggestion, Clyde chuckled. "Well, if you're asking if it's a good idea, I'd have to say yes," he said. "What else can I say? It was my idea. Alan and I were talking about the progress you've made and I told him the one thing I might do if I were you was to get all your supervisors reporting to one manager. You see, Keller's departments have all been improving independently. As they get better, there's a possibility that inventory could accumulate in areas between departments. There has to be a feedback loop that encircles all the others to keep problems from developing in no-man's-land. I was going to suggest this to you myself, but I guess Alan couldn't wait."

That was enough to convince R. D. that the idea was good.

A Cycle Time Graduate

It was also enough to make R. D. realize that Clyde was the real architect of Keller's turnaround. Was it possible that Clyde had put that bee in Cullen's bonnet in the first place? R. D. promised himself to find out someday. In the meantime, one loose end bothered him: If the entire manufacturing operation were consolidated, and if Marketing did not return from Atlanta, what would there be for R. D. Tyrell to manage at Keller? That concern stayed his hand.

He decided to put the matter out of his mind until Keller was back on a five-day, three-shift schedule. That got him off the hook for about a month. Then, one morning, with all shifts working hard to meet the accelerating orders, he got a call from Cullen.

"I wondered if you'd made a decision about reorganizing Keller," said Cullen.

"Almost," said R. D., "but I need to talk with you about my own revised responsibilities if that happens."

"I need to talk to you, too, R. D. Fasglass has its eye on another window company. In Denver. It's an operation that, to paraphrase what you once said about Keller, is about as good as the competition. Which, to paraphrase what *I* once said, is not good enough for Fasglass. If we bought that company, which would take a few months, of course, we'd want to put someone in there who could bring it up to Keller's present performance levels — short cycle times, almost zero inventory, lots of Cycles of Learning, the whole bit — and then grow the business accordingly. Right now we know of only one such person in the whole glass business.

"Would you, uh, be interested in taking a crack at that?"

"Would you, uh, be interested in buying a railroad?" asked R. D.

Keller Wrap-Up: Four Surprises for the Unaware

A year earlier, at the New York management conference, during which Alan Cullen, you, and Jack Betters had shared dinner, Jack had earmarked Cullen as a likely source of information and, possibly, a character in his book. But over subsequent months, Cullen proved reluctant to talk, repeatedly begging off due to business pressures. He did Jack a real favor, however, by referring him to R. D. Tyrell.

Jack's first conversation with R. D. had taken place when Keller Window was halfway between baseline and entitlement. At that time, R. D. sounded unsure of himself, and Jack wondered if Keller wasn't tying itself in knots trying to please Cullen and the other Atlanta bigwigs. He was about to abandon the contact when R. D. got religion and Keller started to pick up momentum. Jack was glad the two had kept in touch.

His final call on the Keller situation found R. D. in Denver where he had lately moved. R. D. was now managing Platte Plate, a slow-moving window factory acquired by Fasglass because of its entitlement potential. As R. D. told Jack, he was recycling his Keller Window experience to lead Platte to entitlement. His voice sounded tired but upbeat over the telephone.

"R. D.," Jack began, "I'm pulling together my notes on Keller. I think that story would be informative to general readers, and I wonder if you could put in a nutshell the important discoveries you made during the Keller turnaround."

Total Cycle Time: Four Surprises for the Unaware

"Well," said R. D., "my feelings about the whole experience were very personal. I know you're looking for generalizations other people can use, so I'll try to put them in an impersonal way.

"Based on experience at Keller and here at Platte, I would say that the biggest bombshell was the importance of outside, objective assistance. I'm here to tell you that a company can be conscientious and hard-working and still be behind the eight-ball. It often takes an outsider to identify that company's most pernicious problems. Clyde Farwell was the outsider at Keller; I'm the outsider at Platte.

"The second biggest revelation was that outsiders can *calculate* a company's baseline and entitlement performance precisely, although the immediate reactions to such calculations are usually disbelief and denial.

"The third revelation was that the data a company uses to measure its performance may be irrelevant. It's absolutely essential to track real, not imaginary, cycle times and real, not imaginary, first-pass yield as performance measurements.

"The fourth revelation was that a company's entitlement is achievable without adding new resources."

"How about taking each of those four points in detail?" said Jack.

Overcoming the Insider Barrier

"Okay. The biggest single thing in fixing Keller Window was the impact of Clyde Farwell, who had never set foot inside Keller until the day he helped me rough out the company's baseline and entitlement. Clyde taught me how to apply the general principles of Total Cycle Time to a particular business. Any business.

"Those calculations revealed a gap between our baseline performance and our entitlement potential you could drive a pickup through. The figures were hard to swallow, to say the least. And when I was told we could reach entitlement without adding any new resources, I found the figures even harder to swallow. They were too good to be true, and I admit they threatened me. I thought I'd been doing a pretty good job and that the change being forced on me was pure harassment from Atlanta.

"Eventually, I realized that the figures were on the level. Eventually, I saw the business through the right measurements: *real* first-pass yield and *real* cycle times."

Overcoming the Denial Barrier

Jack had heard of the denial problem before. It simply didn't seem possible to dutiful managers that their accustomed methods were so far below the entitled performance level, especially when an objective outsider did the estimating. "What overcame your denial, R. D.?" he asked.

"It was the realization that my own data tracking was self-serving and downright wrong. At Keller, we thought we had a grasp of cycle times and first-pass yield, but we were kidding ourselves in both measurements. Clyde showed me the formula to determine real first-pass yield (as opposed to our own rosy estimates), and I suddenly realized that we'd been living in a fool's paradise."

"Can you explain that formula?" asked Jack.

"Not over the phone. I'd need a chalkboard and 10 minutes of your undivided attention to do that. But I'll send you the formula. If you can use it in your book, go ahead. A lot of people will be surprised when they find their yields are a lot lower than they've figured.

Cycles of Learning Overcome Resistance

"One other thing about the credibility of Total Cycle Time thinking," R. D. added. "When I finally made up my mind it was for real, I was over the first hurdle only. I could hardly expect my managers and workers to suddenly buy the concept. They started the trek toward entitlement simply because the boss said to. Later, as results began to show, they bought in."

"Where was the point when acceptance took hold?"

"It started when people identified our new bonus incentives with the new culture. But real understanding came when we cut our setup times by more than 80 percent using feedback from Cycles of Learning. Think of it: A major barrier that we'd lived with for years came tumbling down because we exploited the lessons of experience. Suddenly, it looked as though we could do the impossible."

Cycles of Learning Drive the Experience Curve

R. D. continued: "When you write your book, be sure to make clear that Cycles of Learning can be increased significantly if feedback is systematically exploited in every loop. The more you learn, the shorter your cycle time. The shorter your cycle time, the more Cycles of Learning take place in a given period. You ought to have a diagram to illustrate the process:

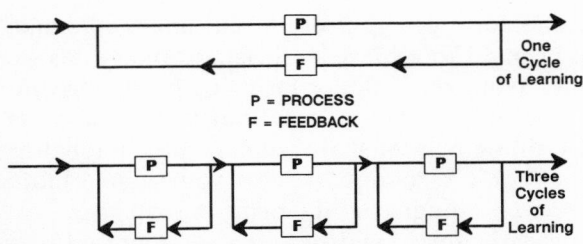

Cycles of Learning accelerate results.

"Also, a very important point that you may need another diagram to illustrate is this: Feedback loops must be used experimentally to shorten the number of Cycles of Learning it takes to make a breakthrough. Using feedback after every cycle, a manager should consider how a different technique might have achieved a better result and experiment with that exact technique. The next time around, the relationship between that technique and its result will be revealed, which in turn permits the setup of another experiment and another set of results from the feedback loop.

"Working that way, a manager can compress the number of Cycles of Learning required and the number of feedback loops within each cycle.

"Another point I want you to be sure to stress is one that Clyde Farwell taught me. It should really surprise a lot of people. Here it is, so listen carefully: *Cycles of Learning have a whopping impact on the so-called experience curve.*"

"Wait," said Jack. "Are you referring to the theory that costs falls by a predictable percentage when cumulative volume doubles?"

"Yes. The theory has it that a company's cost is a function of its cumulative volume. More volume means lower costs, which in turn is supposed to yield bigger market share. In other words, the large can outperform the small because they have the economy of scale. But get this: There is a more important aspect of the experience curve than cumulative volume. By exploiting the feedback from Cycles of Learning, even a small company can accelerate learning and make enough breakthroughs to achieve a crucial advantage. As we learned at Keller Window, Cycles of Learning have more impact on the experience curve than cumulative volume [*as shown below*]. Gaining market share is not so much a matter of volume as speed. It's enough to blow your mind! Little companies everywhere ought to take heart at that!"

"That'll be news for sure," said Jack, who was himself surprised by R. D.'s claim. "Do you speak from Keller's experience?"

"Sure do. Keller Window has the fastest customer response in its field — with the exception of Oklahoma City, of course. The business is growing remarkably, and there's plenty of potential for still shorter cycle times in that plant. Every now and then I revisit the place to exchange ideas with the new management structure there."

"What are you up to in Denver?" asked Jack.

"I'm up to my armpits in the same sort of problems I met

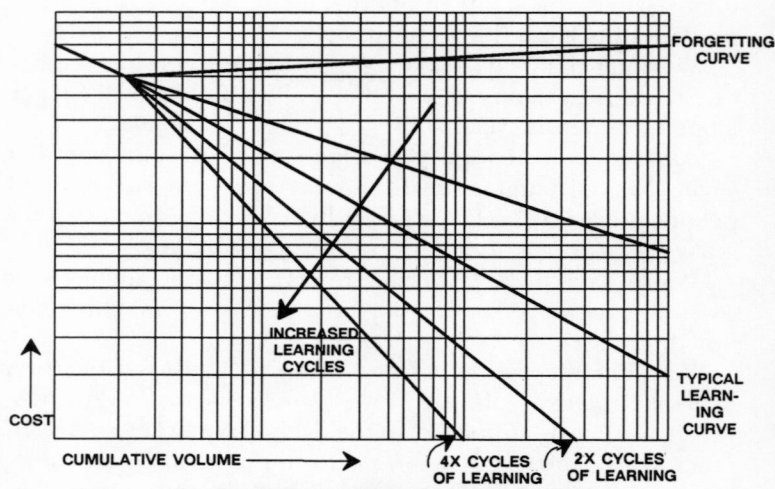

Cycles of Learning impact on experience curve.

at Keller: denial, disbelief. But it'll change, it'll change. No problem. Gotta get off now, Jack. We're about to apply last week's learning cycle to this week's setup. Good luck with your book, and send me a freebie when it comes out."

Jack realized he was amassing quite a long list of freebie obligations.

Jack's Checklist:
Key Barriers Encountered by R. D. Tyrell

1. Lack of comprehension of first-pass yield.

2. The cultural barrier of denial.

3. Poor utilization of Cycles of Learning.

5

The Andy Problem

Attempting to Reduce
Time to Market
of a New Product

Nobody in Contechron expected Hank Petrie to take early retirement, not even his divisional VP. The best of Contechron's three design group managers, Hank was a corporate legend, a relaxed, unstuffy near-genius who had never lost the human touch despite the piles of money his designs had made for the company and, in the bargain, himself. Although he was perennially content to leave upper management to others, he had a nice chunk of founder's stock and had always been well-paid by his co-founding colleagues, in return for which he cranked out the intricate, innovative chip designs that secured Contechron a comfortable niche in the ever-changing semiconductor market.

Although Hank Petrie and Bill Bancroft were about the same age and had started together in the early days of the company, Hank had been reporting to Bill, Vice President for Design, for 11 years. Both were talented designers, to put it mildly; but Bill's chief talent lay in listening to the marketplace and conceptualizing devices that filled needs therein, whereas Hank's stock-in-trade was his ability to translate such concepts into reality. In the last big shakeout at Contechron, much to Hank's relief, Bill's strategic sensitivity had won him the divisional vice presidency. That left Hank altogether free to make technical winners out of Bill's basic concepts. Contechron's other two design group managers, younger men, idolized Hank for his unpretentious affability, his laid-back contentment with his job, and his collegial willingness to share his expertise whenever their own projects bogged down.

It won't be the same without him, thought Bill after Hank had sprung his retirement news, although Bill had to admit to himself that the two had lost touch over recent years. Aside from going back a long way together and knowing a lot about the wide world of analog-to-digital conversion circuits, Bill and Hank didn't have much in common, and they seldom met except at internal meetings wherein each group made detailed, formal progress reports to Bill. Even at those, Hank chose to keep to himself, relying on his team members to present the appropriate data and pep talks.

Hank's reasons for leaving Contechron were mostly personal: his kids were all through college and he was well-fixed financially. The pressure of the old days was off; Contechron had a secure piece of the semiconductor market, and he had reached the point where sailing and puttering at his cottage on Cape Cod were even more fun than they used to be. Hank wasn't getting any younger. It was time, he said, to vacate the Boston area, enjoy what was left of the Cape before developers completely paved it over, and let fresh talent cope with the technological changes necessary to produce Contechron's next line of conversion circuits.

Replacing the Irreplaceable

Bill stayed late that evening to determine how best to fill this unexpected vacancy. Inevitably, he also thought about his own career and whether there was a lesson for himself in Hank's decision. As was his habit, he walked to the window of his Spartan office and stared at the frenzied traffic on Route

128. Whenever he had a problem or was feeling profession-
ally depressed, he had only to look out that window to feel
better about his job. At least he was in here and not out on
128. Any bad day at Contechron was preferable to a single
hour amidst the ruthless kamikaze traffic that hurtled tirelessly around the outskirts of Boston. Bill's home, a 10-room
Georgian-style house with a large mowable yard, was situated
in the sedate, upscale suburb of Wellesley, blessedly outside
that ring of rude, hell-bent commuters.

Surprised though he was, he couldn't quite fault Hank for
his decision. The last of his own kids would be on her own in
a few months, and he too was beginning to see the beauty of
an easier life. But how? Where? He and his wife Emily now
rattled around in their family-sized house, and lots of people
they knew were moving to cunningly tasteful condos near the
water. But to Bill, a move like that still smacked of surrender.
It was too early to pack up his career. Unlike Hank, he'd stay
around to oversee part of Contechron's well-earned financial
security. And the first task in retaining that security was to
find a design whiz to fill Hank's shoes.

Bill was unaccustomed to being caught short. Since its
start-up years of rapid growth, everything at Contechron
moved at a circumspect, deliberate pace with few surprises.
The company did almost $400 million in yearly business and
was an industry leader in profitability. Virtually all of its top
management, Bill included, had been in on the ground floor,
and when Ray Conte and Bill Gendron, the company's
founders, looked across the battered boardroom table at
their senior staff, they beheld a millionaire's club.

Contechron's highly specialized products were developed
by three design groups of about 70 people each, one of which
had been Hank's responsibility and all of which reported to
Bill. Each group included people who simulated the proposed circuits; layout people who, working with computers,
designed them; characterization people who adapted the designs to the manufacturing process; and product engineers
who worried about their manufacturability and cost.

The Making of s Corporate Culture

Thanks in part to Bill's knack for spotting sectors of the semi-conductor market that were too small for giants like National Semiconductor, Intel, Motorola, Texas Instruments, and their foreign competitors to bother with, Contechron had eked out a comfortable piece of the industry for itself. The three strongest elements of its culture were a predilection for rough-and-ready, no-frills surroundings (which reminded the old-timers of their exciting days of struggle and added 2 percent to the company's bottom line), a commitment to pains-taking, innovative design (which preserved Contechron's niche and discouraged interlopers), and a conscious attempt to maintain a collegial, homogeneous white-collar force (which minimized disruptions and empire building).

The Design Division was a model of stability; people came to stay and adapted readily to the environment. Turnover was less than 6 percent. Bill Bancroft didn't have to run a tight ship because he had selected his other team managers on the basis of their compatibility with Hank's style. They, in turn, were free to recruit designers and technicians who fit the mold. All three teams were comfortable with the accepted pace of about two and a half years from basic concept to fin-ished product.

The Right Stuff?

Normally, Bill would have avoided haste in finding a replace-ment for Hank, but the vacancy had appeared at a critical time. Bill had big plans for his newly conceptualized AD-33, which was bound to be a winner, and he wanted a group leader to manage that project from its very inception. Hank had been right: there was a lot of new technology to cope with in the AD-33, so in the interests of a smooth transition, Bill opted for outside help. The Monday following Hank's announcement, he ordered a gold Rolex as Hank's retire-ment gift and then called a headhunter in Phoenix who had tried several times to raid Contechron's talent. That guy, he correctly supposed, would know who was available.

After the usual preliminaries, the Phoenix headhunter set up a meeting between Bill and Andy De Clerck. Andy, a discontented specialist in analog-to-digital conversion, was a little fish in a big pond at NASA in Houston and was scouting around for a smaller pond. As part of his preparation for another job, he would be attending a time management conference in New York. Could Bill catch him before he left? Bill could and did.

On the way into town from LaGuardia, Bill found and salvaged a shopping bag full of New York souvenir T-shirts someone had left in his cab, one for each of his college-age kids. A good omen, perhaps? Bill and Andy met in a room of the Bermuda House Hotel. Bill's first impression was that Andy looked more like a teenager than someone in his mid-thirties. His offhand dress, which included a short-sleeve white shirt and Hush Puppies, bordered on the nerdy. Did he perhaps remind Bill of himself 20 years back? Absolutely not. Andy displayed not one discernible mannerism—that was a little unsettling—and once they had shaken hands, his eyes never unlocked from Bill's, not even when the telephone rang.

But his résumé spoke for itself: bachelor's and master's degrees from MIT (Bill's alma mater), and 10 years working on advanced control systems in Houston. His knowledge was truly state-of-the-art. He expanded upon his résumé by saying he had been part of a successful NASA experiment in shortening design cycles and was eager to perfect those techniques. "What sort of techniques?" Bill asked. Andy replied: "Barrier removal, feedback loops, that sort of thing." Bill wasn't sure exactly what that meant but, being pressed for time, was reluctant to digress.

Speaking personally, Andy said that his wife, another professional (at NASA? he was vague about that), had a life of her own. Andy's hasty assurance that there were no problems about moving made Bill suspect that the De Clercks were separated. For his part, Andy said he was determined to find a spot outside NASA where his management approach would have a direct impact on a project's development, which was why he had attended the New York conference. He added that it would be wonderful to get back to a part of the world where there were four distinct seasons.

Two weeks later, Andy toured Contechron's Design Division. He clearly liked what he saw and was especially pleased by the company's generous salary and stock-option package. The departing Hank Petrie, who didn't have a mean bone in his body, was unlikely to blackball anyone, but he and Andy hit it off especially well. "He's the guy for the AD-33," Hank told Bill. By the end of his two-day visit to Contechron, Andy was adrenalized over his prospects. It was a match and a load off Bill's mind.

New Blood: A Cultural Barrier?

Or was it a relief? Bill began to wonder about a month after Andy took over the AD team. The new man remained an unknown quantity. His acculturation to the company had consisted of joining a carpool commuting from Natick, where he'd sublet a condo in a brutally massive high-rise, and hanging two steel-framed Escher prints in his office. But who was this guy? Nobody really knew as weeks passed. Andy was on the job, often with his door shut, right through customary coffee breaks and occasionally after Bill and the other design managers had knocked off for the day. Then he quit the carpool and started coming into Contechron at all hours. Very early one morning, trudging through new-fallen snow to a senior staff meeting, Bill saw Andy's brown Toyota in its usual parking spot. There were no tracks: the car had been sitting there almost 24 hours.

By the time winter's snow had turned to slush, a lot more parking spaces were being occupied at all hours because AD team members had been dragooned by the new manager into burning the midnight oil. Gossip started around the division about the compulsive weirdo who didn't know when to quit and didn't give a damn about anybody's home life. Some of this grousing reached Bill. He did nothing. Company ethics did not permit managers to beat up on their subordinates, especially new ones, on the basis of grapevine reports. Bill waited and watched to see if Andy would come around of his own accord.

Square Peg Meets Round Holes

Every month, Bill met with his group managers and key team members to hear their progress reports. The mid-level designers who participated therein called these meetings "love-ins" because of the mutually encouraging ambience they engendered. Each group put its best foot forward, illustrating its progress with colored viewgraph slides and, occasionally, a "feelie": a physical representation of whatever device was under development. Often, feelies were schematic diagrams that, with a flourish, a team leader would unroll before his colleagues. On rare occasions, a team might bring along a "macro": a subelement of an uncompleted circuit, wired up to demonstrate that it did indeed perform as hoped. Bill especially enjoyed these moments in a meeting. There was nothing like having a material object on the table to symbolize progress and reinforce intramural spirit.

In deference to the ceremonial value of love-ins, groups vied with one another to make stylish, well-rehearsed presentations. The meetings were seldom marred by embarrassing foul-ups or team failures to keep to projected schedules. After the presentations and wrap-up, all parties usually adjourned to the nearby Spinnaker Restaurant for lunch, courtesy of Contechron. There, amidst brass binnacles, ersatz ship figureheads, and savvy waitresses who knew just how to humor them, they could hash out problems and swap ideas on even friendlier terms.

All but Andy De Clerck, who twice begged off, returning with his resentful team members to work. Inasmuch as Hank Petrie had been a mainstay of the post–love-in lunches, the AD team's absence from the Spinnaker was doubly noticeable. During one of these get-togethers, Bill managed to overhear the BP group leader's incredulous dialogue with a designer at the next table. The two were discussing a reprint of a technical article that had been routed through division mail for all to read.

"I didn't understand that point either," said Ian Forbes of the BP Group, "so I asked Andy to sum it up. That's his field, after all. He told me he hadn't read the article! I said I'd talk to him after he'd read it. He said not to bother, because he'd probably thrown it out along with all the other articles that had piled up on his desk. 'Don't you read any of them?' I asked. 'No,' he said. 'I'm not into defensive reading. I'm here to get the AD-33 on-line, and that takes all the concentration I've got.' I just looked at him; then I had to laugh, because it made me wonder who was dumber: him for deep-sixing the stuff that's pumped through the pipeline, or us for reading it?"

The Reporting Barrier: Rattling the Corporate Cage

Then there was the surprise of Andy's third monthly love-in presentation. Andy was a poor public speaker, and his report was further botched by sloppy, makeshift slides, some of which he clumsily corrected by hand. Feelies? His were confined to diagrams developed strictly in the line of duty. But he was obviously psyched up for this third presentation and it did turn out to be a bombshell of sorts. Andy had chopped 10 months off Hank's schedule for the AD-33! So that's what all the closed doors and midnight oil was about, thought Bill. Why, then, was he not more pleased with the improved business prospect of the new product's early introduction?

Clearly, Andy and a few of his overworked designers were proud of that projection and expected roars of approval. There were none. Shortening the AD-33 design cycle was an accomplishment of sorts, but to what end? Bill made a stab at letting Andy down easy: "You and your team are to be congratulated, but I need to know what you're trying to accomplish by rushing the design that way. We're not in a race; we've got the potential market covered. And by your own admission, you haven't bothered to document your progress with the customary data."

Andy looked blankly at Bill, then responded: "Well, you ask for a prodigious amount of data, month in and month out. And I spend a fair amount of time at these meetings listening to detailed data of the other teams without a clue to what they mean to me. Right now, I couldn't come up with the details you're referring to, I admit.

"It's a matter of priorities. Based upon my experience at NASA, I knew I could slash the design cycle by months, but only by pushing my people very hard at first. To make things simpler for us all, I excused them from keeping weekly tabs on all that stuff. Then I dispensed with biweekly reviews. Instead, I meet informally with key people every other day or so, make whatever decisions are required, and we push ahead on that basis. Things are starting to happen in the AD group, partly because I reduced my requirements for presentations and red tape. In fact, a lot of people who were pretty tired and surly last month are coming in early on their own steam now."

Bill doubted this and was sure the other group leaders did too. To their surprise, they now detected an unexpectedly abrasive side to Andy. Then Ian Forbes spoke up: "Suppose you do cut the AD-33 design cycle. It'll be at our groups' expense, because if you discard your original schedule — I should say Hank Petrie's schedule — you're gonna be crowding everybody else. Manufacturing, Marketing, and the rest of the outfit aren't simply at your disposal alone. When the AD-33's ready 10 months ahead of schedule, it'll be especially bad news to Manufacturing. Are they supposed to drop everything that's running to plan and take on the product? And how is Marketing supposed to adjust its strategies if items start popping up unpredictably?"

"Not unpredictably," Andy replied almost inaudibly, "just quicker." Andy seemed so stunned by the way his bombshell had fizzled that he did not continue.

"I'm sure Andy has considered all this and wouldn't work a hardship on the other groups," said Bill, resuming his control of the meeting, although he was by no means sure that Andy gave a damn about the other groups. Or anything else except getting the AD-33 out as quickly as possible.

Then Andy rallied. "I need the division's indulgence till I'm firmly on my feet here," he said. "Give me two months to get oriented. Then I'll present my data in a way that I'm sure will be meaningful." On that note of accord, they adjourned. Andy and his subordinates tagged along with the others to the Spinnaker but sat by themselves at a single table. Soon they were gone.

Enough Rope

As usual when he had a problem, Bill stared out his window onto rain-slicked Route 128, which was almost a tableau. A multicar smashup in the southbound lanes had brought traffic to a standstill. Northbound drivers, with the morbid curiosity peculiar to Boston, inched past the sight. From a distance, the whole effect was a two-mile-long ribbon of lights, red on one side, white on the other, made even gayer by the flashing domelights of police and rescue vehicles. For a minute or two it distracted Bill from his reverie about how to manage Andy.

There simply were no managerial precedents at Contechron for dealing with such an upstart. Bill's first inclination was simply to order Andy's group to comply with the original projections and measurements. That plus the resistance Andy would encounter from his overworked people would probably get AD back on the right track. But, though soft from years of disuse, Bill's managerial instincts whispered to him to back off. Maybe there's a method to the guy's madness that will teach the rest of us something, he thought. He decided to give Andy the two months of grace he'd asked for.

Barrier Removal Makes Mavericks

Having sent Andy a memo to that effect, Bill braced for the backlash. Instead, quite suddenly, the grapevine gossip reversed itself, saying that the AD group was pulling together again.

For his own part, Bill now noted animated conversations between AD people and quite a few designers whose absorption in their work made them oblivious to quitting time. Bill knew better than to ask such people for particulars, but the word from Ian Forbes and others was that streamlining the documentation and review processes had restored morale. One designer who had asked to transfer to the BP group withdrew his request because, as he put it, "things are different there now. We can spend most of our time designing, which makes us want to spend longer hours on the job."

Andy had little in the way of charisma, nor was he the warm, avuncular leader Hank Petrie had been. He seldom raised his voice or cracked a joke. And he was turning out to be a hard, utterly dedicated driver seemingly interested in little else than accelerating his design responsibilities. As revealed in the love-in presentation, he was impervious to criticism from above or below that he regarded as obstructive to that task. And, as Bill soon learned, there was nothing he wouldn't do to eliminate a barrier to his group's concentration.

Change and the Comfort Curve

One day, when Andy unexpectedly dropped by his office, Bill asked him about his group's morale. "Morale swings are part of the comfort curve," said Andy, whose faraway look made it clear he had something else on his mind. Since Bill had never heard of the comfort curve, he asked Andy to elaborate. "Well," he replied, "when a new kid on the block arrives and starts making changes, people get nervous. In my group's case, the changes I demanded had the objective of shortening the design cycle. At first, everybody had to work longer than usual to get used to my requirements and pace. They hated that, as you probably noticed, and their comfort indices tumbled. It's inevitable in such a situation. After a while, however, the changes began to make sense, and people could see that their discomfort was not simply a matter of humoring a new boss. As I eliminated barriers, my designers had more time to design, which is presumably what they're most interested in. At that point, their comfort curves bottomed out and started to climb. Now that they've seen the psychic payoffs of short cycle times, their comfort level should keep on climbing. But the real reason I stopped in to see you was to get your okay for a conference with the marketing manager. I didn't want to talk to another divisional VP without letting you know."

"Is it something important?"

"I want to get Lou Roberto's input on our proposed designs so I'll know which ones have the most potential."

"By all means get all the free advice you can. But I'm sure every one of your projects will be a winner."

"Sure. But from a sales standpoint, some will win bigger than others, right? Marketing must have a feel for that. Thanks." Andy cracked one of his rare smiles and headed for the door. Then he turned back again.

Measuring Results Against Accepted Form

"Bill," he said, "it's decent of you to give a guy like me the latitude I need to get things done my way, but as you see, I seemed to have reached the limit of my powers to effect change. At NASA, we *had* to cut cycle times, and everyone from the top down was under the gun, so the questions asked there were never *if* but *how*. Here, though, I feel as though I'm swimming upstream. I hope my results will convince you and the other top brass to take a hard look at shortening cycle times throughout the division. Maybe throughout the whole company. But first I've got to get those results." With that, Andy was out the door in a flash.

Prioritizing to Fit Reality

At the next month's meeting, Andy ran through his minimal numbers and, as before, tacked on a contribution of his own device. (By the glances exchanged throughout the room, Bill saw that the other groups' members now expected this to be a regular feature of monthly meetings.) "I've been trying to prioritize my people's assignments," he began, "so I had a long conference with Lou Roberto in Marketing. His advice is going to make a big difference to the group." As heads turned his way to gauge his reaction, Bill nodded knowingly to show he'd okayed the idea.

Andy continued: "Here in Design, it's easy to lose our perspective on the whole process. First of all, Lou was amazed and delighted that I talked to him; apparently it's the first time a design manager has crossed over to Marketing for ideas. He was excited about the AD-33, of course. And because that device is going to make a big splash in the market, he was especially interested in calibrating our other designs to exploit that breakthrough. Lou and I were able to rank-order the 11 projects my teams are presently working on. Obviously, I should bring most of my resources to bear on AD-33 and related devices because, as Lou said, the sooner they see daylight, the better for Contechron. That means, of course, that I'll have to cut back on the number of designs in progress at this time; the least urgent ones will be put on hold. I now think I understand the business a bit better. Lou supplied me with the kind of direction I needed to remove more barriers and smooth the design process further. I think the other groups ought to talk to him as a matter of course. I'll give you all another progress report next month." By the look on his face, Bill could see that Andy was getting to like these reviews.

Sweet Revenge: Blasting a Procedural Barrier

The next morning, Andy was camped on Bill's doorstep. "I need your authorization to buy a midrange copying machine," he said before Bill had hung up his coat.

Bill was taken off guard: "A *copying* machine? Hold it. Contechron's copying center has the best equipment available. Why should you want to duplicate it, so to speak?"

"Because the copying center is one of the biggest headaches my teams have to face, and I'm sick of it." Bill had heard this before, but not put so bluntly. The copying center's equipment was indeed state-of-the-art and it processed orders precisely, but it processed them strictly on a first-come, first-served basis. Time and time again, a group's momentum would slacken as designers and technicians waited and waited for the overburdened, often testy copy people to fill their orders. The wait-stop problem became so acute during the workup of the AD-30 series that Hank Petrie had actually assigned multiple tasks to each team to keep them steadily occupied.

"Before we go any further with this," countered Bill, "have you talked to the center's manager?"

"Of course. Three times. The last talk was more of a shout. I explained to him that dealing with the copy center is a non-value-added step for my people, that the AD-33 is a top priority, that I'm determined to cut the design cycle times in my group, and that four days is too long to wait for requested material."

"And?"

"And he got sore. He wanted to know who the hell I thought I was, he pointed to his notebook full of procedures, and he told me I was entitled to no different treatment than any other group manager."

"He's completely in the right on that," said Bill.

"Of course he is," said Andy. "That's why I want you to sign a voucher for a copying machine. It will pay for itself inside a few weeks and meanwhile I'll be off the copy center's back."

Bill tried not to smile. Another senior manager might have said no to such a renegade idea just to keep peace in his family, but there was something beautiful about circumventing the notorious copy center. He even looked forward to whatever showdown Andy's irreverent act precipitated. "Do it," he said.

Andy did it. AD soon had a new rule: use the copying center only when technical or quantity needs outstripped the capabilities of the group's small machine. He didn't have to ask his people twice.

The other group managers got wind of the copier story when their own requests started to move through the center more quickly. And when the irate copy center manager complained that his responsibilities were being undermined, Bill squelched him abruptly by saying that the entire division might reevaluate the rationale of maintaining a centralized copying facility. Faster response, after all, couldn't be all bad!

That felt good, and Bill resolved to review the copy center issue before the end of the year. Meanwhile, however, he could see that he had a maverick on his hands whose ideas were truly innovative, if discordant. Nobody really liked Andy, nor was anyone close to him, but now, with his honeymoon time expired, his countercultural vigor had turned his group on. The other groups now called the AD people "the Foreign Legion," and they loved it. Inside AD, a lively, skunk-works spirit flourished.

Blasting the Paperwork Barrier: Another Unorthodox Approach

Then came the review at which Andy was expected to align his management with the divisional modus operandi. If the attending managers had expected him to fall on his face, they were in for a disappointment. Andy presented his report in the polished, rehearsed style that was Contechron's accustomed standard. To everyone's surprise and Bill's relief, his viewgraph slides, while different in style and typeface, itemized all the expected points of documentation. After he had done so, however, he added some pointers of his own: "You'll recall that it's taken me three months to come to terms with the type of reporting you've just seen. I appreciate the division's patience, because the fact is I would never have put together such a documentary package on a monthly basis and probably never will. I believe a three-month report is sufficient, and I intend to stay with it. If the other groups cut their cycle times, they'll likewise eliminate the need for such reporting. I urge you people to do that. Meanwhile, I've purchased a software program to run on one of our high-end PCs that makes quarterly reporting a cinch. The time saving to my people has already more than paid for the cost of the software. I'll be glad to share the program with other groups. Of course, the program can't cover all of Contechron's items of detail. That means that about 20 percent of the data you see before you is guesswork, because I've quit keeping precise tabs on some items. I want to emphasize that shorter design cycles eliminate the need for all that data input. *I urge the other groups to cut cycle times.*"

Was this conformity? Andy seemed to be giving with one hand and taking away with the other.

A Linear View of the Business Process: One Team, One Project

"A couple more pointers," he continued. "When I got here, I noticed that every team in my group was working on multiple projects because there were wait stops in each project. When one would hang fire, the team was supposed to go to another. It's that way throughout the Design Division, isn't it? The practice is crazy, and we all should put an end to it.

"Meanwhile, I've reorganized the Foreign Legion into design cells: one team, one project, from start to finish: layout, circuit simulation, characterization, everything. I intend somehow to break the other barriers that keep my people from concentrating on one thing at a time without disruption. My people know I'm serious about this, so they help identify and break those barriers. I meet informally with every team every other day. The team leaders and I have installed a formal feedback system so we can learn from our mistakes and profit from our breakthroughs. I've also instituted a new evaluative measurement: the number of designs per team per year. It's a great motivator. *I urge the other groups to do likewise.* Life in the Foreign Legion can be very exciting.

"A final point. Two months ago, I projected a 10-month shortening of the AD-33's design cycle. With the new software and the new mindset in my group, and yes, with our own copier, along with my absolute confidence that I can break other logjams, I'm going to revise my projection. We can take *14 months* off the cycle. That's about half of the original estimate."

Andy scooped up his viewgraph foils and quickly sat down. This time there was no embarrassed aftermath; he had ceased to expect on-the-spot approbation from his peers.

As he listened, Bill gave up his hope that Andy would ever adapt to Contechron's established procedures. He wasn't arrogant, exactly; he honestly didn't understand the need to fit in. He also assumed that once everyone had gotten his or her gems of AD wisdom, there would be a willingness to do things his way. But why?

The Big Picture: Short Cycle Time as a Counterculture

At the Spinnaker that afternoon, other people also wanted to know why. What was the big deal about cutting design cycle times in a company that made virtually unique items? Who were we racing against? Andy wasn't around to answer, but one of his team leaders, Rube Chappell, took the bait: "Up to now, Contechron has made out very well by working in niches. We've hidden in those niches, developed expertise in those areas, and had the game pretty much to ourselves because we're so good at what we do. We've proven that a little company can outperform bigger ones if it finds its place and stays there. But, as Andy says over and over, there's another fact of life we haven't considered: the fast can outperform the slow regardless of size. That presents two possibilities for Contechron: one's an opportunity, and one's an area for concern. If we taught ourselves to get new designs finished in, say, half the time it now takes us, we'd have twice as much opportunity to introduce new products. In other words, we could deepen our niche if we moved faster. We might even diversify a little. On the other hand, if a potential competitor with shorter cycle times spots our nice cushy niche and invades it, we'll be up the well-known creek, right?"

Culture Versus Counterculture

"Wrong," said Ian Forbes. "If he's bigger than we are, he'll find out that products like ours are more trouble than they're worth. If he's small, he'll find out that speed is no substitute for expertise and decide to specialize in something simpler. End of report."

"But look," Rube persisted, "If the fast can outperform the slow, we could be broadening into more generic fields. Why hide in just one corner of the market if we can outmaneuver clumsier companies on their own turf? Admit it: as specialists, we have enough design know-how to go head-to-head with high-volume companies, but we don't do it because we think Motorola or National Semi or TI will cream us. They'd only cream us if we were slower or sloppier than they were. Don't you get it? What Andy's doing inside the AD group could be the start of something big at Contechron!"

"You gotta be kidding, Rube. Contechron is healthy because we stay out of harm's way. We'd be crazy to get involved in the big boys' chip wars. Who envies them their turf?

Not this designer. And, I'll bet, not this company." Several other heads nodded in agreement.

"Too bad," said Rube. "I'm worried that our know-how may not save us forever, even if we resolve to stay put in our own little corner of the market. So far, thanks to Bill, we've been good at anticipating the next generation of products within our niche. But we don't have a perfect crystal ball. Another company with shorter cycle times and shorter time to market might take its cues from us and still get there first. Maybe there's somebody out there right now...."

"Don't borrow trouble," replied Ian, catching the waitress's eye. "You Foreign Legion guys have your hands full as it is!"

When Less Than Perfect Is Best

The Foreign Legion people did indeed have their hands full for the next two months, and there were no unsolicited lectures from Andy for two consecutive love-ins. But at the next one, Andy announced that thanks to the removal of bottlenecks and the rechanneling of talent, the AD-33 was almost ready for pilot production. Therefore, he said, he might have something interesting to show the division managers in a month's time. "Make that three month's time," Ian Forbes muttered to himself with satisfaction. No one pointed out that backups on the pilot line made Andy's forecast impossible.

The pilot line was the Design Division's advanced minimanufacturing facility. It took developed designs and actually built prototypes. It served all groups, and its manager, John Loos, reported directly to Bill Bancroft. Running a design through the pilot line usually took seven or eight weeks. Because of that, every team at Contechron fine-tuned its designs to perfection before turning them over. Getting the design perfect the first time eliminated the frustrations and delays of going around again and avoided confrontations with the hardpressed Loos, whose territorial sensitivity made the copy center's boss seem like a pussycat. Andy hurriedly turned over the AD-33 design to Loos and commenced the long wait.

A Manufacturing Perspective on Design Barriers

When everyone convened four weeks later, and Andy rose to give his report, he announced that before presenting his usual data he wanted to provide a different perspective on the design and development function within Contechron. With that, Bill could hear feet shuffling and pencils agitatedly tapping, body language that said, "Look out, here comes another sermon from the Rev. De Clerck."

"Before my NASA days," the unflappable Andy began, "I was trained in manufacturing. My Contechron experience has sensitized me to the fact that there are close analogies between the manufacturing and design functions. Inasmuch as I haven't gotten my ideas across effectively during these love-ins — I mean reviews — I wanted to try again by drawing parallels between manufacturing and design." A neatly printed slide flashed onto the conference room screen:

MANUFACTURING AND DESIGN ANALOGIES: LOT SIZE

Manufacturing

Lot size is the most insidious kind of inventory imaginable. A complete infrastructure can get built up around lot size: machines, handlers, information transfer, evaluations, lead times, etc. This makes lot size difficult to change.

Design

In this area "lot size" is called "work package size":
- The natural tendency is toward larger work packages to simplify the review process.
- Large work packages encourage relay races instead of rugby.

"One of the latest manufacturing innovations is to reverse the trend toward large lot sizes. Smaller lot sizes allow a company to respond more quickly to market conditions. Well, in Contechron Design, our groups' work packages could be looked at as lot sizes—large lot sizes. Because of our widely spaced, formalized review schedule, every group juggles a large package of projects because that fits the schedule and the time that elapses between reviews. For my group, however, I took a page from the manufacturing book. I shrunk the work package and switched to frequent, informal reviews. As you know, I was thus able to shorten design cycle times.

"But the lot size–work package analogy isn't the only one that's pertinent," Andy continued, flipping another slide onto the overhead projector.

WAIT TIMES

Manufacturing

- Raw material is waiting to be used.
- Subassembly is waiting to match up with other parts.
- Finished goods are waiting for order.
- Machine is waiting for repair.

Development

- Final design modifications are waiting for prototypes out of the pilot line.
- Engineers are waiting for copies through the copy center.
- A brilliant software concept is waiting for coding resources.
- In development, a lot of wait time involves communications. That's why proximity–physical layout is important.

"Look at these examples of wait times in manufacturing and in development. The circumstances are strikingly similar, except that in a manufacturing context, such bottlenecks would probably be remedied in a jiffy because they are conspicuous and costly. The causes of waits in design and development are pretty much the same. You all know the bottleneck at the copy center, for example, or the wait necessitated on the pilot line, which I'll address in a minute. Ask yourselves why such barriers are more acceptable in a design context than in manufacturing."

Another slide appeared.

MANUFACTURING AND DESIGN ANALOGIES: FIRST-PASS YIELD

Manufacturing

- Think about the causes for yield loss in manufacturing: Unclear customer requirements, unclear specs, improper training, process-spec windows, equipment capability.
  - Do you inspect?
  - Or prevent?

Design/Development

- What causes development-yield loss, delays, rework?
  - Forecast errors
  - Market changes
  - Design execution
  - All caused by cycle time

- A critical measure of development yield is the percentage of products started that are business successes.

"Here are some analogies on first-pass yield. First-pass yield is largely misunderstood by most companies—Contechron included—so I can't point to our own counterparts in Manufacturing as examples. But the *principle* is valid in manufacturing, whether or not it's upheld, and that goes for this division, too. We designers accept yield loss, delays, and rework because first-pass yield is not a divisional measurement. It ought to be."

Up came another slide.

MANUFACTURING AND DESIGN ANALOGIES: BOTTLENECKS/CAPACITY

Manufacturing

- Can't run your manufacturing line any faster than your bottleneck.

Development

- Why would your design/development loop be any different?
- Are barriers to testing creating a bottleneck that impacts the cycle time performance of the whole design/development and make/market loop?
- Are design personnel levels versus designs-in-process overwhelming the cycle time performance?

"What I want to say with this display is that all of us in the division ought to take as hard a look at barrier removal as they do in Manufacturing. Which brings me to my next topic, the one you've probably been wondering about...."

The lights came up, whereupon Andy raised his right hand with the tips of his thumb and index finger touching to form the well-known sign for "okay." Only the thumb and finger weren't quite touching. Between them was a shiny object the size of a cuff link. "A feelie!" exclaimed Ian Forbes in a slightly amused tone.

"Nope," said Andy, "not a feelie. A realie. The AD-33, designed and characterized. It's not perfect, but it's 90 percent perfect."

Mastering the Art of Simple and Direct

Silence. Bewildered expressions. Then Loos spoke: "I don't want to embarrass you, Andy, but that can't be the AD-33. It hasn't even gone through the pilot line yet."

More confusion. "I have a confession to make," said Andy.

"I was able to cut six or seven weeks off the schedule by a bit of creative massaging. When I submitted the AD-33 to the pilot line, John told me on nonnegotiable terms that the wait for a prototype would be eight weeks. Eight weeks. Well, as all of you know, the pilot line's forte isn't speed, although in a real-world manufacturing situation, their collective ass would be grass. Sorry, John. But the main reason they're so slow is that they only run one shift, like the rest of our division.

"Now, as you've heard, I'd been analogizing manufacturing and design. That got me thinking about the real manufacturing operation in Contechtron. I went over there, took a look, and introduced myself to some people. Manufacturing operates three shifts. It so happens that the poor person who's stuck with the second shift thinks she's in limbo, and maybe she's right. But she's really interested in shortening cycle times, and she gets her kicks by being a maverick, something I can relate to. Anyway, I told her about the urgency of the AD-33 and how Design's pilot line takes two months to deliver a prototype. She was amazed at that figure. She was also amazed to see somebody like me in her area. 'You're the first design team manager whose ever bothered to show up in Manufacturing,' she told me. 'And right in the middle of the second shift!'

"To make a long story short, it was pretty easy to talk her into the urgency of the AD-33. She almost volunteered to run it through last-in, first-out with her work in process as a personal favor. Then, between us, we were able to get the first- and third-shift guys to go along with the project. I promised a blowout at the Spinnaker for the shift that had the shortest manufacturing cycle. It was my friend on shift two. That manager is a hero. She really has potential and should be considered for promotion. In fact, you could do a lot worse than hiring her to run your pilot line, John.

"It took 10 days to get the job done. If my calculations are correct, the pilot line's AD-33 should emerge in a month and a half. Meanwhile, here's the AD-33. And it works."

Bill was not easily surprised, but all this astounded him. He would have blown his top if Andy hadn't defused his righteousness by observing the letter of the law: he *had* sent his design to the pilot line. By now, John Loos was three shades of pink. Mercifully, before he could say anything, Ian Forbes spoke up.

"Andy," he began, "I know what you're gonna say: You urge all of us to try this. No thanks. You say the AD-33 is '90 percent' perfect. That's not a bull's-eye. In our book that's a near miss. Maybe if you'd slowed down, the damn thing would work."

"The damn thing does work, now that we've got some experience to build on. And when we tune the design a little, we'll have it perfect 10 days after that—as long as I can use the resources in Manufacturing. That's got to be some kind of record for Contechron, right? And look at the drop the company will have on the competition by getting the AD-33 to market so quickly!"

Form Versus Function

Meanwhile, thought Bill after the meeting, look at the mess this is causing in the Design Division. Everyone but Andy was disturbed by his nonconformity and insubordination. It was a severe challenge to the company's culture, it violated the chain of command (didn't it?), and it shouldn't be allowed to continue unchecked. But—dammit!—by hook or crook, Andy had pulled off an industry design coup. The AD-33 would be ready for marketing just a little more than a year after conception, not two and a half years as anticipated. That packed a lot of profit potential that would make the whole division look good. Bill dialed Lou Roberto in Marketing. Roberto estimated the potential sales increase at $5 million, more than twice Bill's original impact analysis. What happens next? Bill wondered.

Showdown: City Hall Versus
the Foreign Legion

What happened next was as interesting as it was disturbing to Bill: the other group managers began gratuitously to justify themselves. At the next meeting—love-in no longer seemed an appropriate term, even in jest—both managers, having presented their data, stipulated at some length that their teams were working at the fastest reasonable rate, given the special conditions of their assignments. These remarks amounted to a denial that any of the Foreign Legion's techniques applied to them. Forbes added that his yield on first-pass prototypes was 99 percent, as though his own performance were somehow being challenged. Listening to this, Andy was attentive but expressionless and was not drawn into a dialogue. Thank God for small blessings, thought Bill.

Bill skipped the lunch at the Spinnaker that afternoon, and he had the feeling a lot of others did too. He needed some time to sort out the Andy problem before it got completely out of hand. He knew the buck stopped at his desk and now berated himself for his blithe tolerance of Andy's unorthodox methods. Clearly, he had encouraged insubordination.

Nothing so baffling had ever happened to Bill in all his years at Contechron. As he stared out his office window at the cars below, he was overwhelmed by a feeling of envy: Probably at this very moment, Hank Petrie was sitting with his feet up staring out his own window at Cotuit Harbor and thinking happy, trivial thoughts. Maybe it was time....

Bill was startled by a knock on the half-opened door. "Got a minute?" said Andy. Bill waved him in and pointed to a chair. This is as good a time as any to reign him in, he thought, but to save his life he could not think of a straightforward opener.

Truce? Armistice?

"You were right today," he finally ventured. "Your speed on the AD-33 design is a record at Contechron. You must feel pretty proud of that. Lou in Marketing thinks you hung the moon."

"Not really," answered Andy, "and that's why I'm here. It's funny; just now you said I was right, and in the second or so before you finished the sentence, I thought you might mean my methods were right. I realize that's not going to happen here, ever.

"When I interviewed for this job, I thought Contechron's Design Division was a perfect fit. Everywhere there were barriers that were prolonging the process. All I had to do was remove them and the results would blow Contechron's management away. Or so I thought."

"I thought so too, Andy," put in Bill. "And so did Hank Petrie."

"Thanks for saying that," Andy replied. "But first impressions, I guess, can be deceiving. Over the last few months, the AD-33 was done in spite of, not because of, the internal mindset at Contechron. There was nothing really radical in my assessment of design and development cycle times. Every group in the division has enough resources and talent to get every device on-line in less than half the time it's taking. What was radical from my standpoint was that I had to pull every trick in the book to get one device completed within a reasonable time frame: brute force, setting the example, subterfuge, flattery, and even a little bribery."

"Your methods have been quite unorthodox," said Bill. "I'm still not sure you understand how unorthodox."

Countercultural Power: A Few Lessons

Andy replied: "Well, I've learned a lot, and I'm not so cocky as I was. But I'm also not so hopeful. Looking back, I now see my job as a thick forest I had to hack through to reach my objectives. At first, I couldn't see very far into the forest because of the tangle of undergrowth blocking the way: too much data tracking, too many meetings, no clear priorities. So I cut through that tangle and made some real headway. But suddenly I came up against more tangle—barriers I couldn't see from the edge of the woods—and these were a bit trickier to remove: the copy center tangle, the pilot-line tangle, and so on. By that time I was deep in the forest and on my own, so I did what I had to to slash my way to the other side with little, if any, support from above.

"When the AD-33 became a reality, I thought I saw light through the trees. No such luck. What I found on the other edge of the forest was an insurmountable brick wall named Contechron Culture. I couldn't see some of the woods for the trees, and I didn't see that wall until too late. It's bigger than I am. It ought to go, but that would require a lot of top-down effort and dedication at all levels that doesn't exist here. I'm obviously not the man to persuade Contechron to switch cultures. I'm at too low a level and too low on political skills."

"That would be a job for more than one man," said Bill, "if we wanted to switch cultures. Problem is, most of us don't."

"I realize that," said Andy. "I've found out that I can't operate in a vacuum. I've learned that more diplomacy is required than I was prepared to give. I've learned that in an environment like Contechron, a guy can get a lot by asking and a lot more without asking if he's tightly focused. But I've also learned that I can't pull down a wall that everyone but me is happy with.

"Today's meeting confirmed some of my worst fears about corporate mindset. The other group managers were sending me — and you, by the way — a strong message: if it ain't broke, don't fix it. I see that I'm a misfit here, because in my opinion it *is* broke; there are a bunch of little things I see that need fixing. I guess I made a poor case for that. I had hoped that deeds rather than words would get my message across. Anyway, some of the things I resorted to to shorten cycle times can only be done once without a top-down approach to removing the barriers I went around.

Victory? Defeat?

"You probably know what I'm going to say next," Andy continued. "I can't work this way. The Foreign Legion can't buck the wall by itself, and there's no reason to expect any top-down change in the division. Also, the other group managers are dug in. So here is my notice that once the AD-33 is released to production, I'm moving on."

Bill did not reply. He honestly couldn't tell if he were burdened or relieved by the news. Finally, he broke the silence by asking, "What are your plans, Andy?"

"I don't have any clear prospects, and I realize there's a noncompete clause in my contract that'll cramp my style, but there are lawyers who love to handle that sort of stuff. It'll all sort out in due time. I hope, though, that in due time you'll consider what Contechron is forfeiting by indulging itself in its comfortably long cycle times."

Replacing the Replaceable

It was getting dark, but Bill made no move to turn on a light. "I also have to think about who to get to replace you," he said.

"That's a toughie, I admit," Andy replied. "Rube Chappell is the best guy working for me, but he's a convert to my cause. So are most of the people in the Foreign Legion. Ironic, isn't it? You'll probably have to go outside the company or transfer one of Ian's senior people to get someone who can restore the old Contechron culture to my group. But that will happen on its own, if you let it. My group's counterculture is too young to flourish without nurturing. Sooner or later the corporate antibodies will kill it off—unless you get another guy like me. Unlikely, I'd say."

There was nothing more to be said, at least for that day. Bill rose and walked to the window: light traffic was moving briskly. When he turned back toward his desk, Andy was gone.

Leaving the building hours later, Bill noticed that this was the first night in memory that his was the last car in the parking lot.

Contechron: Short Cycle Time as a Counterculture

Four months later, upon calling the usual number at Contechron, Jack Betters was surprised to learn that Andy

De Clerck had left the company. Jack had known Andy since his NASA days. When they had bumped into each other at the Bermuda House management conference, Andy's command of cycle time theory and his stated intention to apply it in his next job had seemed impressive indeed. Jack had also been impressed when Andy told him that Bill Bancroft had made a special trip to New York to recruit him personally. Andy's linkup with Contechron looked like another good story in the making, and Jack's two subsequent talks with Andy had confirmed that. What had happened? Jack wondered.

After quickly scanning his Contechron file as a refresher, Jack redialed, reaching Bill Bancroft. He explained his book project and his need to stay in touch with Andy, whereupon Bill readily gave him Andy's new address. "Andy's been gone four months," explained Bill, whose instincts told him not to let it go at that. "He consulted for a month on his own and then was picked up by a firm of cycle time specialists operating out of Dallas. He's pretty busy, but you can leave a message at his Princeton office. I think Andy has finally found the perfect spot. I was sorry to see him leave Contechron."

"I take it then that Andy's departure was his own idea," said Jack. "Was it a case of a better offer?"

"Andy certainly left under his own power," replied Bill, who was not sure how far he wanted to pursue this topic, "and he's skilled enough to always land on his feet, but I think he found the culture at Contechron unfriendly to his objectives."

Pilot Cultures; Implementing Reform the Hard Way

Jack wanted to know more about that culture and was deciding on a roundabout question when Bill saved him the trouble. "Andy's short tenure here was very instructive, for us as well as him," Bill began.

That was the sort of pregnant comment Jack loved. "I'm

familiar with his early progress in that direction," he said. "Could you tell me the most important insights you gained? I'd like to compare them to Andy's when I next talk with him. Or, if you prefer, I'll keep them strictly confidential."

"No need," said Bill. After a pause, he continued. "One thing stands out. Andy's approach to managing his design team was to create a pilot culture: a microcosm inside Contechron that operated by a different set of values and got things accomplished much quicker than usual. We called Andy's group the Foreign Legion.

"What that experience taught me was that a pilot culture probably won't work in an entrenched corporate environment with different habits. It's like the case of an organ being rejected by the body into which it's transplanted. The rejecting body may need the organ, but...."

"Was Contechron in need of an organ transplant?" asked Jack.

"No! Andy was recruited for his technical ability to continue the work on an important design his predecessor and I had conceptualized. The company, as you may know, is highly specialized and has few competitors.

"From the start, Andy interpreted his responsibilities largely in terms of getting designs to market in the shortest possible time—a laudable aim, but not an end in itself at Contechron, where our expertise has always allowed us to move with meticulous care. Andy moved like the wind. He led by example and became a sort of hero to his people. But he was a maverick hero—a rather abrasive one—and he antagonized his peers, who were comfortable in the sanctuary of the status quo and felt threatened by his contrary example. In any case, his fellow group leaders couldn't see the importance of speed in our rather leisurely, uncompetitive sector of the semiconductor market."

"Could you?"

"Interesting question. Not at first. Partly out of curiosity, I gave him his head for a few months. Andy had a way of cutting through barriers that everyone else accepted as the normal way of doing business, and he held those barriers up to ridicule. He managed design problems as though they were manufacturing problems. He used unorthodox methods. He didn't hesitate to circumvent procedures and whole steps in the design process if he thought it would save time to do so. Meanwhile, he rubbed people the wrong way. Those people outnumbered him, so he decided to seek a more congenial climate."

"Was Andy right?"

"About what?"

"About cutting cycle times. About introducing culture change by example."

"Another interesting question. As far as his results are concerned, he did us a very good turn indeed. We introduced the AD-33 device, on which he spent most of his effort, months ahead of schedule. Thanks to its timely appearance, the '33 became a component in quite a few end products at our client companies where alternate solutions had been considered. With the '33 in hand, designers abandoned other solutions and incorporated its capability. So Andy's speed to market aborted alternative designs and thus opened a wider market for Contechron. Being first also allowed us to charge accordingly. That was a bonus we weren't expecting. In fact, our marketing people are forecasting $5 to $7 million more in sales than we originally expected. I'll bet even Andy would be surprised by that.

"As to whether Andy was 'right' about changing culture by example, as a company man, I'd have to say no. He was insensitive to tradition and collegiality. Psychologically speaking, he set a great example for his subordinates but a poor one for his peers because of his unconscious arrogance. He may have expected me to start forcing his values on my other subordinates, but to do that I'd have had to assault the entire Contechron culture from the top down. There was never any question of that."

"Who's replaced Andy?" asked Jack.

"His likely successor was his second-in-command, Rube Chappell, but Rube left Contechron for a job in Phoenix shortly after Andy. I filled in by assigning another group leader to double duty; then that manager chose one of his own to move up into Andy's slot. Things are back to normal in the AD group. Andy's rapid-fire counterculture has withered away."

Jack thought he detected a note of regret in Bill's voice. "Is that why you said that pilot cultures are too frail to survive in an unreceptive environment?" he asked.

"Yes. Put another way, if this or any company wants to change to a fast-response culture, the change should take place across the board. At Contechron, such a decision and change will probably *not* take place as long as I and a few others are around. Us old dogs aren't about to learn new tricks! That's my view, but be sure you talk to Andy about all this. And give him my regards."

Can a Pilot Culture Be Saved?

Jack caught up with Andy by leaving his home number at Andy's Princeton office and assuring the secretary that he could telephone at any hour whatever. Andy got back to him while he was watching a rerun of *L.A. Law*. The two made a date to meet in one of Jack's deli haunts for an early breakfast the next day.

Jack, a bachelor, lived alone in a house he'd inherited on Bonny Meadow Road, New Rochelle, a short distance from the commuter line to New York. Because he considered his work recreational, he spent little time socializing. He spent a great deal of time watching television and poring over several newspapers daily. If he could be said to have a real hobby, it was the midmanagement book project he'd been moonlighting over these past months.

Whatever Jack was working on, he avoided seeing clients in their offices or his own. Most of his "meetings" took place in his favorite New York hangouts: hole-in-the-wall delicatessens at which he regularly breakfasted (never varying his order from a single poppy-seed bagel with cream cheese and a large coffee). He had narrowed those spots down to three favorites, each of which had a dishy, jokey waitress who knew him by name.

It was at just such a place that he met Andy De Clerck. When they ordered coffee and bagels, Jack noted that Andy was oblivious to the charms of the waitress and the cheery surroundings, so the two got down to cases right away. Jack gave Andy a rundown of his conversation with Bill Bancroft. "That's about the size of it," Andy conceded. "I really don't have much to add."

"Any words of wisdom you'd like to pass along to other folks like yourself?" asked Jack. "There must be quite a few who are swimming upstream against the corporate establishment."

Pilot Cultures Must Make a Big Splash

"Well," Andy responded, "I would say that while it may be true that a subelement of a big company can't force its values on the rest of the outfit, it can do a few things to prolong its life and maybe make a big difference.

"In the first place, a pilot culture should prove its worth by achieving some dramatic results in a hurry and publicizing those. A manager should choose an area where his or her chances of reaching entitlement are very good and shoot the works on that one area. Nothing succeeds like success. The objective is to produce appreciable results fast, very fast.

"And those results, step by step, breakthrough by breakthrough, should be generously publicized. Then it's possible that their merit will be noticed and emulated elsewhere in the company.

"My early successes at Contechron allowed me to make brash promises. But I withheld the details until I could dazzle 'em with a major accomplishment. Intimidate 'em, even. I waited too long. Look here."

Andy snatched a paper napkin from the tabletop dispenser, unfolded it, and, with a felt-tipped pen, roughed out a three-part diagram:

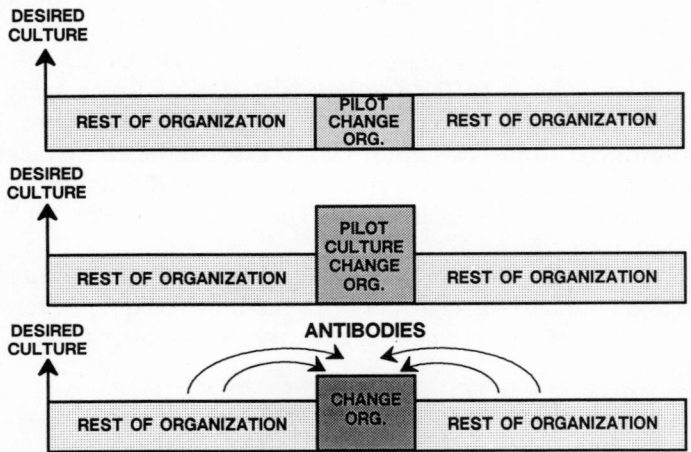

Pilot culture changes typically do not survive the rest of the organization.

"I'm getting so I can't make a move or a statement without a visual aid," Andy admitted, cracking a very small smile. "The point of this one is to show the sequence that all too often overtakes a pilot culture like my Foreign Legion's, surrounded by an organization that's resistant. As soon as it starts to make a difference, the company's antibodies take over and kill it off. That's the story of the AD group in a nutshell.

"Generally speaking, the rules for a countercultural manager are these: Move quickly, don't attempt the impossible, and make sure you share the news with everybody, interested parties or not. Listen: the concept of short cycle time is good in any company, so the problem is one of mindset, not merit. Spread the concept around. Share it.

"Another of my mistakes at Contechron was to talk like a manufacturer in a design division. In my present job, I'm customizing the vocabulary of short cycle time to fit a business where manufacturing lingo is unfamiliar. You could say that at Contechron, I learned a lot of no-nos to avoid in the future.

"But this conversation has accentuated the negative a little too much," said Andy. "Even though my pilot culture was short-lived, its impact was substantial while it lasted." He reached for another paper napkin and drew a diagram [*as shown below*].

"Here's a representation of that impact. By bootstrapping my one little group's performance from baseline to entitlement, I raised the entire company's entitlement potential. And in the meantime, shortening the AD-33's time to market was good for the company—"

"Do you know how good?" Jack interrupted.

"No, but—"

"Bill Bancroft says about $7 million worth of increased sales."

"Seven million?! Wow! You do your homework and you're

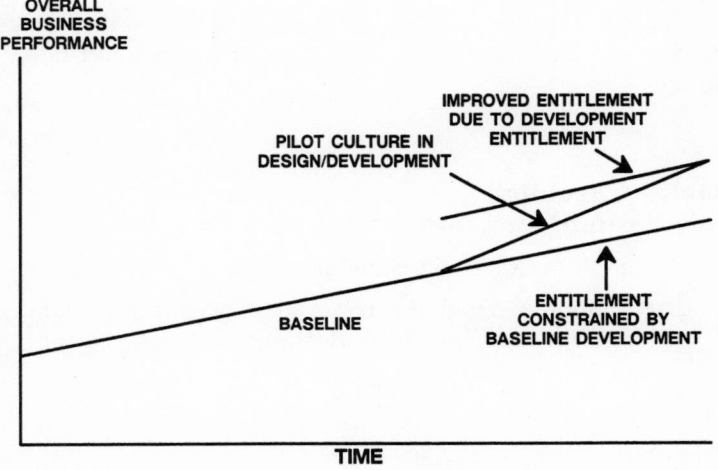

Design/development improves the entitlement for the make/market loop.

way ahead of me with facts and figures. On that I rest my case."

"What kind of work are you doing these days?" asked Jack.

"I've just joined a problem-solving company specializing in the theory and practice of Total Cycle Time," Andy answered. "My first assignment is to coach a major medical instrument company in shortening its time to market."

"Aren't medical instruments a long way from integrated circuits?"

"The products are different but the principles of shortening cycle time and improving performance are the same. I'm excited about working in other businesses where the big profit margins lie in getting products to market quickly. I used to think of myself as a high-powered technical specialist. It turns out that my most valuable specialty is adapting short-cycle-time culture to new situations. You never know. Which reminds me, I've got a presentation to make.

"But now I've got a question for you," Andy said as he rose suddenly and took in the scene. "Why do you meet people in a place like this?"

Jack was about to point to the answer, but the waitress was nowhere in sight. What the hell. "The coffee is good here," he said.

Jack's Checklist:
Key Barriers Encountered by Andy De Clerck

1. "If it ain't broke, don't fix it" mindset.
2. The antibodies from the rest of the organization killing off the improved, but uncomfortable, fast-cycle culture.

6

A Matter of Quality

Considerations of Speed Versus Considerations of Quality

More than a year ago, Jack Betters had noted in the business press the story of how Florida-based Palmetto Computer was dealing with its quality problems and embarking on the comeback trail. Palmetto, he read, had eased out its old guard and brought in new blood to reestablish the company's competitiveness.

Jack promptly contacted Alex Lloyd, Palmetto's head of public relations, for more details. As it turned out, Alex knew of Jack by his reputation. He and Jack hit it off, with the result that Jack ghost-wrote an article for John Dowd, the company's new CEO ("Beating Japan at the Laptop Game"), which was published in a trade journal. During that project, Jack visited Palmetto, where he was squired around by the attentive Alex Lloyd, plied with yacht-club seafood by John Dowd, and given a formal lecture on improving quality by Jerry Lomax, Palmetto's newly acquired quality leader.

In his own proposed book, Jack resolved to use Palmetto's story to illustrate in blow-by-blow fashion how a revitalized business can regain its dissipated market share through improved quality and shortened time to market. Remembering

175

his middle-manager focus, he selected Jerry Lomax as the key protagonist in that struggle and planned to talk regularly with him by telephone. For all other purposes, Alex Lloyd was his inside contact.

Meanwhile, Alex, Vice President for Services at Palmetto Computer, was putting in the busiest year of his career.

An Early Success Story

True to his public relations calling, Alex Lloyd was personable and glib. He could write slick copy in his sleep and insisted that every press release stop at his desk before going to the outside world. Besides his specialty, which he loved, Alex's Service Division included Personnel, Finance, Plant Maintenance, and, lately, Quality Control. He had been at Palmetto computer for 7 of the company's 20 years.

Palmetto was located in West Palm Beach because Eugene Palma, its cofounder and first CEO, had wanted to live there. Accordingly, the company was very much a reflection of Palma's managerial inclinations. The plant site was a carefully landscaped, two-story, flat-roofed concrete structure encircling a central court of greenery. Its driveway approach was lined with the trees that were its namesake. On the grounds was a 2-acre pond, the home of Unix, an alligator who had become the company mascot. (Visitors to the plant invariably enjoyed a brief, shady stop by the pond where they could toss marshmallows into the gator's grinning, ever-ready jaws.) The company had one other site: a bare-bones factory in Juarez, Mexico, which was established five years ago to help reduce costs.

For most of his years with the company, Alex Lloyd had found the story of Palmetto and its colorful CEO a joy to publicize. Palma was a good example of the type that get handsomer and more charismatic with age. A philanthropic, free-enterprise Republican and a member of the local jet set, he attracted enough publicity on his own to impart glamour to his company. He had been a World War II Marine flyer with VMF-114 and still looked as though he could put a Corsair fighter through its paces. After the war, Palma had risen through the ranks at Sperry-Rand. In 1971, instead of simply retiring to Florida, he and a few venture capitalists put together Palmetto Computer and set up shop there. Palmetto soon made a big splash in the minicomputer market with its versatile Amberjack series. Such is the stuff of public relations dreams.

Palmetto grew like a weed and went public, although its profits were never more than marginal. In 1987, in a major strategic thrust, it introduced its Skipjack laptop to a wave of Alex Lloyd's engineered publicity. Skipjack, which had been four years in the making, encountered very rough foreign competition. It was said (though never in press releases) that Palma's military service in the Pacific had imbued him with an enduring hostility to Japan, which was why his company had decided to beat the Japanese in this chosen field.

Quality Crisis

So far the Japanese were winning. Skipjack's liquid crystal screen deteriorated quickly in hard use, and the product got a bad name. Meanwhile, Amberjack's capacity, speed, and weight had crossed the threshold of obsolescence without a ready replacement. So, said a few company directors, had Palma. About a year ago, the board's inside and outside directors alike agreed to bump Palma up to chairman and hire a new CEO to reverse the downward slide. Alex helped Palma draft a short, dignified announcement, whereupon the latter made straight for his boat and steered for the Bahamas and a long incommunicado vacation. Never again did he play a visible role in the company's strategy.

A Man in a White Hat and a Black Ferrari

The board managed to find a new CEO with enough of a reputation to take over Palma's highly visible post. John

Dowd, the person of the hour, was another public relations dream: a well-respected, polished, physically imposing ex–IBM vice president with a track record of performance improvement. It had been a struggle to get a man like him to come to Palmetto, so the new CEO was given a mouth-watering package of perks, including a Mediterranean-style home tucked away behind a security net in Village of Golf, a posh residential country club enclave, transportation of his Hinckley yacht from Long Island Sound to Palm Beach, and membership in Palma's favorite yacht club. But the real incentives, said the executive grapevine, were a very high salary, big potential bonuses, and a stock-option package that would put Dowd on Easy Street forever if he brought off his expected turnaround.

The dark suits, white shirts, ties, and lace-up shoes to which Dowd had been habituated at IBM vanished in the intensity of the South Florida spring. A yachtie-looking blue blazer and striped tie became his trademarks and he never shed them inside the air-conditioned plant. A month into his new job, he arrived at work in a black Ferrari that was immediately dubbed the Batmobile by the company's amused onlookers (although it reminded Alex more of *Miami Vice*). Dowd also inherited Palma's professional goodies: a grand office with windows looking inward to the central atrium's fragrant rain forest and use of the corporate Lear 35. Hearing of the package, Alex Lloyd and his fellow VPs were frankly scandalized. Could anybody be worth that price?

Dowd's selection raised another question: How would the new CEO keep a balance of power among his highly politicized vice presidents? It was no secret that Richard Silva, VP of Research and Development, and Archie Mason, VP of Operations, had been rivals for the CEO position; now their career paths were detoured by the surprise selection of an outsider to run the company. But not for long, perhaps. The best estimate had it that Dowd could make about $20 million on his options if he succeeded over the next five years; then he would almost certainly say good-bye, at which time Silva or Mason would take over. To bystanders like Alex Lloyd, it was interesting how the rivalry between Silva and Mason would probably motivate them to work for the CEO whose appointment they could not but resent.

Strategic Priorities: Quality Improvement, Shorter Time to Market

At his first meeting with his vice presidents, John Dowd sorted out the company's problems and set new short-run objectives. Palmetto was not in serious trouble, he insisted, but it had a number of problems which must be attended to or things could indeed get serious. Obviously, profitability had to go up. Palmetto's sagging credibility in the marketplace had to be restored forthwith, and to achieve that, the quality of its products must dramatically improve. Turning to the company's long-range competitiveness, he wanted to accelerate a line of new products to replace the inferior old ones and diversify the product line. Once identified, said Dowd, such products should take from two to three years to reach the market, no more. That would take some doing. Palmetto's immediate hope for the future was an ultralight laptop, dubbed Bonito. It had been four years in development, and R&D's best guess was that another year of refinement remained.

Quality Improvement: Another Man in a White Hat

Dowd emphasized that quality improvement would require an effort spanning every division. At the conclusion of the meeting he introduced a new, hand-picked member of the executive staff with these words: "We need to mount an organized, systematic program of quality improvement. Since nobody at Palmetto has that specialty, and because quality is a crossfuntional issue, I thought it wise to bring in a crossfunctional expert. Meet Jerry Lomax. Jerry worked with me at IBM. I always thought his contributions went unappreciated there, so I've brought him along to work a few miracles at Palmetto."

Jerry Lomax was about the same age as Dowd, but there the similarity ended. He was slightly chubby, fair, and baby-faced, the sort of person that got perpetually pink but never tan in the Florida sun. He continued to wear his ex-IBM white shirts with sleeves rolled above his peeling wrists and plastic leak-proof protectors lining his shirt pockets. Although he had been selected unilaterally by Dowd, he was assigned to Alex Lloyd's Services Division. When he first heard of the new quality post, Alex questioned whether Services was the place to put it, but Dowd explained that that was the only way to ensure Jerry's crossfunctional effectiveness. "Jerry has to persuade people in R&D, Operations, and Marketing to play ball with him and each other," he explained. "And since your division is, in effect, my staff, Jerry belongs there. I expect to keep in close touch with him — and you too, of course — on the quality thrust." Alex correctly assumed from this that Jerry was the CEO's quality czar and reported to Services on paper only. He accepted this fact and and went back to planning his publicity campaign for Palmetto's new leadership. Jack Betters' ghost-written article had become a part of that campaign.

Jerry seemed well-suited to the role of quality czar. For one thing, he was absolutely convinced that improved quality would pay for itself by yielding long-range benefits to Palmetto. For another, he had the highly focused, unswervable, utterly humorless dedication of the true fanatic. Rumor had it that while at IBM, Jerry had been a bit of a plodder until he attended a quality-training school in Florida. He had returned to Armonk determined to spread the good word and make a real difference, but his efforts were consistently thwarted at the midmanagement level. In other words, he was lost in the crowd and his career was dying on its feet at IBM. Dowd had apparently recognized Jerry as a truly dedicated quality person who would jump at the chance to get his stalled career moving again at Palmetto.

Implementing a Quality Program

One of Jerry's first steps after his arrival was to assemble a crossfunctional team to deal with interdivisional quality issues. From time to time, thanks to Alex, his progress reports made minor splashes in the local press, the trade journals, and *Palmbytes*, the company's newsletter. Inside the company, his motto was the oft-repeated phrase that "Palmetto needs to get its processes under control!" He had stick-on placards to that effect made and distributed throughout R&D and Operations. He persuaded Dowd to make a 10-minute videotape touting the quality approach and saw that it played in the plant's lounges and cafeteria. He spoke to groups in and out of the company, and whenever he took the floor at a senior staff meeting, one could detect in his eyes the gleam of the true believer. While people joked about his "totalitarian" approach, they had to admit Jerry had something. Before long, yellow signs and stickers proclaiming the virtues of quality were everywhere in the plant.

Adding Process Steps: One Approach to Better Quality

To Jerry, getting processes under control was largely a matter of training. Within a few months there were customized classes for every level in every division. Meanwhile, Operations was beginning a statistical process control program whereby the manufacturing flow could be precisely monitored and defects spotted and corrected almost at the exact point of their occurrence. That kind of tracking required major rearrangement of the manufacturing floor and substantial investment in data-tracking software, but the system performed to Jerry's expectations. Remembering that the new quality manager had gone unappreciated in his former job, Alex scrupulously publicized every small victory he won at Palmetto. Skipjack's defect rate went down.

Quality and Short Cycle Time: In Conflict?

Production cycle times lengthened, however, and, over in R&D, so did time-to-market schedules. Jerry's introduction of his program to R&D came at an inconvenient time. Lengthening cycle times there forced the division to reassess its projections for new products. Twice, R&D had to report embarrassedly that the eagerly awaited, lightweight Bonito laptop's design schedule needed an extension. At one such meeting seven months into the quality program, Operations' Mason quipped that Palmetto might someday be remembered as the bankrupt company with the highest quality, which of course got a rise out of Silva. Dowd cut the argument short with the comment that that Jerry Lomax's program was not to blame for most of the problems. Then he added a surprising bit of news.

"I'm increasingly concerned about the lengthening cycle times in R&D," he said. "We absolutely have to cut those. I'm not sure how, and neither is anyone else here, apparently. As you know, I'm a delegator who doesn't like to make decisions for my subordinates. But in this case, my own reading convinces me that we've got to take a formal look at R&D's cycle times. I've therefore hired some outside consultants to have a look around. Maybe they can at least get us back onto the schedule you forecasted when I came here six months ago."

Dowd did not put all his consulting eggs in one basket. Like a patient seeking various medical opinions, he had contracted with two independent parties to observe and advise. The first of these, Marv Allen, arrived from Dallas within a week. Within another week he had completed his study; his report was on Dowd's desk a few days after that. The second visitor was Andy De Clerck, a specialist in engineering cycle times who was free-lancing his know-how after stints at NASA and Contechron. His report was cheaper, and briefer, but took longer to prepare. Both assessments, however, said about the same thing: that Palmetto's R&D cycle times could be cut by two-thirds without adding new resources. One of Marv Allen's conclusions was especially intriguing: "If properly implemented, and with the diligent exploitation of Cycles of Learning, Palmetto's reduced R&D cycle times will *improve* quality."

Dowd knew Jerry Lomax too well to show him those reports. The uphill battles he had had to fight in the past made Jerry mistrustful of outsiders, and he was certain to condemn the notion that speeding up processes could improve quality. Without further discussion, Dowd resolved to add a cycle time specialist to Palmetto. Accomplishing that would equip the company to deal with its problems. After that, the CEO would butt out and let the right people do the right things.

Short Cycle Times: Another Man in Another White Hat

Cycle times were lagging even further when Don Fannon arrived on the scene six weeks later. Don was a greying, somewhat formal corporate executive of 45. His professional specialty was complex electronic switches, a field closely related to Palmetto's technology. He had been persuaded to leave his job in Phoenix where his claim to fame was a series of spectacular cycle time reductions. Finding Don through a headhunter and persuading him to drop everything and come to South Florida ("I can stand the heat, but not the humidity!") had required another package of extravagant perks which amounted to a scaled-down version of Dowd's. Because Dowd was in a hurry, he did not quibble over details, even expensive ones.

Don's reasons for leaving his Phoenix job were personal. He and his wife Fran were childless. They were used to taking vacations in Hawaii, so the prospect of living permanently by a warm seaside had a strong attraction. Here was Don's chance to make up to Fran all the sacrifices she had made as a busy executive's spouse. Shortly after his arrival, as part of his package deal, Don acquired a slightly used Tartan 27 and moored it next to Dowd's boat, courtesy of Palmetto. He had also negotiated generous time-off concessions that permitted him and Fran to take long sailing weekends in various parts of the Caribbean.

It was partly because of the sweet deal awarded him by Palmetto that Don was disappointed, then appalled, by his reception within the company. When he began negotiations, he had expected to be Cycle Time Manager much the way Jerry Lomax was Quality Control Manager, because he was convinced that companies needed to make a total commitment to cycle time reduction. He had been given a few days to look around, had read the Allen and De Clerck reports, and was excited about heading up a Total Cycle Time plan for all business processes within Palmetto. Dowd, however, was preoccupied only with cutting cycle times in the R&D Division. Dowd showed Don the quality-improvement figures of Jerry Lomax and a report by Archie Mason of Operations promising that his division could reduce cycle times on its own once quality was in place. Don was not convinced, and said so. "Short cycle times and high quality are interlocked," he observed. "They shouldn't be separated into sequential programs. Because Total Cycle Time is the driver of all improvement, quality improvement is almost always accelerated. I'd like to work with Jerry Lomax, combining my skills with his to get the best possible products in the shortest possible time."

Dowd could not be persuaded on this point. He did not reveal to Don that merging their skills would threaten Jerry Lomax's territoriality, nor did he state his own doubts that quicker meant better. He did, however, bear down persuasively on the importance of getting designs done more quickly: "We're throwing a hundred million dollars a year into R&D, and we've *got* to get the results I anticipate in a hurry. We've lost time since I arrived, and that alarms me. There simply isn't time or money to work up a corporatewide cycle time commitment now. In nine months to a year, things should be different. Meanwhile, I'd like to bring you aboard as R&D's cycle time manager. You'll report to Rick Silva." After seeing the written offer, Don agreed, on one condition: if he could persuade Jerry Lomax that short cycle times were an urgent matter, Dowd would consider broadening the cycle time approach. That condition was accepted.

Don thus came to Palmetto with his eyes open. But by the time he arrived on the scene, there had been another postponement of Bonito's design debut, and Silva was in a panic. In Operations, Skipjack's manufacturing cycle time was likewise getting longer because of the additional inspection steps Jerry had added to the process. Learning of this, and eager to make a big splash, Don decided to go for broke and see Jerry Lomax right away. Palmetto's chief problem was as plain as the nose on his face: its quality obsession was contributing to—and at the same time camouflaging—its decline!

The Communications Barrier: How Should Quality Be Achieved?

Jerry's second-floor office, like most, overlooked the central atrium's rain forest. Palmetto's standard pastel walls and a jaunty Mexican papier-mâché parrot on a swinging perch completed the tropical effect. Jerry's shelves were literally heaped with fat loose-leaf binders. A framed certificate and plaque bearing the title "SOUTHEAST EXECUTIVE QUALITY CENTER" adorned the wall behind Jerry's desk.

Don, who had never heard of the Southeast Executive Quality Center, sat down uneasily as Jerry leaned back in his chair and smiled. Although he did not know how Jerry would react to his proposal, Don felt he was at a tactical disadvantage. He was a newcomer and, practically speaking, below Jerry in the corporate pecking order. The two managers reported to different division VPs, but it was obvious that Jerry had the CEO's ear. The gap between their ages was probably only five or six years, but the difference in their attitudes was worlds apart. Don wished he'd been able to entice Jerry to his own office to hear his pitch.

What Jerry saw as he looked across his desk was a Lincolnesque figure sitting uncomfortably straight with a hand on each knee and a scuffed briefcase at his feet. Don was in shirt-sleeves but, as was his habit, was wearing a dark tie that he now loosened as a let's-get-down-to-business gesture. Without saying a word, Don reminded Jerry of all the defensive, officious execs he'd been battling for years. Jerry decided to reserve judgment and let Don lead off.

Don's discomfort in such intimate circumstances tended him toward somewhat professorial behavior. He had taken the precaution to construct a preamble that accentuated the positive, however: "Jerry, you and I have a splendid opportunity to coordinate a major breakthrough for Palmetto and fulfill our individual missions in the bargain. You're familiar with my background? Good. To make a long story short, I accelerate results by removing the obstacles to achievement. That's what I'm assigned to do in R&D: smooth out the process so that it moves more quickly."

The Five I's: A Roadmap for Entitlement

Don pulled from his briefcase a packet of charts and outlines for Jerry. He launched into a basic lecture on cycle time theory and systematic barrier removal. Jerry listened but did not follow along using the visual aid packet, so Don was forced to hold up each display on his own, pointing out salient features with his pen. Don didn't realize it, but the outcome of this minitutorial would have a major impact on the fortunes of Palmetto.

"Jerry," he began, "I'm more than a guy who shortens cycle times. I'm a practitioner of Total Cycle Time which, as the name implies, is an all-encompassing business ethic. A company that reaches and maintains its entitled performance level—a Total Cycle Time company—has undergone a five-stage process known as the Five I's [*as shown on the following page*]. The stages are Inspiration, Identification, Information, Implementation, and Institutionalization. Although they overlap somewhat, they are basically sequential.

"Turning a company around begins when people at the top get the spirit, buy the concept, and motivate others down the line the same way. That's the Inspiration part. Once the spirit is willing, Palmetto moves into the Identification phase, in which it zeroes in on the various cycles within its design/

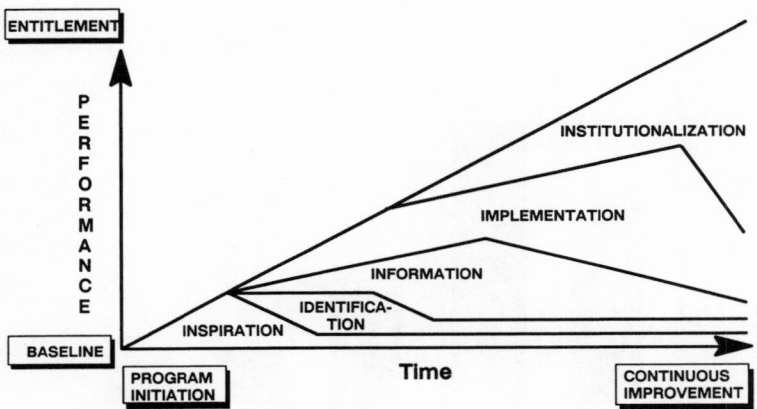

Total Cycle Time: The Five I's Process.

development and make/market loops and identifies the baselines and realizable performance levels in each.

"As that process unfolds, a company begins its Information phase, in which the appropriate skills are transferred to the people as necessary to identify barriers, exploit the lessons of experience, and shorten cycle times. Which, of course leads to action: the Implementation phase in which the barriers are removed.

"The fifth and final component of the Five I's process begins while Implementaion is underway and never really ceases: Institutionalization. Total Cycle Time amounts to a cultural change for a company like Palmetto, so, in the final phase of its turnaround, it must forever embrace the ethic and the habits of the new culture, in the same way as it would have to make quality improvement a way of life. Quality improvement, incidentally, is part of the Total Cycle Time package.

"We're talking about a long and complex process, of course, and managers at Palmetto will need to track the progress of the Five I's using a chart like this one, which tracks the process from Inspiration through Institutionalization against a template of the percentage of completion from the start of the program:

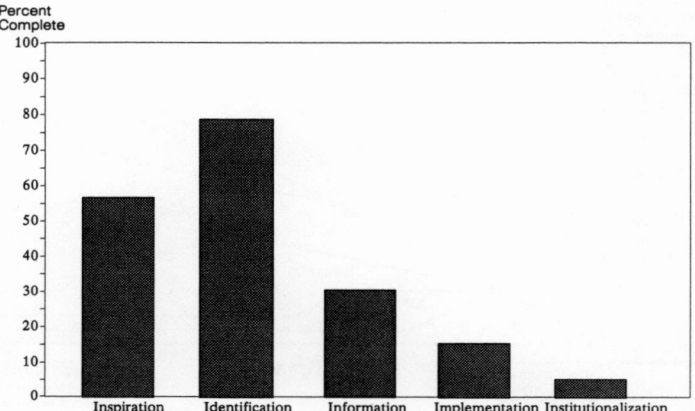

The Five I's barometer chart.

"Jerry, my first purpose in talking to you about all this is to sell you on the general principles of Total Cycle Time. In a minute, I'll get to its impact on quality improvement. Meanwhile, look at these figures, which show improvements in profitability by as much as 14 percent of sales while cash needs are being reduced.

TOTAL CYCLE TIME P&L IMPACT (MANUFACTURING CO. EXAMPLE)			
	Typical cost (% of sales)	Typical improve- ment (%)	Typical impact (% of sales)
Blue-collar	10	15	1.5
White-collar	35	25	8.8
Inventory carrying cost	5	50	2.5
Material	23	7	1.6
Total	73		14.4
One-time cash			10.0

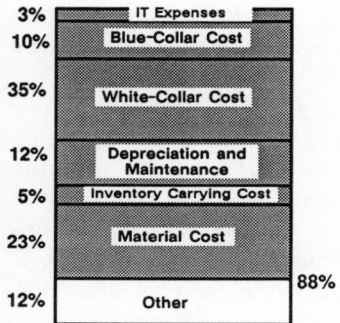

3%	IT Expenses
10%	Blue-Collar Cost
35%	White-Collar Cost
12%	Depreciation and Maintenance
5%	Inventory Carrying Cost
23%	Material Cost
12%	Other

88%

Total Cycle Time addresses a major portion of the corporate spending (percent to sales).

"Pretty impressive, huh? But it's no pipe dream. Palmetto can derive benefits at least as big as these from Total Cycle Time.

"Besides gaining time, we need to raise quality, free up cash from inventory, and reduce white-collar and blue-collar costs. All of that will dramatically raise profitability. And the one-time cash injection of 10 percent of sales is nothing for Palmetto to sneeze at at a time like this."

At which point Jerry riffed through his heretofore untouched aids packet and pulled out the appropriate diagram as Don ran down the figures. Jerry's expression was a mixture of interest and disbelief. Okay, thought Don. That's everybody's reaction at first.

It was time for Don to make his quality pitch. "Now let's consider Total Cycle Time from your standpoint," he said. "When it comes to quality, you might say that I eliminate steps in which something can go wrong and cause defects. That means that you and I are both in the quality business. I'd like you to consider adding my techniques to your own across the board at Palmetto. Right now, I'm assigned to drive down cycle times in R&D only, but John Dowd agreed that I should talk to you about expanding my responsibilities to fit your own. It's a bit awkward, I guess, but John apparently likes his subordinates to work out such issues without his having to get involved. I think he'll take whatever recommendation the two of us make."

Jerry was still reacting to Don's statement that cutting cycle times increased quality. He was also getting a little sore that Dowd had dumped this problem into his lap for a decision. "Before we go any further," he countered, "I want to see where you stand on quality, because it looks to me as if our interests are in conflict, not harmony. When I came here, Palmetto's R&D and Operations divisions were pretty disorganized. In general, problems weren't detected until the last minute, or not at all, which explains why Skipjack's design was inadequate and its production substandard. I'm fixing that by adding steps that nip problems in the bud. For example, if there's a defective component going into Skipjack, we can now detect it and correct the situation right on the line. It's a matter of setting up mechanisms to help Palmetto get its business processes under control.

"All that takes a lot of care. Quality can't be rushed. Now, when you come here and tell me that you're in the business of hurrying everything up, I get uptight. When you say that speedups promote better quality, I get really uptight. Rushing was what got Palmetto into trouble. My guess is that we're in *opposite* camps on what's good for Palmetto, and I can't understand how the CEO could have led you on. Does he want a rush job or does he want quality?"

Cycles of Learning: The Secret Weapon to Achieve Better Quality

"Wait, Jerry," Don interjected. "Dowd's methods may be, um, a bit convoluted, but he's right about short cycle times and high quality. Here's why. As you'll see from my next diagram, cutting cycle times accelerates results, including quality improvement.

> ## THE COMPLEMENTARY NATURE OF TOTAL CYCLE TIME AND TOTAL QUALITY
>
> - In order to improve total quality, an increased number of *Cycles of Learning* is required.
> - *Total Cycle Time* must be reduced and feedback inserted in each feedback loop in order to convert oportunities to learn to Cycles of Learning. Cycles of Learning drive quality improvement.
> - Short-cycle-time companies always have high quality.
> - Total Cycle Time and total quality have been proven to be very manageable through existing quality-improvement teams, with dramatic acceleration of quality results.

"Take R&D: I intend to install a feedback mechanism that people will use to examine and discuss every cycle of activity. They then input what they've learned back into the next effort, using learning to bring down cycle time. Those cycles of learning allow us to improve performance by cutting cycle times further. As times shorten, there are more Cycles of Learning, which means more and faster opportunities to improve.

Achieving Quality Goals Through Improved First-Pass Yield

"I realize that you and I may be approaching quality from opposite methodologies," Don continued. "For example, I noticed that in your reports, you express improved quality in terms of defects per million. You're rooting out defects and correcting them on the spot. My approach is to improve first-pass yield. By using Cycles of Learning to improve the process that caused the defects in the first place, we can increase the percentage of work done right the first time.

"I also noted your quality signs around the company. In my prior job, I worked with a quality manager who used two basic promotional messages. One was "Cycles of Learning Drive Quality." The other was "First-Pass Yield is the Measure of Quality in the Business Process." He had buttons, bumper stickers, and posters up all over the plant to that effect. Well, short cycle times *drive* those Cycles of Learning, and first-pass yield is a very effective measure.

A Total Quality Culture?

"We really are on the same side in all this," said Don. "Obviously, we need to work together in R&D because that's our assignment. But I'd like to see us extend the process companywide. Doing that is a very large undertaking that requires support from Dowd on down. It also involves a universal change of attitude at Palmetto. You're achieving that kind of attitude change in the area of quality-mindedness. Terrific! Couldn't we expand the program to include reducing cycle times and increasing Cycles of Learning? I don't see how Palmetto can avoid having short-cycle-time culture much longer. If we fuse our talents, we'll be saving Palmetto millions and we'll look like a couple of heroes."

Don feared that that last remark sounded like a bald appeal to ambition, especially when paired with his final diagram dramatizing the symbiosis between Total Cycle Time and total quality:

A COMPLEMENTARY PAIR THAT MAKES BUSINESSES COMPETITIVE

Total Cycle Time: total quality

Whatever the case, Don had had the good sense not to mention a future sticking point: his intention to eliminate steps. Jerry's method, obviously, was adding steps which lengthened cycle times. That explained why everything but quality was bogging down at Palmetto and quality was improving so slowly. Don could only hope that seeing short cycle time and Cycles of Learning in action would persuade Jerry that quicker meant better.

Jerry wasn't buying. He had never known the type of culture Don was extolling and he had never heard the phrase "Cycles of Learning" until today. Furthermore, the notion that subtracting steps added to quality sounded positively ridiculous. "Don, I can't throw in with you and take a proposal to Dowd because we disagree about how to improve product quality. I'm absolutely committed to the principle that you can't rush quality. It takes a long, long time—sometimes 5 to 10 years—to develop a quality culture. You can't make quality some sort of by-product of a speedup. And you sure as hell can't send a message like that to employees."

"But Jerry," Don remonstrated, "shorter cycle times would accelerate the move to higher quality!"

"I know you're here to shorten cycle times, Don. I understand that those should be as short as possible, but what's possible varies according to what needs to be done. Right now, Palmetto must get its processes under control to compete. Customers want a higher-quality product. We'll give it to them. And as the defect rate declines, so will our costs. When the quality recovers, and only then, maybe we can go to work on cycle times. Meanwhile, I trust you won't cut any steps in R&D that are designed to promote quality. Sorry, but I have to say no to a team effort." Jerry made a mental note to watch Don every step of the way and did some desktop puttering so Don would realize the meeting was over.

The Leadership Vacuum and Its Consequences

The guy just doesn't get it, thought Don as he left. He was now truly confounded. Back in Phoenix, he had performed his cycle time miracles because, from the top down, his company leadership had embraced the Total Cycle Time ethic and understood that higher quality was a function of simpler, more foolproof processes and the perpetual reinvestment of learning. In fact, as cycle time manager, Don's responsibilities had included quality. It was upsetting indeed to be treated as the enemy of quality here at Palmetto.

He decided to test the leadership waters and make a pitch to his boss, R&D vice president Rick Silva. Silva was very patient and submitted to a chalkboard lecture on Cycles of Learning and their impact upon quality. But he declined to involve himself further in the dispute between Don and Jerry, begging off because Jerry was not his subordinate and observing that Don's job description covered cycle times in R&D only. Anyway, Silva added, Jerry was the resident expert on quality, and if Jerry said quality and short cycle times don't mix, that was good enough for him. Silva also pointed out that, historically speaking, Dowd had prioritized quality before time to market. He thus saw no reason to second-guess the CEO.

Don wrote off Silva's excuses to the company's Byzantine politics. Silva saw himself as possibly the next CEO and wanted to stay on Dowd's good side, so he was not about to jeopardize goodwill by defending a lost cause. Don thought of approaching Archie Mason who, as a manufacturing manager, was more sophisticated about cycle times, but he gave it up as useless. Mason, he had learned, was another contender.

Interestingly enough, Don did talk to Alex Lloyd who, alone among the current VPs, had no ambition to someday replace Dowd. As the company's pundit, Alex was well informed because it was part of his job to homogenize Palmetto's internal problems for external consumption. A few days after Don's abortive meeting with Jerry, Alex happened to pass by Don's office on an informal fact-finding tour. In response to Alex's questions, Don gave a measured account of his failure to warm Jerry to short cycle times. Since Alex was Jerry's nominal boss, Don was careful not to appear to be going over Jerry's head with his remarks.

"Our discussion bogged down on disagreements about how to measure quality," Don admitted. "My emotions are a bit confused at this point. I can't tell if I'm upset because I failed to bring the good word to Palmetto or because, having failed, I now have to confine my activities to shortening Bonito's cycle times. The truth is I'm overqualified for that. I never suspected that cycle times and quality would not be recognized as cooperative issues at Palmetto."

Both knew of the golden handcuffs that now bound Don to the company. Looking for a platitude, Alex could only come up with a bit of irony: "Well, if you're right and everyone else is wrong, there will be lots more assignments around here for a guy like you." He waved and went on about his rounds.

The CEO Barrier: An Empty Room at the Top

Alex's conversation with Don catalyzed some uncomfortable thoughts he had been having about Dowd. The new CEO might be a PR dream, but under his smooth, photogenic exterior beat the heart of an indecisive manager. Old Palma had given his managers leeway, but he never hesitated to provide direction and knock heads together if that was what it took to get a clear consensus. With Dowd it was different, perhaps because of his big-company background.

Dowd had made his reputation in a highly disciplined corporate culture. He seemed to assume that Palmetto, whose former CEO managed from notes on the back of an envelope, was similarly focused. That might explain his phobia against exercising power, thought Alex. He certainly knew of the politically charged atmosphere at Palmetto—every meeting revealed a dash of that. He also had put good men in place to accomplish difficult tasks. But at that point, Dowd seemed content to let various managers settle their territorial disputes themselves. Which meant, Alex concluded with mounting fear, that the CEO was all form and no substance. Here at Palmetto, without the support staff he had enjoyed at IBM (and with problems a good deal more serious), Dowd was letting his hierarchy disintegrate. And it was PR's responsibility to hide that fact from the world.

Shorter Cycle Times: A Man With a Mission

For his part, after sensing the company's managerial realities and analyzing R&D, Don concluded that Palmetto was headed for big trouble unless it undertook a major cycle time effort right away. Before, that had seemed a good idea; now it was crucial. Reviewing his eroding options, he played his last card: his responsibility to report to Dowd on his meeting with Jerry. He steeled himself for the selling job of his life but, to his dismay, he was instructed to report by written memorandum. Jerry had gotten to Dowd first. To avoid further confrontation, Dowd had decided to bury the dispute under paper. Don wrote one of the longest memos of his career, only to see it disappear into the silence of the CEO's office.

One of his recommendations was an off-site conference where all Palmetto executives could receive an intensive introduction to short-cycle-time theory. It would be expensive but, Don was convinced, it would promote general understanding of crucial issues and would thus overcome resistance. At least it would be a start. Several weeks later, he was appalled to learn of an upcoming week-long retreat to teach management more nuances of quality improvement—Jerry's kind.

Damage Control

That left Don with nothing to deal with but R&D's project cycle times, which was plenty. Here were more rude awakenings. In months past, when R&D admitted it was behind schedule on the Bonito laptop, it had rationalized the revised estimates for the sake of short-run appearances. The twice-lengthened forecast, bad as it was for Palmetto's time to market, was far too optimistic. Now it was going to take a miracle just to keep to the revised estimate. In the months that followed, Don performed that miracle, although he was the only one in Palmetto who could appreciate how miraculous it actually was.

Going to work on R&D, Don identified the barriers to short cycle time and broke them down into three categories: subject matter, business process, and culture. The last category was the worst: Palmetto's undisciplined culture had begotten a destructive rivalry between the minicomputer teams (who were trying to replace the old Amberjack line) and the laptop teams (who were redesigning Skipjack even as they labored over Bonito).

Inside the teams, there was no perceivable management discipline, not even a program manual. There was likewise no product contract between R&D, Operations, and Marketing as to exactly what customer needs the proposed design was supposed to meet. Bonito, for instance, had thus entered its engineering phase without a clear definition of its purpose or precise engineering specifications. Starting with Bonito, the company's highest priority, Don froze the project in its tracks until all of the above oversights were corrected and a disciplined approach to development was in place. The project engineers were furious, almost rebellious, because members of other projects were proceeding in the old, less disciplined manner. "Their time will come," said Don, and he meant it, but meanwhile he wasn't sure whether the ingrained cultural resistance was too big to kill.

The first result of Don's actions was that Bonito's progress skidded further. Then it got back on track and made up for lost time.

Meanwhile, as Don eliminated business process barriers, cycle times began to fall.

Damage Control: An Unheralded Miracle

What Don was able to do over seven months was prevent the collapse of Bonito and restore it to its predicted schedule.

Anyone interested in cycle time theory would have recognized Don's turnaround for what it was, but there was no one like that at Palmetto. Silva and, by extension, Dowd saw only that the project had not speeded up. They saw no miracle. By the time Don went to work on the other design teams, his reputation had preceded him and he was up against stiffer resistance. And ahead lay another barrier: the sacrosanct quality steps that Jerry had imposed upon R&D before his arrival. Don could only hope that after he had simplified the process, Jerry would see that such steps were no longer pertinent.

Cultural Myopia: Too Strong to Overcome?

The hardest setback for Don to accept was his colleagues' strong, sometimes snide resistance to the concepts of short cycle time. Yet senior staff meetings at Palmetto were becoming tense and the voices therein shrill because the clock was ticking. At one such meeting Dowd, in a rare fit of anger, slapped onto the table an in-flight magazine he'd picked up on a trip north. In it was a full-page ad for a darling Japanese laptop that was lighter than the struggling Bonito and available in several decorator colors! "Alex, you should have warned us!" Dowd blurted to his stunned PR man. Alex made no reply; he had enough problems these days trying to put a good face on a malingering situation.

Don seized the moment to propose cycle time reduction as first-aid, which struck everyone as gratuitous and did his cause no good. So what, he thought, for once contented to have had a say in things. He cut his remarks short when he saw that no one but Alex and Dowd were listening. Alex couldn't act and Dowd wouldn't act. He sat down.

By the end of his first year at Palmetto, Don brooded constantly about the company's eroding opportunities and, possibly, his own. If he had been given a free hand, he thought, Bonito would be almost ready for its debut and Skipjack would have won back its early acceptance. An expert at barrier removal, he had identified the two biggest cultural obstructions. One was organizational and related to office politics. Don worked for Silva, so Mason was damned if he would support ideas coming from Silva's division. Silva wasn't going to stick his neck out without Mason's support. Jerry, on the other hand, worked for the innocuous Alex Lloyd, so his ideas bore no stigma.

But the real barrier was the CEO himself. Dowd had brought Don into the company and still seemed amenable to a cycle time program sometime after the crunch was overcome. Too bad things were so far gone in R&D that Don couldn't show Dowd a drastic cut in design times. That might have been enough to persuade the CEO to demand what he must suspect the company needed. He did suspect—or did he? That, was Dowd's secret. But it was Don's problem.

Actually, although no one else seemed as alarmed as he, Don was sure it was everybody's problem, and he was increasingly fearful that Palmetto's windows of opportunity were closing fast. Should he dive through one of those windows before it was too late?

Cultural Myopia: Blind to the Passage of Time?

Since he was perhaps a short-timer, Don spent every available hour with Fran on board their boat *Palmy Days*, usually puttering at wharfside in the marina rather than sailing. The press of work being what it was, they hadn't jetted to the West Indies in months. For Don, the best part of these tame weekends was simply standing on the gently heaving deck with a cup of coffee, watching the sunrise and listening to the rigging gently plonging the metal mast. His favorite pelican was sure to be preening on a nearby piling, silhouetted against the early bright.

On one such morning, the mood was shattered by a large, jolly party in preppy nautical attire carrying supplies aboard Dowd's boat, *Lucky Break*. By the look of the provisions being loaded, the Dowds were entertaining in style. Catching sight of Don, John Dowd grinned and waved him aboard for an eye-opener, leading him deftly past the merrymakers to a quiet cabin below. Compared to the snug quarters on Don's boat, *Lucky Break*'s felt like Union Station.

The Dowds and their guests were headed for Grand Bahama, but Dowd had seized the moment of their chance meeting to talk a little business with Don. "As you know," he began, "I'm increasingly concerned that Palmetto's potential market share is eroding. Jerry Lomax has done a helluva job insuring that everything we turn out, old and new, has better quality. But our business processes are more complicated than ever, inventories are building up, and the new products are now so overdue that I'm having to revise my entire strategy for the company. That's a bitter pill after only 14 months." Don nodded and looked out a porthole at his preening pelican.

Dowd continued: "I sense your frustration at the resistance you've encountered here. Frankly, I wish you'd accepted your R&D assignment in better grace. I also wish you'd been able to cut developmental cycle times more than you have. But I want you to know that I realize how hard you've worked. Things in R&D were a lot sloppier than I realized, so just keeping them from eroding further is a victory of sorts.

Quality and Short Cycle Time: A Showdown?

"The trouble with all this," said Dowd, "is that you and Jerry are heading for a major collision. Your reorganization of the design process threatens a number of his quality steps, and you're going to have a fight on your hands if you start to remove those. Is that your plan?"

Now it was Don's turn: "I improve business processes, which requires that I remove barriers. Those are barriers. If I can compress a process to a fraction of its former complexity, there's no need for inspections before and after; they just waste time and money. There are situations like that all over

Palmetto, in Operations, in Services — but you've read all this before in my memos. Getting back to R&D, I guess if Jerry and I deadlock, you'll have to decide how to break the deadlock."

Hobson's Choice

"I don't want any deadlocks at this crucial stage," replied Dowd, "so I want to make a deal with you." Don braced himself. "Your presence at Palmetto is disruptive. I know it's just a matter of time before you fly the coop, and I want to avoid that crisis. I'm taking you out of R&D. I want you to accept another assignment until Bonito hits the market. When that's behind us, I'll entertain a plan for a major cycle time program at Palmetto. Yours."

"What kind of other assignment?" asked Don.

"Well, your mission has acquired a bad name in the company, so I've been thinking that it's going to take some hard evidence to convince Palmetto's management that short cycle times are as desirable as good quality." Don cringed. Dowd still didn't understand that short cycle times accelerated and complemented good quality.

The CEO continued: "To that end, I'd like you to make a star out of the Juarez operation. It's fairly new, its management will cooperate, and it would be a perfect showcase for cutting cycle times. You could score a victory in Juarez."

Victory in Juarez, thought Don. Sounds like an old Hollywood horse opera. A *bad* old Hollywood horse opera. He saw himself on the dusty Mexican plain, bringing enlightened business processes to a seedy, languid factory while vultures circled overhead. The whole idea was so outlandish — and insulting? — he had to laugh out loud. "Look, I could probably still get my old job back in Phoenix," he said. "If this is a way to let me down easy—"

"It's not!" Dowd emphatically interjected. "It's a way of keeping Palmetto on course without losing you. If you're as serious as you say about a Total Cycle Time approach in the

company, you'll say yes to this proposition. We'll cut you a
Juarez deal as good as the one you've got here, and you can
come back to all this in say, 12 months."

"More like 16 months," Don corrected, wondering as he
did so what a good Juarez deal could possibly be.

Dowd smiled; he could see that Don was already toying with
the idea. Dowd walked Don up the companionway and saw him
to the wharf. "I'll be back in the office Monday afternoon," he
said. "We can talk longer then, as long as you like. And Don,"—
suddenly Dowd's face took on an intensely pleading expression—"please stay with Palmetto. When you're done in Juarez,
a real challenge awaits you in West Palm."

Don was too dazed to return directly to *Palmy Days*. He
needed to talk to someone, but he was damned if he knew
who that might be. Obviously, he could say nothing to Fran,
not yet. Maybe Alex Lloyd could give him counsel. Or would
Alex assume his public relations stance, making the Juarez
proposal sound better than it was? Nobody but himself could
sort out this bizarre turn of events.

A First-Class Ticket on the *Titanic?*

Don was, as he said, a barrier remover so, giving Juarez the
benefit of the doubt for the moment, he looked for whatever
barriers existed to prevent a successful turnaround of that facility and a triumphal return to West Palm Beach. There
were four. The first was the possibility that he couldn't put
Juarez on Total Cycle Time. No problem. The second was
his gut reaction that neither he nor Fran should accept the
sacrifices necessary to take on that job. A possibility. If the
job hurt his pride or made life miserable for the two of them,
to hell with it. Working out his ego problems would take
awhile, but he vowed to hash the matter through before be-
laboring Fran with it.

The last two barriers were doozies, however. One, of
course, was Dowd. The CEO was certainly sincere but, reviewing Dowd's history at Palmetto, Dan could see that

Dowd's forte was confrontation avoidance, not controversial new steps. Could he count on Dowd? If so, he might someday become the manager who saved the floundering company. After that....

Which led to the last and biggest barrier to a clear decision: the distinct possibility that there would not be a Palmetto Computer in a year, not at West Palm, not at Juarez, not anywhere. In another sudden flash, he saw himself standing in the hot Chihuahua sun, auctioning off the contents of his well-managed but ill-fated plant under the circling vultures. That, then, was the question: Could Palmetto last long enough to fulfill Dowd's promise?

He might turn up some clues to that question when he met with Dowd on Monday. At the very least, the new proposition would get him one-on-one with the boss at the strategic level. He intended to give Dowd an earful — especially if he decided to turn down the offer — and he was probably the only manager at Palmetto with gumption enough to do so. For the moment, however, he would concentrate on not ruining Fran's weekend.

Picking Up the Pieces at Palmetto

Meanwhile, in the chilly wilds of New York and New Rochelle, Jack Betters had heard several stories about trouble at Palmetto, although such tales did not come from his conversations with Jerry Lomax. The gist of the rumors was that the company had improved its quality but was still behind the competition, still hoping for its market reputation to recover and its overdue Bonito laptop to make its debut. Jack's own file contained press releases promising Bonito's introduction on two successive dates both long passed. He also had two quarterly reports that bespoke serious illness within the company. They showed that building inventory was temporarily boosting the P&L but was draining cash in the process.

One morning, after reading an article headlined "Palmetto Ripe for Takeover" in the *Wall Street Journal*, he telephoned Alex Lloyd, anticipating a different sort of conversation than the neat wrapups he's lately enjoyed with Larry, Bob, R. D., and Andy. All he really wanted to know at this point was what the hell had gone wrong at Palmetto and why nobody saw it coming. He failed to get through to Alex, who, in the wake of the *Wall Street Journal* article, was undoubtedly besieged by the press.

In the week it took Alex to get back to him, Jack roughed out his notes on the Keller Window story. When at last Alex returned Jack's call, the former spoke in the cryptic generalizations of a man who was not free to tell the whole story but wanted to very badly. All he would confirm was that the Bonito was still on hold, that part of the problem was a "management glitch that we're ironing out," and that Jack should "stay tuned." Jack stayed tuned.

Alex called again the day "LBO at Palmetto" ran in the *Journal* and a simultaneous press release ("A New Start at Palmetto") tumbled from his fax machine. "I just got your press release, Alex," he began. "That makes two new starts in 18 months. What happened with the old new start?"

"Now it can be told," said Alex. "Because you're a proven friend of the company, I'll talk to you candidly with the proviso that what I tell you won't see daylight until your book appears. Agreed?"

"Agreed."

"You've heard about our latest management crisis. You've probably also heard that after Palmetto went into Chapter Eleven, a group of retired managers down here put together a takeover package."

"What group of retired managers?" asked Jack.

"Ex-IBMers mostly. The nearby yacht clubs and golf courses are full of 'em. A few had worked at IBM's Boca Raton operation. Like old Alex Palma, our founder, they apparently found time heavy on their hands in retirement.

"The team brought in some high-powered analysts who identified the root cause of the company's problems as its unacceptably long cycle times, which were getting longer, by the way. They looked at the numbers and thought there was a reasonable chance of turning things around — after major surgery. The buyout team also got some inside coaching, notably from Rick Silva, our R&D vice president. Rick, you will recall, was a possible successor to Dowd. At this point, it looks as if he might get his wish."

"And Dowd?"

"Gone. The new team literally walked Dowd out of the building to his Ferrari as I watched from the window. He didn't leave without a golden handshake, of course."

"So Palmetto's quality program wasn't enough to make a difference in the slide? Or should I ask Jerry Lomax about that?"

"Taking your last question first: Jerry has gone the way of Dowd. He was away giving one of his frequent quality lectures when the coup took place, and he won't be back. He may have seen the end approaching before Dowd.

"As to the quality issue itself, that's a complicated story and a PR nightmare because it's so difficult to explain. The bottom line is that Jerry's quality approach added steps and lengthened cycle times, putting us farther and farther behind schedule."

"But," asked Jack, "didn't Palmetto hire a cycle time expert to fix that problem?"

"Yeah. Don Fannon. He was a voice in the wilderness around here. Don kept things from getting worse, which they would have otherwise, but he clashed with Jerry. Don insisted that the road to quality was not the addition of inspection steps, which lengthened cycle times, but the reduction of cycle times so that things wouldn't go wrong. Or something like that. Maybe you ought to talk to Don."

"Where is he?"

"In Phoenix, where he was when Dowd found him. Nothing ventured nothing gained, I guess, although it looks as though Don has the last laugh. Small comfort, I'll bet."

Palmetto and the Quality Barrier

Small comfort indeed, as Jack found out when he contacted Don Fannon the next morning. After reviewing the situation at Palmetto, Jack asked Don to explain what went wrong.

"Three things went wrong," replied Don. "To begin with, Palmetto took a faulty road to quality.

"Quality and short cycle times go hand in hand. Nobody seemed to understand the importance of that point, which is the second big failure at Palmetto. Even Dowd didn't get it.

"That's the third failure: an absence of decisive leadership at the top."

Quality Without Short Cycle Times Is an Illusion

"Why was Palmetto's quality approach faulty?" asked Jack.

Don said, "I'll give you an easy example: manufacturing. Jerry's program reduced the number of defective units that were leaving the plant because the product was repeatedly inspected and bad units were pulled off the line. But that complicated the manufacturing task without getting to the root of the problem. Cycle times got longer.

"As CEO, Dowd could see that the quality program was not going to save Palmetto. That's why he hired me. It was obvious to me that Jerry's program was helping to sink the company, not save it. I tried—God, how I tried!—to demonstrate to Jerry, to the other VPs, and to Dowd himself, that cutting cycle times and raising quality were part of a *single* methodology. It was like this: Palmetto's products were defective, so we had do the job better. We could accomplish that through shorter cycle times which would uncomplicate the process, and—this is important—increase the number of Cycles of Learning by which we could review our business processes and improve upon them."

Executive Power: Sins of Omission

Don continued: "Dowd's biggest mistake, and mine too, I must admit, was to accept Total Cycle Time on a piecemeal basis in one section of the company."

"Looks like Dowd was treating Total Cycle Time as a pilot program," suggested Jack, remembering Andy De Clerck's experience.

"Exactly!" said Don. "A pilot program. When I first arrived, I was sure I could expand that program—boy, was I overconfident!—but from the start I was swimming upstream. I'm used to blasting away barriers, but at Palmetto, the barriers were human."

"Dowd and Jerry Lomax?"

"Among others, but them most of all.

"Because he believed in hiring troubleshooters and letting them do their thing," Don went on, "Dowd let Jerry and me fight our own battles. But he damn well should have intervened when Jerry and I deadlocked. Instead, he tried to smooth out the problem by arranging our assignments in series. First Palmetto would·finish its quality program; then and only then, I could do my cycle time thing. It was totally the wrong approach, especially since there weren't enough months of life left in the company for it to solve its problems one at a time."

"So you quit?"

"Not exactly. Dowd offered me another assignment until Jerry finished installing his program, then I could shorten cycle times. I had to decide whether there would be a company left to work in after Jerry got finished. It was a judgment call. My wife and I decided to go back where we came from.

"Want to hear something funny? Palmetto's new takeover team has been romancing me to come back a second time with the promise that I can implement a Total Cycle Time/ total quality program. That's a system where quality improvement is merged with short cycle times and Cycles of Learning, which in my opinion results in the most competitive corporate culture. As before, they're offering me all kinds of perks including—so help me—Dowd's boat, which they're now holding the note on! But I'm staying put."

"I guess you think Palmetto's a lost cause," ventured Jack.

"No comment," said Don. "Except this: Total Cycle Time is

a major cultural change for a company. It's easy to understand, but difficult to implement. There's not a lot of time at Palmetto for denial, blame, or defending the status quo. I wish 'em luck.''

Quality and Cycle Time: Three Pointers

Because the Palmetto story was still a cliffhanger, Jack had been unable to ask Alex and Don his accustomed question about how they would sum up their recent experiences. He therefore did a little summing up of his own. Generalizing from the scuttlebutt he'd just received, he jotted down these conclusions:

1. The ultimate competitive corporate culture combines short cycle time with quality improvement.

2. Shorter cycle times mean higher quality.

3. Cycles of Learning accelerate quality improvement.

Jack resolved to keep tracking the Palmetto story. Whatever the outcome, it would be a fascinating tale indeed. But whether it would fit into his book without Jerry as its central character was as doubtful as the viability of the company itself.

Jack's Checklist:
Key Barriers Encountered by Don Fannon

1. Lack of top-management support.

2. Inadequate inspiration of the management team.

3. Lack of ongoing barrier removal meetings between top management and the change agent.

7

Negative Questions and Brief Accounts

Cycle Time Dilemmas in Finance and Human Relations Functions

The cycle time expert who had supervised General Widget's turnaround called his quarterly visits "pulse reviews," by which he meant periodic assessments of the revived company's entitlement to make sure its hard-won cultural change was still thriving and that the entitlement potential was continually rising. As the first pulse review drew to a close, the company received a clean bill of health and the expert was about to catch a plane for New York where he was to address some sort of executive seminar. He promised to use General Widget's improvement as an inspirational example for those attending the conference. Before departing, however, he reminded the company's new president that achieving entitlement was no reason for relaxing. "Quite the contrary," he said. "Getting to entitlement has provided you with a responsive Total Cycle Time culture. You now have the means means of *continual improvement*. Entitlement is a moving target, not a fixed point. With the right mindset and the help of Cycles of Learning, you can and should be improving your performance steadily. I'm looking forward to next quarter's pulse review. Until then, good luck."

Hardy Sellers, President and Chief Operating Officer of General Widget's Philadelphia operation, was a major beneficiary of the company's recent revival. Six weeks earlier, after a corporate reorganization, General Widget's CEO, Victor King, had appointed himself chairman and chief executive of a newly created Genwid Holding Company and moved into the beautiful but small Genwid office suite in Center City. Much to his surprise, Sellers, then VP of Marketing, had been tapped to take over most of King's former domain. King was a detail man with years of manufacturing experience but, as he told Sellers on the happy day of his promotion, the company now needed direction from someone "with a fresh slant on things and a low tolerance for excessive procedures. That's you, Hardy."

It was. In fact, Sellers had been far quicker than King to see the competitiveness potential of Total Cycle Time and the need to adapt the entire company to the new culture. But his first act as president was to send himself and Suzy on the trip to St. Thomas they'd been planning for the better part of a year. It might be their last chance to get away for quite a while. The trip had done him good. He now felt really relaxed, his acquired tan flattered his handsome face and greying hair and, if he held his stomach in just a little, nobody would notice the slight addition to his inconspicuous paunch.

The admonishment he'd just received joggled his need to put his own imprint on the company. Immediately after the pulse review, therefore, Sellers had his secretary set up a meeting with his assorted vice presidents: Butch McMills of Manufacturing, Witt Tinker of Design and Development, Prudence Cash of Finance and Human Resources, and Ernest Greenbach, who had moved up to his own old slot in Marketing.

After Total Cycle Time: The Search for New Barriers

The scheduled meeting took place in Sellers' handsomely appointed office, which until lately had been King's. Sellers had not had time to do the room over to his taste and the walls still showed shadowy rectangles where King's sporting prints had once hung. Coffee was served, one cup per person, because Sellers had a personal rule against meetings that lasted longer than it took to nurse a single cup's worth.

He was sure that rule would be okay with Butch McMills, a tough, old-line manufacturing type who had come up the hard way and had a low tolerance for administrative chatter. McMills, another new VP, still doubled in his old job as manufacturing manager. He was built like a fence post and looked a little bit like one. He chain-smoked unfiltered cigarettes down to miniscule stubs, though not in the boss's office. Since his recent promotion to VP, Sellers noticed, he had let his crew cut grow out and had adopted long-sleeved shirts that covered his tattoo. Witt Tinker, a talented, academic designer of the elbow-pad-and-horn-rim variety, had lately become a convert to short cycle time but had not shed his apparent love of long meetings. The trick was to avoid giving Tinker the floor.

Prudence Cash was the class act of the senior executives. Competent, calm, and chic (Suzy had identified her suits as St. Johns), she ran a smooth operation and enjoyed great respect among her subordinates. Because his relationships with business associates were strictly professional, Sellers suppressed a flirtatious impulse when Cash complimented him on his tan. Ernest Greenbach reminded Sellers of himself 15 years ago, and for good reason: like Greenbach, he had been a happy-go-lucky northeastern sales manager before being tapped for the frightening position of Marketing VP. Sellers could sense Greenbach's self-consciousness over attending his first high-level gathering. No matter; he would work out fine.

After greetings and niceties, the meeting began. Being a natural salesperson, Sellers was loquacious, which is why he had made a second rule: to reduce everything he wanted to say to an outline that would fit on a 3-by-5-inch card. The card read:

- Congratulations.
- Stay on the curve.
- Macromanager — me.
- We are our own customers.
- Prepare for growth.

The first item on the card had mostly been covered in the various hellos, but Sellers made a general comment praising the divisions for the stirring accomplishments of the last year and a half, during which sales had climbed from a flat $600 million to $762 million ($115 million of which had found its way down to pretax profits) and cycle times had dropped from 110 to 42 days in Manufacturing and from 30 to 18 months in Design and Development.

Then came point 2, with which he passed along the warning made at the pulse meeting: "Having reached our entitlement, we have not won the right to sit back and watch the competition flounder. We have the responsibility to keep our performance curve climbing past the old entitlement figure, because we now have the understanding and mechanisms to identify barriers, remove them, and continually exploit the lessons of such experience."

Point 3: "You were probably as surprised as I was by my appointment to the presidency of this outfit. One reason for the appointment is that I'm a macro-, not a micromanager, which is what the new culture calls for. I'm admittedly not comfortable with or even competent to interpret the technical data blitz that still permeates the company and piles up in my office, although I do know how to read bottom lines. I want to reduce that blitz. If you and I agree on the cultural priorities at General Widget, and I think we do, you'll be running your own show. I plan to concentrate on developing a strategy to utilize our superior responsiveness to further accelerate our growth."

Point 4: "My sales background has conditioned me to view business relationships in terms of our customers. I intend to bring that kind of thinking to internal transactions between General Widget managers. I want each of you to consider the other divisions with which you interact as *customers* and yourselves as *suppliers*. Witt, you supply Manufacturing with designs; hence Butch is your *customer*. Design, Marketing, and Manufacturing are all *customers* of yours, Prudence. This is not a word game or a gimmick. As we learned over the last year or so, effective and timely response to customers while using minimum resources is the key to competitiveness. Let's apply that thinking to our intradivisional relationships and eliminate the barriers to effective, timely response. I'm especially sensitive to this matter and will be watching to see that you follow through on it.

"My last point is this: You must prepare for growth. We've spent almost two years positioning ourselves for a surge. The surge is upon us. I project that we can probably grow 22 to 25 percent this year because of our improved customer response and our timely introduction of the Widgerino. Prudence, your Human Resources department will have to get hopping. Historically, General Widget's white-collar attrition rate has been 5 percent; so, adjusting for our improved productivity, my guess is that we'll be hiring 15 percent more people over the next 12 months. Talk about a challenge!"

But to everyone's surprise, he did not talk about it. The president seemed to be through! And as at the conclusion of the Gettysburg Address, the assembled listeners sat silent for a moment before they realized there would be no more. Rising, Sellers walked the small group to the door, presenting each VP with a firm handshake and a 3-by-5-inch copy of his five-point outline to inspire them further.

A Mandate for Barrier Identification and Removal

Prudence Cash, who had been with General Widget 12 years and had been VP of Finance and Services for 5, realized that Sellers had used her division as an example for a reason. She had a clear understanding of life under the old regime; but she also had acquired a grasp of short-cycle-time theory. Lately, when asked, she had helped managers develop the apparatus to report the new system's measurements. Somehow, it had not dawned on her that her own division should take the initiative, but Hardy Sellers had left no doubt that the time had come to do so.

Leaving the meeting in Sellers' office, she walked immediately to her own to do some thinking. A collector of Shaker furniture, she had furnished her inner sanctum at General Widget with modern adaptations of Shaker designs that were amazingly functional, startlingly handsome, and conducive to relaxed concentration. In this environment, it did not take her long to sort out a few priorities to pass along to her subordinates.

Getting Started: Pushing Responsibility Down From the Top

Within 24 hours, Lonnette Quarles and Neal York were sitting in Prudence's office, getting the message that had trickled down from Sellers. Although their specialties were quite different — Lonni was Director of Human Resources and Neal was General Widget's Chief Accountant — both knew and liked each other and felt entirely comfortable with their boss, which was a good thing, because the day's meeting packed a wallop.

Prudence did most of the talking. Being a detail person, she took a good deal longer than Sellers to make her points. But with characteristic clarity, she had sorted out the challenge into two neat sections, one each for Neal and Lonni, and backed up her comments with a packet of diagrams and figures. The first of these was a chart that Lonni and Neal had seen before, displaying an upwardly inclining line which plotted the company's dramatic improvement in recent months.

"Not bad, huh?" said Prudence, holding up her copy. "Now look at the next chart." Lonni and Neal did so; on it the rising line continued its ascent past the achieved goal to future heights. "That chart," Prudence continued, "makes the point that the company has no intention of resting on its laurels. It also quantifies the next objective. Hardy Sellers is determined to maintain our momentum. In other words, General Widget's entitlement is a moving target edging continually upward. We're expected to cut our cycle times in Finance and Human Resources.

"Hardy Sellers gave another order yesterday that applies more to us, I think, than any others. The gist of it is that we should regard ourselves as suppliers of business services and the divisions we serve as 'customers' and treat our transactions with them as responses to 'customer needs.' Since then, I've been figuring how Finance and Human Resources can reconcile those two responsibilities. Let's start with Human Resources." Lonni, whose energetic manner was contagious, perked up even more than usual, something Neal would not have thought possible.

The Impact of Entitlement on the Hiring Process

"Lonni," said Prudence, "the new word from on high is really going to shake up Human Resources unless we make changes. Yesterday, Hardy projected a 15 percent increase in white-collar recruiting over the next 12 months. I think he's a little optimistic—he always is—so I did some refining and came up with a figure of about 10 percent; the exact numbers are in your packet. Are your people braced for that kind of a work load? And can you shorten the recruiting process so we can respond faster to the needs of our divisional 'customers'?"

Lonni didn't answer but nodded her understanding of the problem. Prudence then turned to Accounting.

The Impact of Entitlement on Accounting; Eliminating Measurements and Controls

"Neal," she said, "I want you to review the way your department supplies our divisional 'customers' with the financial data they use to track their operation. In the old days under Victor King, when I managed Accounting, the data requirements became very, very burdensome. King liked data, so the divisions learned to cover themselves by tracking and reporting everything under the sun. Accounting obliged them. When the Total Cycle Time team came in, they required us to add new measurements and controls. Again, Accounting obliged them. They also encouraged us to drop old measurements. We gave that suggestion lip service only, and ever since, your department has been cranking out what amounts to a dual system of macromeasurements: one for old time's sake and one that's new.

"Enter Hardy Sellers, our new president. Hardy is indifferent to picayune details and death on effort that adds no value. For his own part, he's content to monitor only the new measurements. That means that the old data we've been generating no longer has support at the top. Neal, I want you to strip out as many of those old measurements as you can. I'll bet that if you check, you'll find that a lot of those items we track and report aren't even looked at. Let's identify them and drop them."

"Well," said Neal, a bit perplexed, "dropping them is not a decision I can make. Last year, when Tinker got the bug to cut paperwork in the Design Division, you and he simplified our reporting system and I just followed orders. Manufacturing is where most of the data now goes. Maybe if you and Butch...."

"No. *You* and Butch. I'm delegating to you the task of approaching Manufacturing. Get a consensus about what those people can live without, and drop it. You might as well come on strong, so start with the proposition that we'd like to cut the measurements at least in half.

"As you can both see, it's our division's turn to get on the short-cycle-time bandwagon. Lucky for us we have Hardy in the driver's seat; that widens our options considerably. As always, this door is open, but I want you both to see what you can come up with. Think big. And think fast!" All was suddenly quiet except for the point of Prudence's jiggled pencil excitedly clicking on the tabletop. The meeting was over.

Second Opinions on Barrier Removal

It was a short walk to their respective offices, but Neal and Lonni took a long time getting there, each hoping for some moral support from the other. Neal, the older by half a generation, had always had an avuncular feeling toward Lonni and thought he should come up with something that sounded wise right now. "Let me tell you," he ventured, "It's going to be a lot harder than Prudence thinks to 'strip out measurements' or 'shorten the recruitment process,' because we're both at the mercy of the other divisions. Let's make a deal: when either of us hits a brick wall, the other will listen and make suggestions. Our skills may be different, but we're both in the same boat this time."

"You've got a deal," said Lonni with a smile. "Meanwhile, we each need to do some woodshedding." Which was okay with Neal, at least for a day or two. Lonni and Neal went their separate ways, both bent on rooting out barriers to better performance but somewhat in doubt about how to begin.

The Buck Stops in Personnel

Lonnette Quarles had grown up in Darby, a seedy district on the outskirts of Philadelphia, where she enjoyed no benefits, not one. She seemed to have grasped this fact by the time she was a teen, at which point she turned her assets to her advantage. These included an ability to absorb information like a sponge and an altogether engaging personality that stopped just short of being cute. Underneath the perky exterior, however, was a tough mind and a driven soul. Accordingly, she graduated at the head of her high school class with a four-year scholarship to Penn.

Moving up the hard way had made her reverently uncritical of the psychological and sociological truisms she had digested in college, and she was hooked on How-To-Be-A-Better-You type books. The shelves of her summery office bulged with dog-eared paperbacks on anger, intimacy, assertiveness, feminism, complex relationships, and the psychological secrets of better management, any of which she would loan to colleagues at the drop of a hat. Her grim background had also left her with a soft spot for anyone with a problem, which, tempered by her keen and otherwise unsentimental brain, made her a crackerjack personnel director.

Charting the Business Process in Personnel

The next morning, passing her office on his way to the coffee machine, Neal looked in and beheld Lonni chewing on a ballpoint and frowning at a desktop flowchart she had made entitled "RECRUITMENT." "Come in here," she said, "and give me some advice." Neal got his coffee, came back, and peered at the chart.

"Ever since Prudence put us on notice," explained Lonni, "I've been trying to get the kinks out of Personnel's recruiting sequence. You remember that she'd paired Sellers' recruiting estimate down from 15 to 10 percent because Hardy is optimistic? Well, I think Hardy is right on the money, and I'm figuring on 15 percent. Since the Total Cycle Time thrust began, the company's been on attrition, and recruiting has been really slow. I've been looking forward to a change and now it's here. And how! It looks as though we'll be adding 750 white-collar people within the year. Anyway, I've plotted out the recruiting sequence and its long, long, long! I can see several barriers.

"The first is the way we identify candidates. We list most of our vacancies with headhunters. Do you know that it can take a month before we get a response? When we do get a name or two, we encounter another problem: scheduling a definitive interview. By the time the necessary schedules are coordinated, another month has usually gone by. When at last we fill the slot and the new employee shows up, it takes another two or three weeks for that person to be oriented and trained. In other words, if I hear about a vacancy today, with luck we might have the right person on the job in three or four months! In the light of what Sellers forecasted, that's enough to make my skin crawl."

The Headhunting Barrier

Not knowing much about recruitment, Neal kept quiet and let Lonni continue. "I guess the place to start is at the front end of the process, she said. "There's a standing order at General Widget to do what it takes to get a good match when we hire so we don't have to repeat the process. That means we rely heavily on professional headhunters. Since your department signs the checks, you may have noticed that we have 31 headhunters on a minimum retainer. We've retained them through the lean recruiting years because we didn't want them to lose interest altogether."

"How did you decide which ones to keep on retainer?" asked Neal.

"Past performance or expertise in some obscure specialty," Lonni answered. "Price isn't the deciding factor. They all seem to know each other's minimum rates, and their commissions are about the same, too. But they can take forever, because they're working with a lot of clients who lately have been more active than General Widget. My problem, now that we're under the gun to speed up the process, is to figure a way to jump-start the headhunting process."

Neal thought for a minute. "My department's records will indicate which headhunters have earned the highest commissions," he said. "If you want to simplify the process right off the bat, why not keep the top performers and drop the others?"

Lonni nodded and smiled. "Is this a pitch to simplify your accounting tasks with another internal customer — me? Nice try, but simpler in this case might not be better — or faster. Up to now, we've used the-more-the-merrier as our approach because the best headhunters, who are very busy, sometimes take weeks to act on our announced vacancies. Weeks we ain't got."

"So what would be wrong with breaking the headhunters' mold?" asked Neal. "Let's identify those five or six who have outperformed the rest. Why not offer them *higher* retainers and commissions than their standard rates? It would have the same effect on them as sending a check with an order. I guarantee that'll get their attention and put General Widget's needs on the top of their piles. And since you'll be retaining just a fraction of the former number, it will probably cost you less."

"Fabulous! You made my day!"

"No charge. We're in this together. I'll pull out the names of the top 10; you take it from there. Incidentally, I don't know if this is relevant, but your department uses up an awful lot of money in airplane tickets for visiting applicants. That suggests to me that simplifying the interview process would grease the wheels a bit."

"Barrier number 2," said Lonni, touching a block on her flowchart. "I'll get back to you on that one."

The Interviewing Barrier

And what a barrier it is, thought Lonni after Neal had departed. Lonni had already done her interview homework. To begin with, she had calculated the cost in worker-hours to complete the number of projected interviews over the upcoming year, which had astounded her.

True to its familial cultural values, General Widget expended much time and effort on finding the right people for the right jobs. Accordingly, it was customary for white-collar candidates to undergo 5 one-on-one interviews before a decision was made. Two of these took place in Personnel (Lonni herself was one interviewer), with at least three more in the division concerned. For example, in Design, where the needs were the most technically complicated, Witt Tinker, a group leader, and one other designer with a specialty similar to the applicant's was the regular slate, although it was not unusual to include one or two more specialists in the sequence. Coordinating the schedules of five to seven busy people with an applicant's arrival and departure often necessitated two visits. And after the elaborate, expensive process was completed, too many potential hirees seemed to slip through General Widget's fingers.

On the day after Prudence had alerted her to the company's increasing labor needs, Lonni toted up the tab in terms of time. Experience told her that each one-on-one interview required a total of about 3 hours for preparation, execution, and review, making for a 15-hour overall effort per candidate. Because General Widget's hit rate was about 50 percent, she doubled the figure of 750 new hirees and multiplied by 15. Filling the vacancies was going to require 12,000 managerial hours, not counting the distraction factor, which might well double or triple it. "That's criminal!" she said aloud, staring at all the zeros.

Lonni decided to attack that problem first in Design, where the recruiting process was longest. There were two routes of attack: the division could cut the number of interviews per applicant or learn to interview more effectively so that fewer candidates got away. Lonni's hopes for the first tactic weren't high. Last year, Design VP Witt Tinker had dropped the ceremonial interviews that various bigwigs felt obliged to conduct as a professional courtesy. Speaking for herself, Lonni thought that the usual number of 5 was not extravagant. That left the second option, improving the effectiveness of the interview process itself.

Negative Interviews and Barrier Removal

Witt Tinker was a zealous guardian of his divisional autonomy. But he was also unsure of his managerial skills and suggestible under the right approach. Lonni was a master of the right approach. It wasn't difficult for her to get Tinker's permission to sit in on the next few routine interviews in the name of improving her ability to serve the division.

Those interviews confirmed Lonni's worst fears about the process. One recent case in particular stuck in her mind: a NASA engineer named Andrew De Clerck. De Clerck's opaque personality gave no clue about whether he could lead, and his credentials suggested he was overqualified for the job in question. But because he was experienced in the theory, practice, and lingo of short cycle times, he had Tinker eating out of his hand without having to crack so much as a smile. (No doubt De Clerck had drawn an unfavorable impression, because he withdrew his application a few days later.) Something had to be done to sharpen the process, and Lonni, a sharp interviewer in her own right, was determined to take action.

When, after a very long day in which two engineers had run Design's recruiting gantlet, Tinker asked her her opinion, she saw her chance. "Maybe it's just me," she ventured, "but I prefer interviews where the applicant doesn't call the shots. What I heard today was too positive."

"How could 'positive' be a drawback?" asked Tinker as the two relaxed over coffee.

"In interviews it can," replied Lonni, flipping open her briefcase and withdrawing a xeroxed magazine article she just happened to have with her. Its title was "Getting to Negative," and the byline was hers. "I wrote this little piece for a trade organ last year. 'Negative' is probably as loaded a term as 'positive' when it comes to interviews, but the article has a few pointers on how to *manage* the process."

By now Tinker's managerial insecurity was taking over. "Is it possible that Design could manage its interviews better?" he asked.

Bingo, thought Lonni. "Not only possible, but easy," she answered. "Hey, we're all involved in selecting the right people to fill vacancies, and I'm here to tell you we'll be run ragged unless we can strengthen the process." She showed

Tinker her estimates on the worker-hours required for General Widget's anticipated growth. He whistled through his teeth at the bottom line. "More than ever," Lonnie said, "we have to make the right choice the first time and keep our turnover to a minimum."

"In line operations, that's called raising first-pass yield, Lonni."

"Whatever. But since we have the same goal, why don't you let me run a few classes for your top people on interview techniques? It won't take long. And it will save *me* time in the long run. Besides, its fun. Try one of these classes on for size. If you like it, we'll expand them." Tinker couldn't say no. He even agreed to let Lonni begin a class after tomorrow's late afternoon staff meeting.

The Interviewing Barrier: Getting Negative

That first class included only Tinker and his group leaders. For an introduction, Lonni expressed the view that the division's screening process was too collegial: "As I listened, I noticed that the interviewers did most of the talking. They seemed to want to tell the applicants about the company instead of getting them to tell about themselves. In one case, the applicant asked interesting but complex questions that took most of the allotted time to answer. It was as if she were interviewing us!"

"Wait a second," said Tinker defensively. "Your department screened these people, and their credentials had been circulated to each interviewer. There wasn't that much more to find out other than whether or not they were compatible with General Widget."

"Finding that out isn't a matter of *them* chatting *you* up, though. It's a matter of getting negative."

"Getting negative?"

"Yep. For instance, you should ask a candidate what he or she is worst at on the job. As you said, the paperwork has already spelled out what he or she is good at; so have the references. Ask for negative references: names of people they clashed with for one reason or another."

"What if they deny they have such negative references?" asked a group leader.

"Well, I wouldn't consider such a person further for a responsible position. Statistics show that every successful white-collar type has had a personality or policy deadlock somewhere along the line. It's part of doing the job right. Asking for such details is not a game designed to make an applicant feel uncomfortable. When you get those references, follow up on them. Most of the time, negative references will describe some characteristic of the candidate that isn't really a minus. Maybe the person was a workaholic, or too focused on goals, or an overachiever. Whatever you find out, you'll have a much more real-world idea of who you're hiring.

"If the applicant looks generally attractive, ask that person to rate him- or herself on a scale of 1 to 10 in various categories. If the person's honest, he or she will come up with a low number here and there. That'll provide food for discussion and give you a balanced picture of the person's strengths and weaknesses. Of course, how the subject answers the question is almost as important as the information itself. My rule is don't bother with anyone who can't or won't admit deficiencies. There ain't no perfect 10s out there. Now, let's get some practice by doing a little role playing. I'll play the interviewer and you, Witt, be the interviewee."

The amazing thing about the role playing was how Lonni, whose technical knowledge was insufficient for her to program a VCR, could smoke out a three-dimensional profile by negative questioning. It thus didn't take much imagination to see how a specialist armed with such techniques would fare. The others grew immediately enthusiastic and wanted to role-play long after quitting time.

The Interviewing Barrier: One Final Question

When the games were over, Lonni had a final point to make: "Interviewing a candidate for employment in the Design Division is a lengthy process. In principle, five to seven interviews is a good idea, but only when each interviewer produces some informative feedback afterward.

"After a sequence is over, each of you should ask yourself, 'If my job depended on this individual, would I hire him?' and rate the applicant accordingly. That's a generic *him*, by the way. Witt, you should turn that question on every interviewer: 'If your job depended on it, would you recommend this individual? Why?' Because, of course, it might. If each of you have a firm answer for that question, you've probably gotten to the nitty-gritty.

"When you have these techniques down pat, you may want to double up in interviews. Two heads can be better than one, and the process will move faster. We really do need to move a lot faster." The rest of the session, which went far beyond normal quitting time, was spent in questions and answers.

The Training Barrier: A Solution?

The next day, Witt Tinker was on the phone to coax Lonni into designing a recruiting course for his division. Lonni had a course in her bottom drawer that everyone in Personnel ran through. She could easily adapt it for Design and, when that was done, Manufacturing and Marketing as well. She was saying as much to Tinker when her eyes fell on another block of her flowchart: training. Next to identifying and hiring new people, training them was the biggest bottleneck. "Witt," she said in a burst of sudden inspiration, "I've just had a fabulous idea. Could your people help Personnel develop a computer-based orientation packet to train incoming design people—one good enough to modify for other parts of the company? If we had such a packet, new employees could train by themselves in a very short time without having to wait for the orientation schedule to roll around again. We might be able to shave a week or two off the time it takes to get new employees ready for work." Tinker said he would

take it under advisement; but Lonni knew that when he saw
the knockout job Personnel did in the recruiting course, he
would be glad to play ball.

Inside of a week after getting Prudence's mandate to improve customer response, Lonni had spotted three major
barriers and three possible ways to remove them: streamlining the headhunting process, sharpening the interview process, and making the training process more flexible. Suppose, as seemed likely, she could shave a week from each of
those steps. That was a one-third reduction in time right
there. Lonni was sure she could do better. Beautiful! Sitting
back to enjoy the moment, she wondered if Neal was making
similar progress.

Accounting for Accounting: Too Many
Measurements

As a boy comic book freak, Neal York had found Clark Kent
a more interesting character than Superman, and had
shaped his own life accordingly. He had spent 34 years in Accounting at General Widget, having joined right after grad-
uating from Temple. The job had looked good because it was
convenient to his parent's home in Drexelbrook, a postwar
development in suburban Upper Darby, just a few miles but
a world away from Lonni's neighborhood.

Neal roomed with his parents for two years, then put a
down payment on a Drexelbrook row house for himself. Like
many accountants, he felt almost obligated to be "sensible
about money" and had lived up to that obligation. For years,
he rode the trolley and the el to work, just as he had as a college student. Meanwhile, by judicious investment and the in-
heritance of his late parents' modest estate, he had acquired
several other pleasant suburban houses, which he rented out,
and a summer cottage in Avalon, New Jersey, on which he'd
made a killing when that ramshackle seaside town was
gentrified. Neal also knew a thing or two about the stock
market, although he had sense enough not to ruin friend-

ships by expounding upon such knowledge. Now, at 53, he had a sizable nest egg aside from his salary earnings. He was happily, blandly married, with two kids on college scholarships. All the Yorks were devoted 76ers fans. In his leisure time, Neal read fantasy and science fiction and planned someday to write a few such books of his own. He owned a vast, well-catalogued collection of pulps and comic books, many of which he'd saved religiously since boyhood. They were now worth a small fortune.

Because his personal satisfactions were not mortgaged to his job, Neal had watched Prudence Cash, a whiz kid 10 years his junior, be promoted over him to Chief Accountant and then to VP of Finance without surprise and with little envy. When, upon Prudence's promotion to VP, he had made Chief Accountant, he realized that he had reached his limit of career advancement. He accepted that. Recently, watching her adroit management while the entire company reinvented itself, he felt glad that it was Prudence and not he who ran the division. It had not occurred to him — or to her either, apparently — that Accounting would have to make some drastic changes. Well, that day had arrived.

Eliminating Measurements: Simple Subtraction

Neal brought little of his imaginative reading tastes to his work. He tended to take and follow orders literally, and Prudence's recent instructions were no exception. So, closing the door behind him, he had his PC print out a directory of the data Accounting reported to Manufacturing. There were 30 different items on the list. Prudence had said to cut them in half. He therefore would have to convince Manufacturing that they could live with 15. But which 15? Obviously, the five new cycle time measurements were taboo; Sellers had made it clear he would be reading those to run the business. Neal needed to retain five others just to keep Accounting legal. The other 20 were fair game. He printed multiple copies of those 20 measurements and set off for Manufacturing the next morning.

Butch McMills sometimes appeared to be afraid somebody would take advantage of him unless he put up a gruff, no-nonsense front. Listening to Neal's announced plan to streamline reporting, Butch professed sympathy because, he said, he was a hip-pocket manager who hated red tape. Neal wasn't convinced; that was the sort of thing everyone said, especially in the company's new culture. "Tell you what," said Butch, passing the buck a little, "Talk to my supervisors and maintenance managers. If they can live without some of this stuff, I can live without it. Tell 'em I said so."

But where and how was Neal supposed to tell 'em Butch said so? He dreaded making presentations even in his own department, so he was appalled at the idea of approaching manufacturing people. Suddenly he remembered his deal with Lonni Quarles. He doubled back to her office.

"Facilitating" Crossfunctional Barrier Removal

"I had a feeling I'd be hearing from you," Lonni said as Neal sat down by her desk. "The answer is no, I don't have any idea how to trim your reports to Manufacturing."

Neal smiled at this. "I have to meet with McMills' people. Maybe you have some pointers on how I can make an effective presentation to a bunch of manufacturing types who have better things to do than listen to the likes of me."

"The first pointer is to demonstrate that there's something in it for them," said Lonni, automatically taking a suspiciously short paperback (*Moving a Group Your Way*) from her shelf and sliding it across her desk to Neal as she talked. "Convince them that lightening the load of unnecessary data will make their tasks easier, which is the truth, after all.

"The second is to prioritize the items you want to dump. Find out from the group which items are eyewash—some of them must be. And be sure everybody's on your wavelength by giving them clear, simple handouts, nothing too slick. Also,..."

There seemed no end to this cavalcade of pointers, but already Neal was demoralized. "Maybe you oughta do the presentation," he quipped. "I'll stay here and fire a few people."

"That's not a bad idea—the first part, I mean," answered Lonni. "I won't make your pitch for you, but I can attend as a facilitator."

"What's a facilitator?"

"You don't know? It's one of my specialties. When General Widget managers gather to hash out big decisions, I go along in case the proceedings deadlock over a personality problem or a point of order or a turf issue or whatever. As an outsider (and, I suspect, as a woman, although you didn't hear that from me), I can sometimes come up with the right procedural suggestion to move matters along smoothly. When Witt Tinker and Prudence had to work out new measurements for the Design Division last year and neither were familiar with the modus operandi of the other, I facilitated. When Victor King reorganized the company and passed out the promotions and reassignments, I facilitated that, too."

"How do you facilitate matters that are all outside your specialty?"

"The same way I spot good job applicants. Because I'm not a vested specialist, I can see the woods instead of the trees. You might say that as a facilitator, my specialty is not having a specialty. Part of the trick is training; the rest is intuition. Trust me on this, a meeting like the one you're proposing would be a snap. And then I could call in the favor if I ever got into trouble with Accounting. By the way, do you do income taxes on the side? Just kidding!"

Neal wondered if this conversation was an example of how Lonni broke tensions at such meetings. "You're on," he said before she could change her mind.

Crossing Divisional Lines to Slash Paperwork

The meeting went so smoothly that Neal almost enjoyed himself—or was that Lonni's subtle assistance again? Whatever the case, it was a cinch to persuade the participants that the cause was just. And there were a few measurement indices on Neal's hit list that the group unanimously agreed it could live without—the cost of accidents, for instance. Another item, the per-person cost of operating the division's cafeteria, actually brought laughter because only one person in the room besides Neal had ever heard of such a measurement. Several other items, however, proved more controversial. A debate began about retaining the traditional numbers on work-in-process inventory. But McMills' assistant pointed out that a new inventory measurement added by the cycle time experts included the material covered by the old measurement and provided a truer overall picture of work in process besides. All then agreed to drop the old one.

Some measurements were so arcane that the meeting stalled as participants tried to guess the original rationale for including them. "There must be some good reason or they wouldn't be there," said one. Just as matters were unraveling into irrelevant speculation, up popped Lonni with an ingenuous question: "When was the last time anyone here used the cost of absenteeism to make a decision?" Silence. "Here's another one I don't understand: labor-rate variance. Is that helpful?" More silence. "I wonder," she continued, "if it would make sense to put a time limit on these items. If, for example, nobody's used a measurement during the last year for any purpose, maybe it should be discarded." Several people, Neal included, looked gratefully at Lonni.

Using that criterion, it was impossible to defend 9 other items. Adding them to the 5 already dispensed with gave Neal 14 expendibles; 16 stayed in place. Close enough, thought Neal to his intense relief. He thanked the group for its cooperation, ran back to his office, typed out the results of the meeting, and E-mailed them to Prudence and Butch. The next morning, when he read his own E-mail, he felt like Superman for the first time. Prudence's electronic response was "Well done! You're now the resident expert on barrier removal." Butch, a man of few words, had answered with "Good riddance." Neal thumbtacked copies of both messages to his bulletin board and stared happily at them for several minutes. He also sent copies on to Lonni, who was the unsung hero of the day.

A New Barrier: What Will the Auditors Say?

The sweet smell of success, however, lingered but a short time. Having eliminated one set of barriers to better performance, Neal had unwittingly exposed a second. He was still swiveled back in his desk chair, feeling a glow of satisfaction, when Prudence popped in. "I wanted to thank you personally for your *spectacular* performance with Manufacturing," she said. (*Spectacular* was a word seldom heard in Accounting.) "I do think, Neal, that you'd better inform the outside auditors of your intentions. We don't want to take them by surprise. And don't make a move until they say okay." With that, Neal knew that his troubles were just beginning.

General Widget was audited by Andrew Elder, Inc., one of the Big Eight accounting firms. In Neal's opinion, Andrew Elder's reputation was overinflated, although all he really knew of the firm was the type of accountants it sent out to go over his books, people he classified as young squirts. He was damned if he was going to wait for one of these shavetails to come in and jump all over him, and he said as much to Prudence. "Well," Prudence answered, "go beard the lion in his den. The lion's name is Carter Welles Swain, no less. He's a senior partner, and his office is in Kennedy Plaza. You'll have to go to him, he won't come out here."

Neal had a lifelong suspicion of people with three names; most of the ones he'd met were stuffed shirts. "We'll incur expenses," he said. "Those guys charge like lawyers and they'll treat this as a consultation."

"So be it, but try to take as little of his time as possible."

"You took the words right out of my mouth." Neal drew up a detailed letter of his plan to eliminate 14 itemized measurements, explained that the move was part of General Widget's revitalization, and posted it to Swain. Swain responded promptly with a request that Neal appear at his office five days hence.

Barrier Removal: Bearding the Lion

The offices of Andrew Elder, Inc., were relatively new but designed to look like old money, complete with oriental rugs and gigantic European landscape paintings. Neal felt like a brown shoe at a black-tie formal. Carter Welles Swain's office commanded a view of the Benjamin Franklin Parkway and the distant Art Museum. Swain was a ruddy-faced, patrician Ivy Leaguer with a firm handshake and a firmer opposition to Neal's plan.

"Mr. York, I would be remiss if I gave my approval to your plan," he began. "Please don't think me peremptory. Our firm has been auditing General Widget since before the war [Swain meant World War II], and I'm quite familiar with the company's recently improved performance. As you may know, I meet personally with your top management every quarter. I might add that I was a classmate at Haverford of your chief executive, Victor King. We still lunch together regularly at the Union League, so my understanding of General Widget is, shall we say, sophisticated.

"General Widget's improvement is a case of management having adopted a more aggressive set of values to keep competitive. The turnaround has taken place in truly rapid fashion. As you've indicated, your wish to simplify accounting is part of the company's instant makeover.

"With all this in mind, I'm afraid that the new values may be more apparent than real and that the company will be in for some tough sledding now that its improvement program is complete and the novelty is wearing off. You can thus appreciate, I trust, that the company may want—need—to fall back on its traditional systems, and that includes accounting. So Andrew Elder must give thumbs down to your proposal."

Neal was feeling like Clark Kent again, but he wasn't about

to roll over and die on Swain's Bokhara carpet. "Mr. Swain," he said, assuming the formal diction of his host, "With all due respect, my notice to you was not a 'proposal' because Andrew Elder is not part of our management. It was an announcement. As a fellow accountant, I need only remind you that the company is retaining the required statutory items and has implemented new elements that cover all the management essentials within the new culture." That 'fellow accountant' remark had been too familiar. He could see Swain stiffen, but he went on: "A short-cycle-time company has no use, no need, for the sort of accounting data we're discussing. I assure you that simplifying our procedures at this point is consistent with our improved status."

"Were you specifically told to drop all those labor-related measurements?" asked Swain.

"I was delegated to simplify my department's tasks. The choices were mine, in conference with our Manufacturing Division. Next week, I'll be meeting with representatives of Marketing to discuss stripping out unnecessary accounting items in that division. I'd like to continue the momentum of the reforms —"

"Reforms?" exclaimed the astonished Swain. "Let me give you the benefits of my perspective. I supervise the auditing of several other corporations quite similar to General Widget. Two, if I may say so, are much larger and to date have been more profitable. None of those companies has seen fit to 'strip out,' as you call it, the measurements you so blithely want to discard. Could it be that you are overeager to please your superiors? As your auditor, Andrew Elder cannot endorse moves that appear to be potentially harmful, however expedient they may look on the surface."

"That's final?" asked Neal.

"I will take the matter up with my associates, and you will have our rendered opinion shortly in writing." Sure you will, thought Neal, then you'll bill us for five consultations instead of one. But the answer will probably be the same.

"But the answer will probably be the same," concluded Swain.

Fallout From the Lion's Den

Within two weeks, Neal had the auditors' verdict in writing. The letter mentioned "potential loss of control," "new expectations not being realized," and "established procedures for similar manufacturing-based industries." Worse, to add insult to injury, Swain had pointedly sent copies of his letter to Prudence Cash and even Hardy Sellers. The multiple copies were doubtless intended to put the kibosh on one small, eccentric idea and, possibly, one small eccentric accountant.

That Friday afternoon, before Neal had had time to get upset about the matter, he and Prudence were summoned to Hardy Sellers' office. The new president was in a high dudgeon when they walked through the door. "What's going on with Andrew Elder?" he demanded.

Prudence told Neal to explain. I've had it, Neal thought. Gathering himself, he reviewed the assignment he'd been given, his decision, and the auditors' reaction to it. The explanation did little to calm Sellers, but the president's next remarks certainly calmed Neal.

"Look," he said, "I want to make it clear that you two are not on the carpet. As far as I can see, you were following up on my general instructions of last week. And you were moving damn fast on those instructions, which is a plus. About this Andrew Elder barrier: I'm the first to admit that I don't know the whys and wherefores of labor-rate variances and costs of absenteeism. That was the kind of stuff that my predecessor liked to pore over, and I suspect that it was retained for Victor's interest, not Manufacturing's. If Manufacturing says we can kiss it off, we can kiss it off. Who the hell's running this company, anyway, Andrew Elder?"

Far be it from Neal to go to bat for the auditors, but Prudence interjected one point in their defense: Andrew Elder's job is to keep us out of trouble. They've learned how to read our old system, and they're probably afraid that if we junk it for a new one, they'll be unable to spot problems before it's too late. And, of course, they don't want their signatures on an annual report that their other customers can't read."

Now Sellers was fuming. "Let me handle this. I'll get back to you." Prudence and Neal beat a hasty retreat. Neal spent an uneasy weekend rereading Lovecraft's *At the Mountains of Madness*, one of his favorites, but for the first time was totally unable to concentrate.

Tigers Versus Lions: Who's Tougher?

On Monday afternoon, Sellers called Neal and Prudence back to his office. "I've had quite a day," he began. "I got Victor King to take me to lunch at the Union League. That's not my favorite stamping ground, and the feeling is mutual. Victor and I had a very short conversation about General Widget's accounting. It went like this: I told him about my five-point instructions and about the resulting tussle with the auditors after Accounting decided to drop the old measurements. I was particularly irate about their implication that General Widget might be getting out of control. I showed Neal's list of expendibles to Victor. He looked at it and smiled. 'Are you going to lose control of the company?' he asked me. 'Of course not!' I answered. 'Then drop the measurements,' he said. 'They're holdovers from my era, and if I'd known then what I learned in the last two years, most of them would have been gone long ago.' Then he added, 'Even if that were not true, you're running the show, and the holding company supports you.'

"Which was all I needed to detour to Swain's office as soon as lunch was finished. Our conversation was likewise very brief. You'll both get copies of the letter I'm about to send him because turnabout is fair play. Basically, it makes three points: that I am authorized by Genwid Holding Company to manage General Widget, that I have mandated the removal of accounting barriers, and that our audited annual report is our responsibility, not the auditors'.

"What's not in the letter is the last thing I said to Swain in person. You'll like this, Neal. I told him if Andrew Elder is uncomfortable auditing our books, it might be in both our interests to 'reappraise the relationship.' I even mentioned the dreaded name of their competitor, Albert Small Associates. Swain gulped. Then he said that in view of my strong feelings on the matter, he'd confer once more with his colleagues and get back to me. We all know what the new decision will be."

"Yes," said the relieved Neal, "but leave it to Swain to wring one more billable conference out of the incident."

"This time it's worth it," said Sellers, laughing. "I just wish I could be at the Union League the next time Swain sits down with Victor. But back to business. Prudence, if Neal's plan still has your support, you may as well get the ball rolling right away. This has been mighty fast work. Thanks to you both. And Neal, when you start stripping measurements from Marketing, I think the pathway will be a lot smoother."

Another Accounting Barrier: Is Labor Just Overhead?

Before taking on another division, however, Neal had a few chores to attend to. The next morning, he hiked over to Manufacturing and tapped on Butch McMills' office door. McMills looked up from his cluttered desk. "I heard you got along with my people just fine," said McMills, as usual skipping the hello.

"Yeah. And I've gotten the green light to cut those 14 indices," said Neal, making a long story short. "But running over that list, I noted that most of the items are tidbits which track various blue-collar costs. So are some of the ones we've left in. That got me to thinking about something the cycle time experts told me last year: that labor could be considered one aspect of overhead, pure and simple. So, glutton for punishment that I am, I'm here to put that bee in your bonnet. What do you say we drop *all* the separate labor measurements and simply roll total labor cost into your overhead category?" With that, Neal handed Butch a single sheet of paper entitled "A Proposal to Modernize Accounting at General Widget." Butch looked at it and winced.

"Just chew on it for a while," said Neal. "After that, I'll bet we can both sell it to Hardy. I'll bet we can even sell it to the auditors.

"Gotta run now Butch; Prudence Cash is taking Lonni and me to lunch."

Life After Entitlement: A Few Pointers

Six months after Prudence, Lonni, and Neal lunched together, Jack Betters read an article in the latest *Fortune* that featured a color photograph of shirtsleeved Hardy Sellers sitting on the corner of his desk and smiling confidently as he fondled a shiny Widgerino, his company's ticket to greater market share. "Turnaround at General Widget: An Old Business Finds New Glamour" was the caption. The article discussed General Widget's reawakening as it had moved from baseline to entitlement. Although the story stuck to the decisions of top management, there were enough details to capture Jack's interest.

General Widget's well-oiled public relations office (a component of Prudence Cash's division) proved most cooperative when Jack identified himself and his project by telephone. The PR director sent Jack a complete set of promotional materials on the General Widget turnaround and even threw in a kit prepared by the company to acquaint a novice with Total Cycle Time values. General Widget is nothing if not messianic, thought Jack as he rooted through the kit's contents like a kid with a Christmas stocking. There was, he knew, book material in there somewhere.

He found it in the form of several introductory guides that would fit neatly into his proposed appendix. One was a warning against the resource-hungry alternatives to adopting Total Cycle Time (TCT):

WHY IS TCT SUCH AN OVERWHELMING OPPORTUNITY IN TODAY'S BUSINESS ENVIRONMENT?

- The effectiveness of any business process can be measured by:
  - Cost
  - First-pass yield (quality)
  - TCT
- Pressure to improve cost comes from:
  - Competition
  - Management
  - Customer

  Solution is to throw resources at the problem with little understanding of TCT impact.

- Pressure to improve quality comes from:
  - Customer
  - Competition
  - Management

  Solution is to throw resources at the problem with little understanding of TCT impact.

- No pressure to improve TCT; it has never been managed. It has always been the squeeze point of poor performance.
  - Put time in inventory/action in process to respond
  - Delay schedules while controlling quality and meeting budgets

---

Besides fending off the wrong baseline impulses about improving performance, that chart underscored the point that getting to entitlement almost never required the application of additional money, people, or equipment.

Jack also found a handy-dandy form which had been used successfully at a General Widget internal workshop addressing the company's make/market loop divided into subloops, each of which had to develop its own time-phased entitlement goals and identify its respective barriers [*as shown on the following page*].

He paired that form with another from the same workshop wherein the make/market barriers could be quantified as to impact upon productivity. The point of both these forms, he

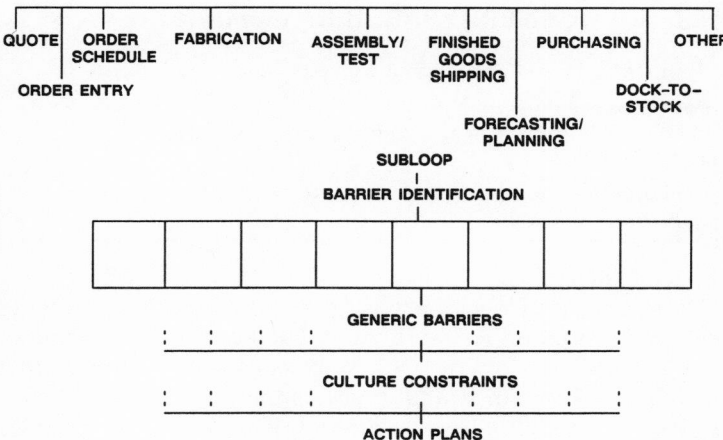

Develop time-phased goals from baseline to entitlement for each subloop and in total (make/market example).

thought, was to dramatize how shortening cycle times was a predictable, trackable exercise. A list of conspicuous generic barriers — the type most companies might expect to encounter — rounded out the series.

GENERIC BARRIERS

Work-in-process manipulation. Attempt to adjust output by changing schedules and priorities.

Nonlinearity. The relative use of resources by time period. Usually starts with end-of-period revenue push and ultimately affects the whole business process.

Inspection (including sign-offs) versus prevention. Inspection is the act of observing results, not achieving them.

Transportation. Time to transfer from one process to another. Can be large in some functionally organized white-collar areas or remote-location plants.

(Continued)

GENERIC BARRIERS (*Continued*)

Wait time. Holds/queuing, not using 24 hours and 7 days.

Poor process design. Non-value-added steps: duplication, needless complexity, workarounds, serial vs. parallel, value added too late.

Inadequate communication. Delays caused by unclear or absent communication.

More goodies: General Widget's kit contained a pamphlet titled "Questions and Answers about Total Cycle Time," most of which was by now old hat to Jack except for one question that had occurred to him several times, namely, What were the effects of Total Cycle Time turnarounds on employee morale? The pamphlet had a neat, almost pat explanation: "It is important to recognize that employees will find the demands placed upon them by Total Cycle Time stressful at first. High cycle times breed matching levels of comfort because the pressure is low. When cycle times start to descend, however, so do employee comfort levels, and managers should be prepared for this occurrence. Moreover, until Total Cycle Time is institutionalized, employees are apt to revert to old habits if faced by new and stressful challenge—a downturn in the market, for example, or a change at the top, or the introduction of a competitive product by a rival. However, once Total Cycle Time is institutionalized and employees derive their psychological comfort from fast response, their comfort index climbs past its previous level to a much higher plane." To complement the explanation, the booklet provided the inevitable diagram [*as shown on the following page*], which Jack tore out and filed in his appendix folder.

Usable forms and lists were not the only goodies Jack received from General Widget. Included with the packet was an offer from the company's Public Relations Department to put Jack in touch with whatever senior managers he might wish to interview for his book.

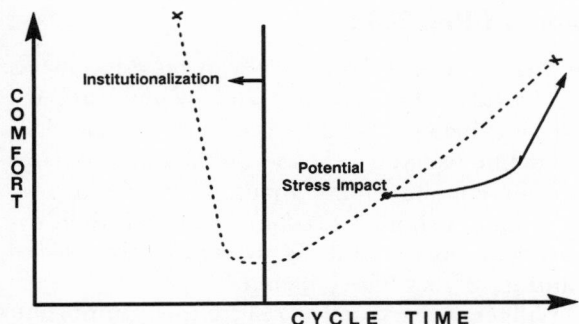

Typical comfort curve.

Not long after, while catching up on correspondence in his tiny New York office, Jack was very surprised to receive a call from Hardy Sellers himself. The man's powerful, upbeat personality positively leaked through the phone lines. "I've been briefed on your book project," Sellers said. "We'd like to get our oar in that water. What do you say to a trip to Philly so you can meet face-to-face with some of our people?"

Before Jack could think of a polite way to say that he avoided junkets, Sellers added, "You could have a few minutes to fire questions at me; just the two of us. Then you could meet with people down the line. Of course, the story of how we implemented Total Cycle Time has been pretty well covered in the media, as you saw from the PR packet you received. But I think there's another story to tell: how a company keeps its momentum up after reaching entitlement. That's what we're working on now." Jack accepted.

He, of course, paid his own way—most of it, anyway. Detraining at 30th Street Station, he was met promptly but unceremoniously by a General Widget driver in a shiny middle-aged Chevy, which spoke volumes about the company's corporate self-image. Forty-five minutes later, he was swept into Sellers' office by the smiling CEO himself who, true to his word, gave him a few minutes, no more, no less.

A Postentitlement Pep Talk

Sellers hooked one leg over a front corner of his desk just as
he had for the *Fortune* photographer and beamed as Jack
reached for pad and pencil. "Glad you're here," began Sellers, "because someone like you needs to publicize the part of
the speed management movement that's been overlooked,
namely, what companies should do *after* they've cut their cycle times and are lean, mean, and highly competitive. We're
at that point, and it's a very big challenge.

"At General Widget, we've come to realize three important
facts about Total Cycle Time." Jack's ability to take notes
without breaking eye contact served him well at moments like
this.

"I'll give 'em to you quick," continued Sellers.

"First—and this is so fundamental it can easily be overlooked—when a company reaches its entitlement, it is on a
continuous improvement curve. It does not pause. It must
continue to exploit Cycles of Learning faster and faster to
improve performance and stay ahead of competitors.

"Second: at entitlement, a company must review all of its
business processes because, inevitably, its achievement of Total Cycle Time has probably been less than total. In other
words, there are always a few key areas which have escaped
the new culture. In our case, we neglected Finance and Services, where there was and still is a lot of room for improvement.

"Third—and this is a special baby of mine—the various divisions of an entitlement company have to regard their internal transactions in the same light as customer relations. They
use each others' services; therefore, they are each others' customers and each others' suppliers. If the mentality of quick
customer response is applied to internal relations between divisions, all sorts of removable barriers will surface."

So far, Jack had not asked a single question, nor did he
ever get to ask one. He also need not have taken notes because, as he finished, Sellers took a printed 3-by-5 card from
his pocket and pressed it into Jack's hands. It read:

RECIPE FOR STAYING COMPETITIVE

Maintain the improvement curve *past* entitlement.
Spread cycle time culture *everywhere* in the company.
We are our own suppliers and customers.
Practice customer responsiveness.

Sellers steered Jack toward the door. "I've arranged for you to meet my Finance and Services VP," he said. "Her division is a perfect example of the pointers I just gave you. Thanks for your interest."

Barrier Removal in the Services Sector: Four Pointers

Prudence Cash was waiting outside Sellers' door. As she walked Jack back to her office, she outlined for him how her division had lately applied Total Cycle Time ideas.

"While the other divisions were moving toward entitlement with our help, Finance and Services was not addressing the need to simplify its own business processes," Prudence said as they sat down in her office. "Suddenly, there was Hardy Sellers, a generalist, assigning me the general task of barrier removal without giving me a clue as to where the barriers lay. I had to make some quick and important decisions."

Out came Jack's pencil. "What were they?" he asked.

"You're taking notes?" said Prudence. "In that case, I'll be brief.

"I identified the two top priorities as barrier removal and simplification, not the automation or enhancement, of existing procedures.

"I recognized that removing barriers involved specialized expertise, so I pushed the responsibility down the chain of command to my subordinates in Personnel, Accounting, or whatever.

"I recognized that barrier removal in a service division

must take place in accord with the other divisions it services (our internal customers, if you will).

"Finally, I learned that there are times when barrier removal can blow up in someone's face. An idea may be good, but the power to enact it may exceed that of the assigned manager. When that happens, senior management must provide help to maintain momentum, and do so with short cycle time.

Automation as the Last Priority

"Let me explain those ideas a little further. Most of our task in Finance and Services was a matter of simplification. My people had already learned the principles of short cycle times from the outside problem solvers who helped us understand how to become more competitive, and by helping the other divisions reach entitlement.

"My first impulse was to go the high-tech route: to automate further with new software and that sort of thing. At first glance, automation always looks as though it will simplify tasks such as accounting. But it was obvious to me that we were awash in recordkeeping, data-tracking, and reporting—practices that had multiplied in the preentitlement years. Automation was therefore the *last* thing we should be considering. First we had to remove barriers and develop fast, more effective ways of doing things. Otherwise, we'd be automating obsolete, possibly useless processes."

Prudence pointed to the wall behind her Shaker-style desk. Hanging there in an antique grain-painted frame was a decoratively lettered document which at first glance looked like Early American folk art, but wasn't. It read

FIRST YOU SIMPLIFY.

THEN YOU AUTOMATE.

"That's a pretty elementary little motto," admitted Prudence. "But you'd be amazed how many companies get that order reversed. To prevent such a thing from happening here, I had copies made of that motto and personally sent one to every middle manager in the division. When they saw I had put mine on the wall, a lot of them did, too.

Where Is the Responsibility for Barrier Removal?

"Taking first things first," Prudence continued, "I figured that the best approach was Hardy Sellers': move decision making down the line to the specialists in the various accounting and service fields. Make sure they understood that simplification is keynote, but let *them* identify the processes to simplify.

"But remember, it's a service division's job to grease the wheels of the other divisions. I therefore impressed upon my subordinates the point that barrier removal must occur with the blessing of the divisions affected by such changes. It was an interdisciplinary exercise. Sometimes, crossing divisions is a formal matter of committees and such; other times it can be a piece of cake. For example, Lonni Quarles, our personnel director, eliminated a major recruiting bottleneck in Design simply by assembling a clever training package, making it fun, and personally demonstrating it during regular business hours.

"Not everything was a piece of cake, of course. I had to be prepared to step in when the backlash got heavy. For example, our chief accountant, Neal York, caused a major flap with our outside auditors when he revamped the reporting procedures. The auditors would have beaten up on Neal if Hardy hadn't got wind of it. Believe me, he put a stop to that right away.

"The moral of that story is that when a barrier removal problem escalates beyond a middle manager's power to deal with it, upper management must be prepared expeditiously to use its muscle to break the logjam. A quick decision at the top can eliminate months of midlevel wrangling. Anyway, my division is making impressive progress. And we're not only scuttling a lot of obsolete practices; as I've said, we're coming up with some time-saving innovations."

Up and Out at General Widget

"I'm particularly interested in the two examples you gave involving middle managers," said Jack. "Could I have a word with your chief accountant and personnel director?"

Prudence buzzed her assistant and asked him to find Neal York. "Your timing is perfect in one case and awful in another," she said, smiling. "Neal York is about three weeks from early retirement. He's on his way over to meet you. Lonni Quarles has left the company."

Jim's brow furrowed and Prudence read his mind. "No, neither of them are under a cloud," she added. "Quite the contrary. Neal has made exciting contributions around here lately. He just wants to attend to a few personal objectives on the outside.

"Lonni was a firecracker who also knew the art of gentle persuasion. She got an offer she couldn't refuse. The training program she put together compressed the time-consuming interview process and improved its reliability. It also improved the hit rate of a major headhunter firm that works with us. They were so impressed that they hired her away from General Widget! Competition in the headhunting field is awesome, so that firm is extending its customer service beyond the procurement of candidates to include courses in interviewing and developing business processes for hiring and improving the effectiveness of new people. Lonni's perfect for that. Too bad you didn't meet her. Oh, here's Neal."

After good-byes and the obligatory exchange of business cards with Prudence, Jack followed Neal York down the hall to the coffee machine. He was feeling pretty good about his writing project, which had commenced as a casebook on midmanagerial competitiveness but was assuming a human interest dimension as well. He decided to save General Widget's postentitlement tale for his final chapter.

Over coffee, Neal gave Jack one last human interest story: the ups and downs of streamlining General Widget's reporting system. "I'd been a by-the-book, green-eyeshade accountant for 34 years," said Neal by way of a closer, "Then BAM! Along came this new requirement to strip out old measurements. It turned my way of looking at accounting upside down, and I've never had so much fun!"

"But Prudence — Ms. Cash — said you're leaving," put in Jack.

"True. For several reasons. One is that 35 years is long enough to push numbers around this plant. Another is that it's a good time for me to bow out at General Widget. Over that last year, I've accomplished a few reforms that the company will come to realize were very innovative. General Widget Accounting doesn't just operate on a simplified basis. It operates on a Total Cycle Time basis. For example, all direct labor is now carried as an overhead line item. And get this: all overhead is allocated by cycle time. Those are substantial changes. When I got them in place, that seemed like a good note on which to make my exit.

"I also have a personal agenda. I want to do some fantasy writing. I'd put that off for years because, I now realize, I was too inhibited to really exercise my imagination. This last year at General Widget brought my imagination out of the shadows and lowered my inhibitions. I'm going to pull up stakes and move out beyond the suburbs to a college town with a decent library and a nice view: Carlisle, maybe, or Gettysburg. And there's one more thing...."

"Yes?"

"I'd like to take some of my know-how and put it to work at other companies. America has plenty of uncompetitive businesses whose accounting procedures are full of cobwebs. Hell, the country has plenty of uncompetitive businesses whose procedures, top to bottom, are full of cobwebs. That's gotten me thinking about how to reach such businesses.

"As an accountant, I've become sensitized to the incredible amount of cash most companies keep tied up in long cycle times. Here, look at these computer graphics I ran off the other day. I call them resource effectiveness profiles. The numbers should really impress you." Neal handed Jack a simple chart. It looked like the figure at the bottom of the page.

The upper bar in this graphic represents a typical R&D cycle time in a large company: three years. The amount being spent on R&D in this case is usual: 12 percent of sales per year. Now look at the lower bar, which represents a 10 percent reduction in spending but—this is crucial—a 50 percent reduction in cycle time. In the latter instance, the total cash tied up in the cycle is only 16.2 percent of annual sales, versus 36 percent in the former. Now if that's not an incentive for lowering cycle times, I'll eat my hat.

"This example of a resource effectiveness profile can be extended to an entire company, showing the difference in resource effectiveness between baseline and entitlement. Such an analysis shows huge potential for improvement.

"Anyway," said Neal, "I'd like to see these advanced accounting exercises make a difference in corporate thinking outside General Widget much as your book will reach a wider audience. Now that retirement is staring me in the face, I'm wondering if there isn't some firm that could use me one or two weeks a month as an occasional problem solver."

Jack reached in his briefcase for his address book and

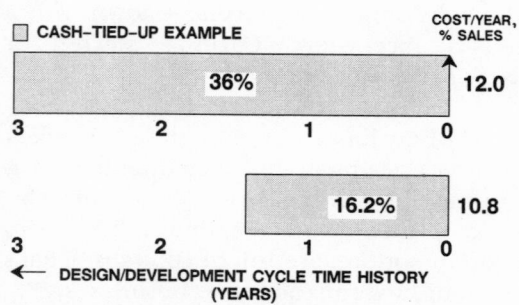

Total Cycle Time resource-effectiveness profile.

flipped a few pages. He put his finger on Andy De Clerck's Princeton address.

"Got a pencil?" he asked Neal.

Jack's Checklist:
Key Barriers Encountered by Neal York

1. Outside vested interests attempting to perpetuate noncontributing measurements and controls.

2. The comfort curve in changing to new measurements.

8

The Years to Come: Where Are They Now?

Lessons Learned in a Change to a Realizable Competitive Performance

Key lessons learned by the characters in this book are similar to lessons learned in changing the competitiveness performance of over 100 operations. Reducing them to the essence of the experience of over 20 years results in the following conclusions:

First, let's look at what works:

- Top-down commitment, including the CEO or top managers of each entity
- Top-level active involvement
- Change through current operational management structure
- Involvement of outside objective team players with hands-on experience

- Well-trained internal facilitators, working with outside help
- Frequent (monthly) top-management/outside-change-agent barrier removal meetings
- Simplifying and revising measurements to a minimal responsive set that drives competitiveness
- Monthly incentives tied to progress
- Communication, communication, communication

Now, let's look at what doesn't work:

- Self-medication (which typically stalls at 25 to 30 percent of potential)
- Lack of top-management involvement
- Assigning responsibility to internal staff as leaders of the competitiveness culture change
- Continuing with today's measurements
- Program-of-the-year type of focus
- Edicts of performance change

The people impacts of Total Cycle Time are very significant:

- Initial reduced comfort—a lot of initial resistance
- Final high comfort
- It is hard to recruit from and easy to recruit to a short-cycle-time culture
- Very high morale prevails when short-cycle-time performance is the norm
- People accomplish much more, learn faster, and have higher job satisfaction
- Most people can change (experience has shown that less than 5 percent of management cannot make transition and must be replaced or reassigned)
- Bottom-line impacts on people are very positive.

The competitiveness impacts are probably the most significant — so significant that they frequently cause disbelief. The real lessons learned in this area are indeed hero making. Competitiveness impacts include the following:

- Pretax profit increases of approximately 10 percent of sales
- Inventories are reduced by half, freeing up cash of 10 percent or more of sales
- Responsiveness to customers is dramatically increased; often response time cut to one-third or less
- Time to market of new products is cut in half or better
- Return on invested capital is raised by 2:1 or 4:1
- Very high quality
- Gains in market share and happy, loyal customers.

One of the most fun things about changing the responsiveness of businesses is thinking through the answer to the question, "What do you do with it when you have it?" Responsiveness strategies are:

- When a company enjoys superior responsiveness, its potential is virtually unlimited
- Specific strategies must be developed that exploit superior responsiveness as a market differentiator
- Such strategies often encourage customers to demand faster responsiveness and shorter cycle times, and to change their mind

Most importantly, a lesson learned over the last 20 years that should motivate any middle manager in a company, big or small:

THE BIG DON'T OUTPERFORM THE LITTLE.

THE FAST OUTPERFORM THE SLOW.

Now finally, what happened to each of our key characters?

- After serving on the companywide crossfunctional team, Larry Coile returned to Retrospace Purchasing and eventually succeeded the Godfather, a step up which gave him enough financial clout to buy a comfortable home in San Juan Capistrano.

- Bob Landon taped what was left of his record collection after the earthquake, sold the originals, and bought another boat with the proceeds. Meanwhile, he had a close call while commuting to and from Chicago, but managed to remain single. Because he insisted on staying in San Francisco, another member of Slumbertech's Marx Brothers, George Finlay, was groomed to be Vice President of Marketing.

- R. D. Tyrell remained as permanent manager of Platte Plate, a company that out-responded its regional competitors and grew accordingly. On weekends, he helps operate the historic, full-size, live-steam Georgetown Loop Railroad in the Rockies west of Denver. Every Christmas, he sends a gross of Kit Kat Bars to Clyde Farwell·in Oklahoma City.

- Bill Bancroft took early retirement from Contechron and moved to Phippsburg, Maine, where he became active in the local historical society. He and his old Contechron buddy, Hank Petrie, rekindled their youthful friendship and often visit one another. In July, the two compete in the Kennebec River Bluefish Tournament.

- Andy De Clerck continued to work with the Total Cycle Time specialists. Operating out of his Princeton office, he became a kingpin in that company's competitiveness programs, changing quite a few cultures over to the quick-response mentality. He also took a turnaround assignment as CEO of a outfit acquired by his employer's holding company, availing himself of stock options and doing a very good job of raising the value of that stock.

- After Palmetto's LBO went sour under the debt load and

the company was still "digging itself out of trouble," as he put it, Alex Lloyd took a job at an advertising firm in Boca Raton.

- Don Fannon became a vice president of a major semiconductor manufacturer in Phoenix. He and his wife take at least one sailing vacation a year in the Virgin Islands.

- Jerry Lomax was last seen on the lecture circuit.

- When General Widget acquired Unigadget, a Baltimore competitor, Hardy Sellers made Prudence Cash CEO of that operation.

- Lonni Quarles became a partner in the New York headhunting firm she'd joined. She now operates a branch office of the firm in Philadelphia.

- Neal York moved to an antique farmhouse in Adams County, Pennsylvania, to exercise his literary imagination. His first fantasy story, "Bridging the Walls of Xtar," was rejected by 11 publishers, but his work as a specialist in competitive accounting techniques (working as an associate under Andy De Clerck) has kept him too busy to write a second.

- Jack Betters is still working on his book.

Index

About the Author

Philip R. Thomas is founder and chairman of Thomas Group, Inc., an Irving, Texas-based business turnaround firm. His Total Cycle Time system is the result of 20 years' work at Texas Instruments, General Instruments, Fairchild, and RCA. Since 1978, he has successfully introduced TCT-based management to improve corporate competitiveness and streamline operational and new product cycle times at companies ranging from Fortune 10 firms to entrepreneurial start-ups, from the aerospace industry to financial services.

This book was written with **Kenneth R. Martin**, who is the author, coauthor, or writer of numerous books on business and maritime history. He lives in Woolwich, Maine.

Mr. Thomas is also the author of *Competitiveness Through Total Cycle Time*, which shows CEOs how to plan and successfully implement TCT strategies in any kind of company.